Accelerated Disruption

Eric Lefkofsky

Easton Studio Press

Copyright © 2007 by Eric Lefkofsky

Published by Easton Studio Press

ISBN-10: 0-9798248-2-6
ISBN-13: 978-0-9798248-2-1

All rights reserved. No portion of this book may be reproduced in any fashion, print, facsimile, or electronic, or by any method yet to be developed, without express written permission of the publisher.

Books are available at special discounts when purchased in bulk for premiums and sales promotions, as well as for fund-raising or educational uses. Special editions or book excerpts can be created to customer specifications. For details and further information, contact:

Special Sales Director
Easton Studio Press
P.O. Box 3131
Westport, CT 06880
(203) 454-4454

www.eastonsp.com

Printed in the United States of America

First Printing: November 2007

Cover Design: Steve Polacek
Book Design: Lisa Liddy

Dedication

To the most beautiful woman I know, my wife Liz, who in addition to filling my life with wonder has given me four of the finest gifts the world has to offer: her unconditional love, a boy named Sam with a mind and soul that dazzle me nearly every day, a little girl named Stella whose authentic beauty and captivating personality have grabbed a hold of my heart and a little boy named Quinn with sandy blond hair and a smile that makes even the toughest days manageable.

Contents

Dedication	iii
Acknowledgments	ix
Introduction	1
What does it mean to disrupt a business?	3
Our work	4
Chapter 1: The Law of Accelerated Disruption	9
How fast is fast?	10
Disruptive technology	12
What makes a business process disruptive?	13
What we've learned	15
Technology and timing	16
A revolution isn't enough—there must be evolution	19
The Disruption All-Stars	20
Chapter 2: The Law of Ubiquity	25
Ubiquity begins at home	28
Data drives disruption—and dollars	29
How will today's industry leaders destroy themselves?	34
Finding that tipping point	36
What ubiquitous technology really means	37
Chapter 3: The Law of Need	41
Spotting pain in existing industries	43
Creating the solution	46

The value of people in a world driven by technology	48
Pain and the point of commonality	57

Chapter 4: The Law of Convention — 59
Finding a fissure for revolution	61
Is experience overrated?	62
Looking for blue ocean	63
Great blue ocean innovators	68

Chapter 5: The Law of Objectivity — 71
Moving from idea to industry-destructive model—or not	73
Testing for value	75
When great ideas fail—for the right reasons	76
Famous flameouts	78
Learning to say no	80

Chapter 6: The Law of Informational Advantage — 85
The value of information	86
Solving the mystery of ad spend	96
Information gains clarity over time	99

Chapter 7: The Law of Adoption — 101
Value starts with knowing your customer	102
Technology accelerates the Law of Adoption	104
Making adoption happen	107
Functionality is everything	111
Send in the clowns	112
Our next adoption challenge	112

Chapter 8: The Law of Space — 119
Find the ocean, not the lake	121
The markets we've attacked	122
How scalable is your idea?	127
Space is the only frontier	128
The Exception to the Rule	129

Chapter 9: The Law of Ignorance — 133
Ignorance is the first step	136
Finding the "soft middle"	136
Think like an eight-year-old	139

Learn how to listen ... 141
Ten key questions to disrupt a business ... 142
Turning the Q&A around ... 143

Chapter 10: The Law of Awareness ... 145
Learning from failure ... 147
Learning from criticism ... 150
Learning from listening ... 153
Learning from transparency ... 155
Learning from adjustment ... 157

Chapter 11: The Law of Arbitrage ... 159
Creating value that moves an industry forward ... 161
Arbitrage is addiction ... 162
Real innovation results in real arbitrage ... 164
Arbitrage is (pleasant) surprise ... 165
Arbitrage is an innovation tool ... 168
Arbitrage at ThePoint ... 170
Those that fail to find arbitrage…fail ... 172

Chapter 12: The Law of Velocity ... 175
If you're not moving at warp speed, you're not moving ... 178
The new innovation paradigm ... 179
Balancing speed and accuracy ... 180
When giants sleep ... 183
Lightning cycle time ... 184
Speed leadership ... 186

Chapter 13: The Law of Promotion ... 189
When the unexpected dominates ... 190
Advancing without a script ... 192
Your beliefs are your message ... 193
Overcoming the Law of Convention, Part II ... 196
Building passion into a disruptive idea ... 197
Convince others by convincing yourself ... 198

Chapter 14: The Law of Experience ... 201
Andy Grove was right ... 203
Protecting a disruptive idea ... 204

Debt: the not-so-silent killer	206
What is business wisdom?	207
Constructive pessimism attracts capital	209
Chapter 15: The Law of Accretion	**213**
Simple solutions require complex thinking	214
The design process for our solutions	215
Real-time software development	217
Scale is everything	220
Lots of little adds up to a lot	222
Chapter 16: The Law of Automation	**225**
Identifying pain	226
Humans should be thinking	227
Putting process under a magnifying glass	231
Revolutionizing your customer's supply chain	233
Creating an automated business from start-up	235
Chapter 17: The Law of Privilege	**239**
The simple lessons	242
Understanding what the business needs	243
What you'll be asked by investors	245
The baby steps of funding a business	247
The funding models for our technology businesses	249
The value of a convertible	252
Chapter 18: The Law of Risk	**255**
Parting the Red Sea	268
Selected Bibliography	**271**
Endnotes	**275**
Index	**279**

Acknowledgments

You have to pick a strategy when acknowledging those who have helped your cause or in some way touched your life. You have so little space and so many to thank. The process is much the same as an actor who gets on stage at the Academy Awards knowing that the orchestra is going to begin within 30 seconds telling him that he is out of time. My strategy is to highlight with words only a small sample of those to whom I owe undying gratitude and to hopefully cover the rest throughout my life with actions.

I first want to thank my wife and kids for putting up with me not only as I wrote this book but in general. There is a mad-scientist nature to those who endeavor to build something that does not exist, and the real medal belongs to my wife who has been my partner and soul mate for the past twelve years.

I also want to thank the rest of my immediate family: my parents (Bill and Sandy) and my brother and sister (Steve and Jodi). I have been molded for 38 years by not only their unwavering support and unending guidance, but also their infinite love, and for that I am both eternally grateful and forever in their debt.

I want to thank Brad Keywell, my business partner and trusted kinsman. Brad and I have been on a roller coaster ride since the day we joined forces and I can honestly say there is no one on earth I would have rather had by my side through it all.

I want to thank Scott Frisoni, Nick Galassi and Orazio Buzza—three of the finest operators I have ever seen in action.

I want to thank Rich Heise and Barry Friedland who have believed in me and our work from the beginning.

I want to thank John Walter for being the consummate Chairman, in business and in life.

I want to thank a few of our managers: Steve Zuccarini and Eric Belcher from InnerWorkings, Doug Waggoner and Vip Sandhir from Echo, Vlad Karpel and Anne Marie Checcone from MediaBank and Andrew Mason from ThePoint.com.

I want to thank several of our Directors for their time and effort: Jack Greenberg, Sam Skinner, Lou Sussman, Peter Barris, Betsy Holden, Linda Wolf, Dipak Jain, Harry Weller, Sharyar Barardan and Tony Bobulinski.

To Pat Garrison and Mark Desky who both have carried more water than they were supposed to in terms of my class, this book and my everyday life.

To those who have always supported me: Sarah Adelman, Esther Bernstein, Bernie Bernstein, Kevin Neff, Melanie Lefkofsky, Andy Sommers and Gabe Karp.

To those whose work was invaluable to the creation of this book: Lisa Holton, Bob Saldeen (a great technology pioneer), Sheila Saldeen, Steve Polacek, Kate Rockwood, Luz Lopez and Lisa Liddy.

And finally, I want to thank the nearly 900 people who make up InnerWorkings, Echo, MediaBank and ThePoint. Your hard work, dedication and passion are the driving force behind all our accomplishments and I am both amazed and honored to work with such a talented group of folks.

Strange is our situation here upon Earth. Each of us comes for a short visit, not knowing why, yet sometimes seeming to divine a purpose. From the standpoint of daily life, however, there is one thing we do know: that we are here for the sake of each other, above all, for those upon whose smile and well-being our happiness depends, and also for the countless souls with whose fate we are connected by a bond of sympathy. Many times a day I realize how my own outer and inner life is built upon the labor of others, both living and dead, and how earnestly I must exert myself in order to give in return as much as I have received and am still receiving.

—Albert Einstein

* One hundred percent of the proceeds from the sale of this book will be donated to Children's Memorial Hospital of Chicago, a place where kids come first and where a small cadre of people still believe that they can make the world a better place one healthy child at a time.

Introduction

Every day, we see evidence of a world that's changing faster than we can imagine, faster than any historical precedent: [1]

- ✔ Last year, human beings produced more transistors (and at a lower cost) than they did grains of rice.

- ✔ There were 108 million websites in 2006 delivering nearly 30 billion pages on the World Wide Web.

- ✔ In the last 10 years we have delivered nearly 50,000 exabytes of disk storage into the market. An exabyte is a billion gigabytes. Five exabytes would be enough to store all human speech since the dawn of time.

- ✔ In 1993, there were fewer than 300 users of the World Wide Web. Today, the Web is growing exponentially to a current level of 1.1 billion users worldwide.

- ✔ It is estimated that 100 new Internet users are added every minute.

- ✔ According to the U.S. Department of Labor, the top 10 jobs that will be in demand in 2010 were nonexistent in 2004, meaning we are now preparing students for jobs that don't exist with technologies that haven't yet been invented.

- ✔ One out of every eight couples married in 2006 in the United States met online.

✔ The number of text messages sent and received each day exceeds the population of the entire planet.

This is a book about innovation in a rapidly changing environment where business models can disrupt entire industries in a matter of years or months or days. It's about taking a longstanding, predictably profitable and conventionally accepted way of doing business and re-engineering it in a manner that seems counterintuitive to most people and then reassembling the best working parts to redefine an industry.

It's about Accelerated Disruption.

The companies we've founded are living, breathing evidence of these principles. Here, you'll see an in-depth view of four companies that are revolutionizing some of the oldest industries and practices in America—printing, transportation, media buying and activism. Industries evolve in increasingly shorter time spans and as we'll explain, today's hot idea may end up morphing or dying in a remarkably compressed period of time.

The four companies (InnerWorkings, Echo Global Logistics, MediaBank and ThePoint.com) which we'll discuss in detail throughout the book are growing at exponential rates as they convert old-industry customers into enthusiastic early adopters of unique systems and models we've developed and deployed. But in our experience, not even the most revolutionary of ideas is safe and that's why today's innovative companies have a shockingly short shelf life without planned evolution. We watch great ideas fail because management fails to break down its core business into its most fundamental elements and value drivers on a regular basis.

Racecar drivers are constantly tearing apart and rebuilding their engines for maximum performance. Today's successful business models require that same ongoing vigilance for latent defects or emerging opportunities.

We realize that *our* businesses will ultimately fail if we lose sight of this.

Accelerated Disruption is not only the initial act of breaking and rebuilding dated business models, but acquiring the skills, perspective and instinct necessary to do it on a daily basis as business opportunities, technology and customer needs evolve.

What does it mean to disrupt a business?

Disruption means to send something into disorder. In business processes even a generation ago, that would have meant something terrible. Today, disruption is the primary tool that can keep a company in a constant and necessary state of reinvention and growth. Accelerated Disruption means that you are managing change; change isn't managing you.

Disruptive technologies have been around as long as markets have been open to free trade. Innovation is often the end result of new methodologies and technologies as they gain acceptance in an industry. Accelerated Disruption is the state in which this process occurs in compressed time due to the rapid deployment of market-changing technologies. It's about understanding what speed and velocity can mean to a business concept as technology pervades all of its functions.

We've entered an age in which technological innovation has moved beyond the newest product launch to the revolutionizing and re-engineering of the entire ecosystem in which particular businesses reside.

Historically, technological innovations have been used to wreak havoc in new products that were introduced into the manufacturing sector. But today, technological advancement is increasingly affecting the service industry that now makes up a majority of the U.S. economy.

A June 2007 piece in *BusinessWeek* put the transition this way:

> When most of us think of innovation, user-friendly products such as the sleek iPod come to mind. But leading companies, innovation consultants and academic researchers are shifting their focus from products to services. Service employment is booming: Thanks to increased demand for services and the

difficulty of automating tasks, service industries are projected to account for most U.S. job growth between 2004 and 2014, generating almost 19 million new jobs.[2]

Traditional service-oriented business models evolve over decades or centuries, often taking on the characteristics of the local, regional or national culture in which they're incubated. They're typically antiquated and slow to react to the changing dynamics that technology and automation force upon their environment. As the service component of our economy has grown, for many companies, the ship has become harder to steer from its current course—a bit like turning a large vessel.

The evolution of technology, aided by the Internet and the digital universe in which we now reside, is creating an opportunity to build systems that can and will fundamentally change the basic mechanics of many service-oriented business models. This will have a profound effect upon our entire economy. A technological leap in how a tennis racket is manufactured, for example, is great, but in the end, it might only produce a faster serve for a small number of skilled players. But when you begin to radically enhance basic services, from insurance to banking to health care, the effect is far more profound.

We are witnessing the convergence of two powerful and typically opposite market forces—service and automation. Service moving slow and automation moving fast has created tension and instability in many markets that can be exploited as companies find ways to deliver new value using new tools. This phenomenon can be seen at work as we examine InnerWorkings, Echo, MediaBank, and ThePoint.com, the disruptive models we founded in older, traditional service industries.

Our work

To introduce myself, I'm president of Blue Media, LLC, a Chicago-based private equity and consulting firm focused on applying technology to service-oriented business models. The best way to describe what I do is to describe what I don't do. There's a classic scene in the John Cusack film *Say Anything* where he says, "I don't want to sell anything, buy anything or process anything as a career. I don't want to sell anything bought or processed or buy anything sold or processed or process anything sold, bought or processed or repair anything sold, bought or processed."

In my first decade at work, I had the opportunity to touch many different industries: retail, distribution, manufacturing and real estate. Fortunately or unfortunately, I realized I wasn't cut out for any of them and came to focus on service-oriented businesses that could be radically improved by technology.

I came to the conclusion long ago that I wanted to focus on businesses where you could literally celebrate EBITDA (Earnings Before Interest, Taxes, Depreciation and Amortization) at the point of revenue generation—which basically means that once you get the order, you can count your money. Given my experience in helping launch InnerWorkings, Echo and MediaBank, I now focus my limited technological attention span on hybrid business models that are half driven by people and half driven by technology.

As I mentioned, I have played a role in founding and nurturing many businesses. Some have been wildly successful and others have failed, leading up to our present portfolio. Here's a more detailed look at what they do:

InnerWorkings Inc. (www.iwprint.com) provides print procurement services to more than 2,000 corporate clients in the United States—without owning or operating a single printing press. The software and database system allows them to store, analyze and track the production capabilities of more then 6,000 suppliers in their network. They store quote and price data for each bid they receive and print job they execute. InnerWorkings was founded in September of 2001, went public on the NASDAQ in August 2006 and is currently trading under the symbol INWK. As an aside, throughout this book I'll refer to InnerWorkings in the third person due to the fact that I am no longer involved in the day-to-day operations of the company. I want to be clear that my insights are about their past or are from the outside looking in.

Echo Global Logistics, Inc. (www.echo.com) solves a critical supply-and-demand imbalance in the transportation industry—finding the best and most economical transportation solution at the exact moment a customer needs it and a carrier has it. Echo was founded in February of 2005. We created it because we were spending too much money on shipping due to a market shortage of licensed truck drivers at the time. We found ourselves wondering whether we could develop a cost-effective solution to locate trucks going the way our shipments needed to go at any particular moment. Fortunately, my longtime business partner Brad Keywell had been thinking for some time about forming a technology-enabled logistics business. We decided to combine our original idea with Brad's and Echo was born, resulting in a proprietary online solution that matches client shipments to available shippers with real-time efficiency and proprietary market intelligence to optimize the market. Today, Echo employs over 300 people and is adding roughly 25 people a month to its talented and pioneering team.

MediaBank LLC (www.mbxg.com) is an electronic exchange, database and order management suite that automates the purchase and management of traditional and emerging advertising media. The problem that sparked its creation was that there was no single technological solution that could tell a customer what the best advertising prices were on all local, regional and national media at every moment in time and no automated order management system that integrated analog and digital media seamlessly. Media buying is still a people-centric industry, but we have built a revolutionary tool that we believe will forever alter that process. Our application is currently being used by several of the largest media procurement agencies in the world.

ThePoint.com is an online network of people working together to solve problems. While the Internet is full of people protesting various issues, in our opinion there's never been a specific online tool that allows various people of like minds, skills and agendas to come together and develop campaigns or solutions to problems of an economic, political, employment, social or corporate nature. ThePoint.com is an organizing engine for all that online frustration that we believe will get hundreds, thousands and even millions of people to go beyond complaining to unification and specific action on any issue.

These companies reflect our approach to innovation and the pace of change we see coming in all industries, not just the ones we're presently redefining. In the next 18 chapters, we'll present philosophies, thoughts and tactics that entrepreneurs and business leaders can use to establish new business models, recast their current operations and redefine entire marketplaces.

In a world evolving more rapidly by the second, we believe that companies will need every tool they can find to sustain advantage and maintain relevancy.

CHAPTER 1

The Law of Accelerated Disruption

Understanding the true speed of innovation

In the mid-fifteenth century, books were handmade and would cost as much as a house in town or a small farm. Books were so rare that the most precious books in a church's library were actually chained to the reading tables. But that was all about to change.

Johannes Gutenberg, born in 1398, had the idea to transform a wine press into a printing press by carving letters into a soft metal like bronze and then arranging them on a frame that could be pressed onto paper. The inventor's method of printing from movable type allowed for the first mass production of printed books, culminating in the production of the 42-line Bible, often referred to as the Gutenberg Bible.

Eventually, someone came up with the idea of forming the letters in steel so the metal wouldn't soften after multiple uses and smudge. Hundreds of years later, the printing press would become automated, first by hand crank and eventually by electricity. The lettering process would change again and again as well. In early days men with magnifying glasses would place letters with tweezers on a frame; later Linotype machines would place type onto those frames with a keystroke. Eventually, computers would replace dozens of workers along the food chain, not only automating the entire prepress process but advancing the printing press itself.

There have been hundreds of advancements to the printing process in the last 500 years and we expect it will continue to go through technological changes as more and more of the process is migrated to digital formats that continue to squeeze cost and time out of the process. But will the process itself be disrupted by technology? Retailers now sell nearly 5 million e-books annually in the United States and the industry is growing at nearly 40 percent a year—no printing press required. Even more staggering, China's e-book sales volume is over 10 million books annually.

Welcome to the Law of Accelerated Disruption.

Social and digital change are revolutionizing and reinventing industries at a pace unparalleled in our history.

With each passing year, businesses that were once leaders in their field find themselves paralyzed by the sheer speed of these developments. Technology is the cause of this change and businesses must manage and manipulate these accelerating conditions. To succeed, companies will have to do much more to embrace the ubiquitous computing world in which we live (which we'll talk more about in Chapter 2).

There is really no way to separate a revolutionary business concept from the technology needed to deliver it.

This is the essence of Accelerated Disruption. It is business disruption taking place at literally the speed of technology, which no longer doubles every two years—the old Moore's Law paradigm—but increases exponentially over time. Trying to measure the speed of technology is like trying to measure the velocity at which a ray of light travels across a room.

How fast is fast?

To put the pace of change in perspective, futurist and inventor Ray Kurzweil wrote in a 2001 article that society wouldn't experience 100 years of progress in the twenty-first century, but "more like 20,000 years of progress (at today's rate)."³ With advances in technology, the ever-increasing rate of power on computer chips alone, there will be "exponential growth in the rate of exponential growth." Further, he adds:

> Within a few decades, machine intelligence will surpass human intelligence, leading to the Singularity—technological change so rapid and profound it represents a rupture in the fabric of human history. The implications include the merger of biological and non-biological intelligence, immortal software-based humans and ultra-high levels of intelligence that expand outward in the universe at the speed of light.

Kurzweil writes that the first technological steps—sharp edges, fire, and the wheel—took tens of thousands of years and in fact it took until 1000 A.D. for things to start speeding up noticeably. By then, "progress was much faster and a paradigm shift required only a century or two." In the nineteenth century, the world saw more technological change than in the nine centuries preceding it. "Then in the first 20 years of the twentieth century, we saw more advancement than in all of the nineteenth century. Now, paradigm shifts occur in only a few years' time." The following chart illustrates that pace and ends with the advancement of the Internet, circa 2001:

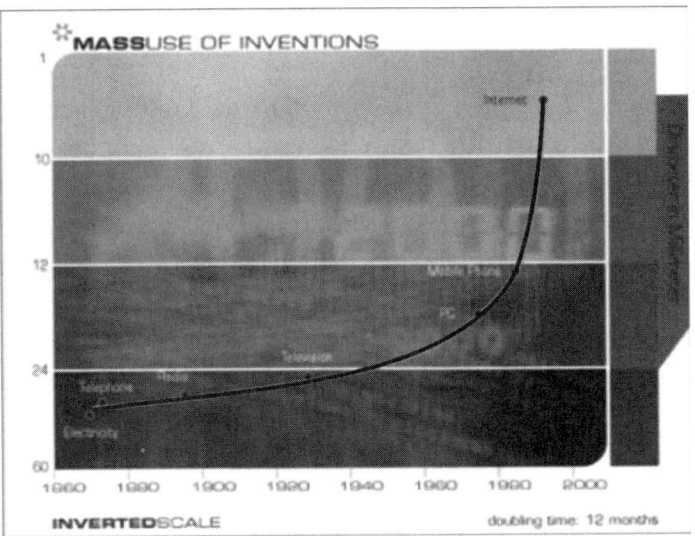

Fig. 1.1: The Mass Use of Inventions
[SOURCE: Raymond Kurzweil, The Law of Accelerating Returns, 2001]

Whether you accept Kurzweil's worldview or not, we believe all entrepreneurs and business leaders need to accept one key tenet of his hypothesis—that technology is changing and developing far faster than we can presently imagine and those advances will open a constant array of business opportunities that emerge, develop and hopefully evolve based on how you identify the smartest uses of technology within a given market.

One person can now create an entire company, launch it, come up with a brand identity program, make business cards, find a factory on the Web, build a website from an online template and launch a business within weeks for maybe a few hundred dollars. Only five years ago, that process would have taken months and cost considerably more. In the next few years, that process will take days and at some point in the not-so-distant future, possibly minutes. All thanks to the advancing speed of technology solutions.

Disruptive technology

Astronomer Carl Sagan, in his book *Billions and Billions,* said: "The prediction I can make with the highest confidence is the most amazing discoveries will be the ones we are not today wise enough to foresee."

Ten years ago, the term *Disruptive Technology* made its first appearance in *The Innovator's Dilemma,* a book by Harvard University business professor Clayton M. Christensen. Christensen wrote that disruptive business models based on technology—even technologies that are inexpensive and unoriginal—could work their way under the radar screen of established industries and disrupt them partially or completely in a very compressed time period.

In an overview of disruptive growth businesses, Christensen described disruptive innovations this way:

> Disruptive innovations either create new markets or reshape existing markets by delivering relatively simple, convenient, low-cost innovations to a set of customers who are ignored by industry leaders.[4]

When Christensen coined that term in 1997, the dot-com boom was still in relative infancy and nearly every late twentieth-century industry seemed poised for disruption. The Internet pioneer Netscape had gone public only two years before and the futuristic discussion at that moment centered on how Netscape would be the new Microsoft, essentially making traditional software manufacturers obsolete.

Not every disruptive idea worked as predicted back then or now—in fact, disruptive thinking is sometimes wildly off-target. It's fairly common for a disruptive idea to overshoot or undershoot a market before an entrepreneur or business leader eventually finds the right path.

But every disruptive idea makes its mark in some way. Microsoft today is very much alive, but it is a much different company than it was in 1997. Netscape still exists in a modified version, as its roots have made their way into Mozilla which created Firefox. But today, the word is Google.

But will the word be Google two years from now? Five? Ten?

By building and/or adopting technology solutions that are designed to re-engineer an existing business process, the very framework of that process can be disrupted, revolutionized and then exploited. Disruption creates *arbitrage* in the marketplace that allows a new business to scale at a greater rate than the rest of its competitors and achieve operational efficiency that can be used as a beacon to attract and retain employees, suppliers and clients.

What makes a business process disruptive?

Despite the success and growth of the companies we've started, we haven't invented new industries. We didn't have to. We simply took existing processes and asked, "If we could infuse technology into the established marketplace, could we produce an outcome that is materially better than what exists today?" We believe in great new ideas, no question, but we believe that short of a truly revolutionary concept or proprietary mathematical algorithm, most great business ideas are around in some fragmented sense; all you have to do is recognize how to use technology to build something better out of those fragments.

InnerWorkings, Echo and MediaBank are businesses that deliver the same end products to customers as their more established competitors do: printed materials, transportation services and tools for media buying, respectively. But what differentiates each is technology that finds excess capacity or pricing advantages in their respective and deeply fragmented markets, while offering customers exponentially more information on their strategy and total spending.

This technology and the information it provides was the missing formula of the value equation in each of those marketplaces. Customers needed this data desperately, whether they realized it at the time or not.

Actually, that's a point worth a quick pause. Need is a critical concept in this book (and we'll be focusing on it in Chapter 3) because as technology accelerates, businesses need to stop asking, "What do our customers need right now?" and start asking, "What will our customers need one year, three years or five years from now based on what emerging technologies can or will deliver?"

Need is a far less useful measurement when seen only through a present tense lens. It must become anticipatory, even clairvoyant.

For example, look at an industry in one of the most high-profile current states of disruption: The recording industry.

Back in 1999, the highly profitable recording industry could count on CD sales at a significantly higher price point than the predecessor vinyl albums brought in during their heyday. Granted, the entire industry pumped significant promotional dollars into the music video industry, but the result was exponential returns in CD sales and concert revenue from that joint investment in onscreen exposure.

Enter an obscure website called Roxio, which later changed its name to Napster. At the time, the music file-sharing community was thought of as little more than a bunch of teenage pirates downloading music and swapping it online—until the rapidly expanding community of Internet users (including people well beyond their teen years) discovered file sharing as well. The number of music download sites exploded with names like Kazaa, Gnutella, LimeWire and many others entering and exiting the fray.

The music industry had not anticipated the customer need that would be met by the ability to capture music online, one free song at a time. Since then, the music industry has averaged sales losses in the neighborhood of 20 percent annually.[5]

And despite Apple coming to the rescue with the creation of iTunes and its pay-per-song concept in 2003, between 2003 and 2005 alone, traditional record store closings averaged 550 a year. The Recording Industry Association of America continues to protest loudly about the measures it's taking to thwart the wide sweeping changes in the industry. But with the lights dimming, this industry is now a stark example of the disruptive power of technology and the accelerated pace of its adoption.

Perhaps you have your favorite tunes playing on your iPod while reading this. If so, you're in direct personal contact with one of the most striking business cases in recent history that underscores how technology ignorance—or avoidance—can sink an entire industry.

What we've learned

In each of the industries our companies have entered, we have made the most opaque and accepted parts of those businesses transparent and more cost-effective for the customer—an idea both simple and pioneering. We couldn't have done it without adopting the latest technology at every stage.

However, to break in, we didn't spend a lot of money in relative terms on technology or process by design. At InnerWorkings, Echo and MediaBank, we built our early technology application by modifying off-the-shelf rapid application software tools (FileMaker Pro, etc.) while letting our customers advise us on what was working and not working with those solutions during our earliest days of operation.

Once we got to the point where we had the best working model for our customers, we invested more dollars in scalable, secure and highly customized technology. We let our customers do our most cost-intensive R&D for us while we were building our revenues and business. In most high-growth businesses, there tends to be heavy technology spending before the first sale is ever made, a practice that we try at all costs to avoid.

Questioning conventional practices in something as fundamental as software development is just one aspect of what we believe makes a successful disruptive business succeed. It's not just about the idea—it's how you manage the idea and bring it to life.

Every business we've launched shares these common attributes:

1. A fragmented industry with hundreds, sometimes thousands of companies providing services.
2. The opportunity to unearth and collect proprietary information not typically available in a particular market that can be used to create advantage for the customer and arbitrage for us.
3. Unprecedented transparency into each stage of the customer's order from bid to fulfillment.
4. A hybrid of automated and human processes that make our businesses both profitable and flexible.

We will touch on these attributes in greater detail throughout the book. While this list is not comprehensive, it does serve as a foundation of characteristics to look for inside a market that is ripe for disruption.

Technology and timing

Back in 1999, literally the last surreal days of the Internet boom, my partners and I wrote a business plan for our first technology endeavor called Starbelly.com. Between 1993 and 1998, we had been in the licensed apparel business—embroidered and screen-printed clothing—and there we learned quite a bit about putting print or artwork on pretty much anything you could put print or artwork on. That led us into the promotional products business, where you do the same thing on products such as a mug, a pen or a golf ball for anyone looking to promote their brand. At that time, the promotional products industry was largely a catalog and door-to-door salesman kind of business—very people-intensive, very old-fashioned.

As the Internet grew and online retailing began taking its first serious steps, we began thinking about migrating the promotional business online. What would happen if customers could see the best-selling printed mugs, caps, polo shirts or pens online so they could bulk-order products directly from the manufacturer without going through a sales representative or distributor? We could reduce the reliance on a sales force, increase sales volume through an edited selection of key products and there it was—an opportunity to re-engineer an entire industry via the Web.

That's how Starbelly.com was born, named for a Dr. Seuss book where the main characters, the Sneetches, were constantly trying to one-up their neighbors by adding and then removing stars on their bellies.

We assembled a small team and began building the site and instantaneously, we were in the middle of the Internet frenzy. We wrote Starbelly's business plan in March of 1999 and the company got funded by May of that year at an enterprise valuation of $10 million. Looking back now, the number seems almost incalculable for a business that was less than two months old. But it was a real reflection of the times.

Over the next few months, we achieved several milestones. We hired a bunch of people and began building up the technology and then we received our second round of financing in July, three months after our first round of financing, from Chase Capital Partners and Flatiron Partners. They put money into our business valuing Starbelly at $40 million. In those days, the accepted norm (and we'll be talking a lot about accepted norms in Chapter 4) was to reach for the stars, designing technology applications and models that if fully deployed would completely re-engineer an entire market. We were hiring the best of the best, at a rate of two or three developers a day. Money was no object because at that time the most abundant resource was capital in search of good technology investments.

By December of that same year, only 10 months after we typed the first word of the business plan, we had reached an agreement to sell the business for $240 million in cash and stock to a public company, Halo Industries.

By the following April, the NASDAQ imploded. Technology models went from being red hot to ice cold and Halo was left with a technology business that would have required tens of millions of dollars to complete. Yet by then, the capital markets had caught the last train to the coast and capital was no longer plentiful. To make matters worse, Halo itself was a failed roll-up of over 30 companies and Halo had seen its own stock price drop from a high of over $30 per share to around $5 per share months before they announced the acquisition of Starbelly. Since Halo had its own problems to worry about, the timing of the acquisition turned out to be disastrous.

There were many lessons learned from that experience, but among the most lasting was an understanding of what I'll call hybrid technology models—businesses that are really half people and half technology solving critical structural problems within existing industries while considerably lowering the overall cost of doing business.

You see, when you have a process that is either complex or esoteric in nature (like promotional products), it is very difficult for technology alone to automate what humans do—at least using the technology that is out there at the moment this book goes to press. Instead of fighting this reality as many companies do, we now embrace it, something we didn't do back in the days of Starbelly. We now construct technology applications that are not only dependent on human involvement, but actually enhanced by that involvement. In other words, if you remove people, the technology is useless and if you remove the technology, the people are useless. The solution only works when both are connected in a symbiotic manner. We have developed an expertise at applying technology to service-oriented problems at critical moments of need. Identifying and executing solutions for those needs has become a key component of our success, as we'll highlight in greater detail throughout the book.

A revolution isn't enough—there must be evolution

Accelerated Disruption is at the center of the long-term viability of any business that has broken the mold and revolutionized its chosen industry. It may be a struggle to remember the many iconic names from the 1990s and even the more recent past now buried in the corporate graveyard. But most of them disappeared for a simple reason: They didn't understand the inertia of disruption. In other words, the forces of acceleration overtook them.

Clayton Christensen describes six lessons that help managers and entrepreneurs understand disruption:

1. *Disruptive innovations spur growth.* As Christensen says, companies "have two basic options when they seek to build new-growth businesses. They can try to take an existing market from an entrenched competitor with *sustaining* innovations. Or they can try to take on a competitor with disruptive innovations that either create new markets or take root among an incumbent's worst customers." Disruption gets his vote.

2. *Disruptive businesses either create new markets or take the low end of an established market.* Christensen points to the early days of the transistor and minimill industries as technology innovations that secured a small end of the market (radios and teen Baby Boomers; lower-end steel production) before redefining all the products in their industry.

3. *Disruptive opportunities require a separate business-planning process.* "All innovative ideas start out as half-baked propositions," Christensen says. They then go through a major metamorphosis as they reach senior management. "When firms have a single process for all the various forms of innovation, what comes out the other end of the process looks like what has been approved in the past and it all looks like sustaining innovations."

4. *Don't try to change your customers—help them.* Christensen identifies "faulty market segmentation schemes" as a way to explain the stunningly high rate of failure in new-product

development. Most companies define markets in terms of product categories and demographics. We just don't live our lives in product categories or in demographics. When companies segment markets this way they often fail to connect with their customers.

5. *Integrate across whatever is not good enough.* Firms have to decide when creating an innovation-driven growth business, what its optimal scope is. In other words, what activities can be managed internally and what can be safely outsourced?

6. *Be patient for growth but impatient for profitability.* "Managers inside new-growth businesses often feel tremendous pressure to quickly ramp up sales volume. But disruptive businesses can't get big very fast. The only way to make them grow quickly is to cram them into large, obvious markets...As long as their core businesses are growing healthily, companies will find it easier to wait for the disruptive businesses to find a foothold market and slowly build commercial mass."[6]

These are just thoughts to consider. While the book is filled with dozens more, in the end, there is no secret formula or prophetic wisdom that one can follow to launch a disruptive business model in today's technology-driven environment. But you can obtain tools that will assist you in the process.

The Disruption All-Stars

Most of the following are company names you know. They are businesses that revolutionized the industries they're in largely due to the technology decisions they made to support their internal operations or their customer experience or both. Each company below mastered the lessons Christenson described above.

Apple Computer: Remember the Newton? Fortunately, Apple has never forgotten the significance of single-handedly creating, then losing, the entire market for personal digital assistants (PDAs). The year was 1993 and Apple would keep the Newton on the market for six years while criticism swirled about its price (over $1,000) and larger-than-pocket size. Ironically, Steve Jobs killed the Newton in 1997 when he returned to the company he founded 20 years earlier. Since then, Apple has scored with the omnipresent iPod, a device that some might imagine the Newton may have become had it lived. At this writing, the company had just entered the wireless communications business with the iPhone, another iteration of the iPod and by extension, the Newton.

Of course, you can't stop there. As we mentioned above, Apple has actually managed to disrupt an industry that's still in the process of disruption with the creation of iTunes. Mingling hardware (the iPod) with pure technology (the iTunes Store, an online music, video and podcast retail outlet) Apple has not only provided the gadgetry to fuel innovation, it has defined a market in its own image and managed to create a successful business out of a dwindling revenue stream in a market it had never operated in before—the entertainment industry.

Wal-Mart: In 45 years, Wal-Mart has redefined the balance of power between traditional discount stores and their suppliers. Before the ascent of Wal-Mart, manufacturers held the keys to the kingdom, setting strict parameters on price, promotion and distribution. Wal-Mart reversed the established norm by flatly refusing to stock merchandise above its price targets for those goods. To make its case, Wal-Mart was an early adapter of state-of-the art information technologies that closely monitored customer behavior and product movement and it used that data to bring suppliers to heel. The information that Wal-Mart would share with its suppliers would eventually change their manufacturing practices and many of their product lines. And as customers responded favorably, Wal-Mart pressed its suppliers harder. And the cycle continued.

While Sears, Roebuck and Montgomery Ward had more than a century to hone their leadership positions, Wal-Mart was able to reach No. 1 in 28 years.

Though Wal-Mart is now facing competitive obstacles that come with the reality of being the largest target in the world, its ascension to No. 1 in 1990 is a classic case of business disruption on the largest scale possible—disruption across not one major industry, but in nearly every industry it touched.

Southwest Airlines: In the 1970s, Southwest Airlines' founders took the model of the successful airline and turned it on its head. At that point in the industry's history, airline travel was an upscale activity with profit centers based on expensive transcontinental routes such as New York to Los Angeles or Chicago to Washington, arriving at the top airports in those cities. Major airports left behind smaller, secondary terminals in favor of size and scale. Southwest focused on those orphaned locations for landing rights, realizing that value-minded customers wouldn't mind flying out of an uncongested airport as long as the price was right.

Today, Southwest is the nation's largest domestic air carrier. It has definitely made the skies egalitarian—too egalitarian, some might say—but it has also taken ownership of the latest innovations in efficient aviation, including the use of the Internet to drive revenue and customer convenience.

BlackBerry: The Canadian company Research in Motion (RIM) introduced the wireless handheld device in 1999 and between 2004 and early 2007, the service went from 2 million subscribers to 8 million. While concentrating first on ubiquitous, real-time e-mail access through any wireless network in most countries around the world, the device gathered a messianic following from its earliest days—leading many to refer to the addictive product as "Crackberry." Since then, the BlackBerry has added mobile telephone capability, text messaging, Internet faxing, Web browsing and many other wireless features in addition to traditional PDA applications like address book, calendar and to-do lists.

Why was the BlackBerry disruptive? In its earliest days, most cell phones didn't have e-mail access and most PDAs didn't have the widespread e-mail or phone access the BlackBerry had from the start. During the week following the attacks of September 11, 2001, news reports said BlackBerry customers were among the few with consistent phone and e-mail access during the tragedy and the days following.

Like the other companies mentioned here, BlackBerry has seen other competitors flood the zone where it established its truly disruptive formula. Yet its main goal is to continually offer best-of-breed technology to its true believers to keep those true believers recruiting converts.

James Burke in a passage from *Connections* describes the pace of innovation:

> The moment man first picked up a stone or a branch to use as a tool, he altered irrevocably the balance between him and his environment…While the number of these tools remained small, their effect took a long time to spread and to cause change. But as they increased, so did their effects: the more the tools, the faster the rate of change." 7

When you look at companies like Apple and BlackBerry, it is clear that we are living the effects of this change today.

SUMMARY:

Accelerated Disruption is the future of business innovation—it means that managers and entrepreneurs will have to learn to innovate at the anticipated pace of technology so their own leadership positions won't be disrupted by others.

NEXT CHAPTER: The Law of Ubiquity describes a world where virtually every aspect of our lives will be linked to a computer that we'll access effortlessly. In the next chapter, we'll examine how this passive, all-enveloping technology will influence successful business models in the years to come.

CHAPTER 2

The Law of Ubiquity

Our movement into a world submerged in data

Edwin Land was just a kid in the 1920s when he started experimenting with light. He was obsessed with kaleidoscopes and stereopticons (a predecessor of the modern motion picture camera). As he grew, his chosen area of study was light polarization: while normal light is made of waves that vibrate in various directions, polarized light is trained in a single direction. The manipulation of light and images became his life.

After dropping out of Harvard after one year to start a company with one of his teachers, Land would become a prolific inventor—his 533 patents are second only to Thomas Edison. He became an expert on military optics, manufacturing glare-controlling goggles, tank telescopes, gun sights and flight training machines—all items common to military and private industry today.

But it wasn't until 1943 when his three-year-old daughter Jennifer asked him why she couldn't see the picture he had just taken of her, that he stumbled upon the invention that would become synonymous with his name—instant photography. By 1948, the Polaroid Land Camera was on the market. Land had created film that was essentially its own darkroom, coated with chemicals that sprang into action once the film was exposed.

Granted, not many people are walking around with Polaroid cameras around their necks today, but instant photography is everywhere as virtually every cell phone today takes a digital picture that can be immediately sent around the world. Land created something bigger than film. He gave the world an insatiable desire for faster, sharper instant images for commercial purposes and certainly for fun. Had he not died in 1991, it's arguable that Land would have been part of the digital revolution that once again redefined his beloved territory of light and image.

For an invention to be universally adopted you need one part innovation and two parts desire—it starts with a great idea and takes off with insatiable demand in the market. Through technology, this process is often accelerated as the deployment of the innovation is more rapid and the effect it can have on the user is more extreme. Through technology, great ideas or products can achieve an omnipotent status in a short period of time.

Welcome to the Law of Ubiquity.

Some say that by 2013 a supercomputer will be built that exceeds the computational capabilities of the human brain and that 25 years after that milestone, an ordinary everyday computer will exceed the computational capabilities of the entire human race.

The Law of Ubiquity describes a future in which technology is so pervasive and advanced that its profound effects, while subtle, will usher in an era of unprecedented disruption within our markets.

Consider the following: [8]

- ✔ The worldwide Internet population in 2004 reached 934 million.

- ✔ It's estimated that a week's worth of today's *New York Times* contains more information than a person was likely to digest in a lifetime during the eighteenth century.

- ✔ Roughly 1.5 exabytes (that's 10 to the 18th power) of unique new information will be generated worldwide this year, more than was created in the past 5,000 years.

- ✔ The amount of purely technical information is doubling every two years. This means, of course, that by their junior year, most college students will have learned material that is already obsolete.

- ✔ Third-generation fiber optics have already been tested that push 10 trillion bits per second down a single strand of fiber—equal to 1,900 CDs or 150 million simultaneous phone calls every second.

And we haven't even begun talking about the implications of Web 2.0—the next generation of Web-based functionality that's already here—or what Web 3.0 or 4.0 could bring.

We have entered an era in which people can use wireless networks to connect computers, appliances, machines and almost any other device by using a mere mobile phone that can command our environment with a keystroke hundreds of miles away. Until recently, this kind of society existed only in people's dreams, but now it is about to become reality. As Chairman Yoshitoshi Kitajima described in Dai Nippon's annual report some years back, "the society we live in is gusting forward in a wave of change."

Traditional business models evolve over decades or centuries, often taking on the characteristics of the local, regional or national culture in which they're incubated. They are often slow to react to the changing dynamics that technology and automation force upon our environment.

As we said previously, the evolution of technology, the Internet and the digital universe is creating an opportunity to build systems that can and will fundamentally change the basic mechanics of many traditional business models. From insurance to banking to health care to brokerage and beyond, we are witnessing the convergence of two powerful and typically opposed market dynamics—service and automation.

Automation—becoming exponentially more powerful year by year—is a disruptive force with the potential to re-engineer any existing business process.

We briefly mentioned the concept of arbitrage in Chapter 1. Arbitrage in our definition is the discovery of hidden profitability—value— within an existing business process aided by technology-driven activities. Customers may pay less, get more or both through the operating efficiencies created by this particular application of technology. Automation fuels arbitrage in just about any business.

Service on the other hand has historically been removed from automation. You can't automate compassion or care or attentiveness. At least you can't in the year 2007.

Ubiquity begins at home

The average American household owns 25 consumer electronics products and spent an annual $1,200 on electronic devices based on early 2007 data.[9] The Consumer Electronics Association reports those numbers are up a full 25 percent from the previous year and rising at unprecedented levels.

For the moment, such devices—computers, televisions, digital recorders and cell phones—lead largely separate lives. But not for long.

Chances are you've already heard about convergence—the combination of voice, data and video applications onto a single network with devices increasingly built to handle these combined technologies. The classic example of technological convergence on the consumer level is the cell phone. Our mobile phones are not only becoming our primary verbal communication devices, they're handling our e-mail, our music, our appointments and contact lists. Increasingly, they're becoming our personal entertainment centers away from home, displaying our photographs and videos and allowing us to watch our favorite movies and TV shows.

As time goes on, convergence will reach us everywhere with devices so subtle we won't even notice them.

What we hold in our hands will eventually drive the structure of the businesses we operate, the businesses we work for and the businesses we choose to do business with. Convergence will be a tough habit to break.

It's a habit we are trying to feed at our own companies. With our online capabilities, we are planning for the day our applications move from the desktop to the handheld—or to the plasma TV in our customers' living rooms. Already, the connectivity of business has reached unprecedented heights with a keystroke and a wireless connection. This trend will not only continue, but will dramatically accelerate in the decades ahead.

The Law of Ubiquity will increasingly allow us to gather and dispatch information wherever, whenever and to whomever. Most of us believe we are completely surrounded by technology at this moment. The reality is that we haven't scratched the surface of what is to come.

As Bill Gates wrote, "In 2001, according to the Semiconductor Industry Association, the world microchip industry produced approximately 60,000 transistors for every man, woman and child on earth. That number is expected to rise to one billion by 2010."[10]

As technology becomes more ubiquitous, it will also fuel Accelerated Disruption.

Data drives disruption—and dollars

In the last chapter, we examined Ray Kurzweil's theory of the Singularity—the expectation that by mid-century we will see non-biological intelligence outrun the horsepower of the human brain. Kurzweil doesn't mean that human existence is going to go the way of *The Matrix,* but his theories suggest that unless entrepreneurs realize how fast the world is moving, they'll be left standing still.

Gordon Moore, a former chairman of Intel and one of the pioneers of integrated circuits, said in the mid-1970s that it was possible to add twice as many transistors on a chip every 24 months. And since electrons have less distance to travel, the circuits on that chip will run twice as fast, leading to an actual quadrupling of computational power. With faster chips comes more power to crunch data, each year, faster and faster, exponentially so. The number of transistors in a chip has increased from 29,000 in the 8086 microprocessor in 1978 to 7.5 million in the Pentium in 1998; the microprocessor's capability has grown ten-thousand-fold over the same 20-year period. This exponential improvement stems from Moore's Law.

According to Bill Gates, "To put Moore's Law in perspective, if products such as cars and cereal followed the same trend as the personal computer, a mid-sized car would cost $27 and a box of cereal would cost a penny."[11]

The companies we've founded are living, breathing examples of Moore's theory given the value that they derive from the proprietary data that they gather and store driving all of their operations. Each day, actually more like each minute, InnerWorkings, Echo and MediaBank collect and store pricing data that creates real-time value opportunities for their clients who buy printing, shipping and advertising around the world.

We are becoming smarter about these marketplaces and their particular advantages for our customers. As our suppliers respond to our constant need for real-time value for our customers, they are changing their own business models to meet that need. We believe we are forcing efficiencies and operational advancements on businesses in our supply chain that have never been forced to consider such advancements before.

If they don't join us, will they become obsolete? Maybe not. But they certainly won't have access to the new markets we can provide them at the touch of a keyboard.

Data is the currency that drives the growth of all of our businesses. As the tools available to us become more powerful and more ubiquitous with each passing day, our ability to collect, store and manipulate data increases. Of course, none of that means anything unless we are able to deliver superior customer service and products. But data is the primary engine that fuels these businesses.

Here's how we've used computational power to our advantage:

- ✔ At InnerWorkings, we gathered and used data to determine who had open capacity at a given moment in time by capturing millions of bits of price data that our suppliers sent to us every time they bid on a job. We were also constantly going into the market to determine which suppliers had optimal equipment profiles to be able to produce a given job. When specifications came in from a client, we matched those specifications against historical price data and current equipment data to help our buyers find the best suppliers in the market. This process is a perfect example of using data, actually vast farms of data, to influence a human decision and thereby producing a superior market outcome.

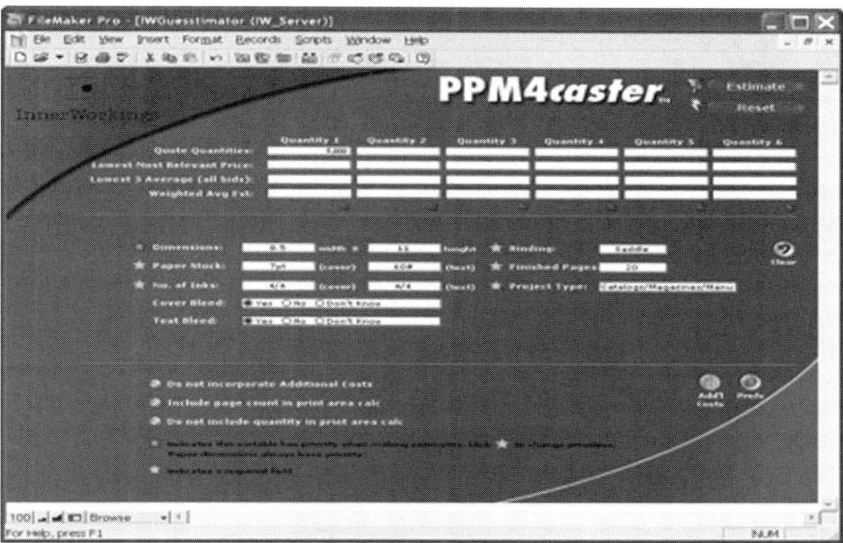

Fig. 2.1: An early version of InnerWorkings' "4caster" application

The above graphic shows our "4caster" module that allowed our staff to predict pricing for selected items by accessing our database of proprietary pricing data that we believed was the largest such database of independent printing knowledge in the United States.

✔ At Echo Global Logistics, we use data to determine where trucks, planes, trains and ocean liners are going, how much empty capacity they have and how economically they align to our current needs. Given the many opportunities we have to collect and post data for our shipping clients, we realize that making all aspects of the transportation process transparent is part of the value proposition that makes us unique in the marketplace. Our technology application helps us find the right carrier which is moving in the right direction at the right moment in time.

Our employees come from many of the nation's largest carriers, some of which helped create the tariffs that drive the pricing algorithms of the transportation industry. So in addition to data gathering, we consider the expertise we've drawn to our company a key factor in the insight and intelligence that Echo can offer to its clients.

Fig. 2.2: A historic version of Echo's Lane IQ technology that allows Echo to find open carrier capacity and match that capacity to a customer need.

Fig. 2.3: A historic version of Echo's Lane IQ technology at a later stage in the process where the system has now pinpointed the optimal carrier.

✔ At MediaBank, we offer media-buying and planning tools that streamline the data collection and order management of complex multimedia campaigns for global advertisers. MediaBank provides a secure forum that allows media buyers and planners to access data on nearly every conceivable form of media available in the market—from publications to direct mail lists, from online advertising to newspaper FSIs (Free Standing Inserts), from transit advertising to sponsorships, from place-based advertising to traditional outdoor. MediaBank provides an electronic exchange whereby advertisers are aligned to the most appropriate media in the market to achieve optimal buying.

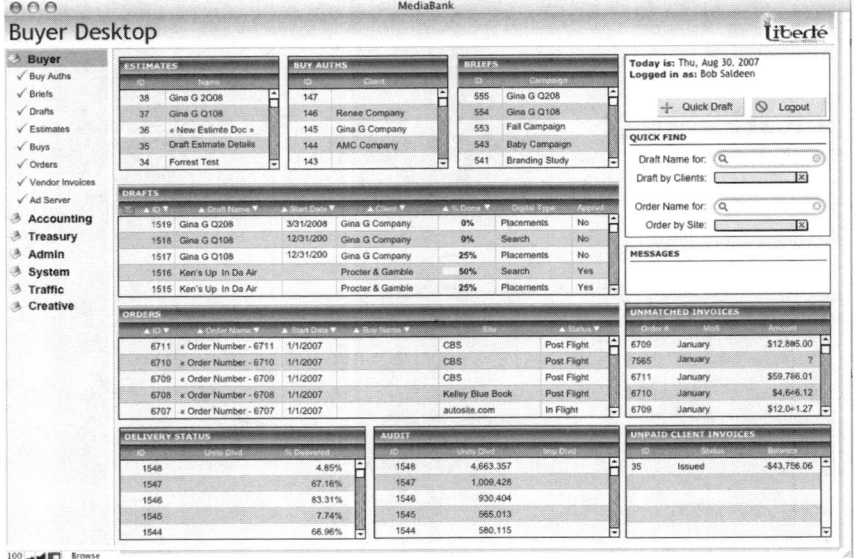

Fig. 2.4: MediaBank's first iteration of its digital module home page whereby digital media can be purchased through a system that is integrated with analog media.

How will today's industry leaders destroy themselves?

Google has monetized the concept of search in ways no one could have anticipated 10 years ago or for that matter, three years ago. It continues to evolve. Yet even Google has kinks to work out of its system. For instance, a search of the word "Saturn" will give you results for a car, a planet or a dozen other locations of various meanings.

So, despite the magnificence of Google, it is still deeply flawed by Kurzweil's mid-twenty-first-century standards. It returns lists that are too large and must be culled by ever-more specific keystrokes. That's fine for our present nation of grateful Americans who are just happy not to have to get in the car and head to the library. But will it satisfy us five years from now? Perhaps the next Google frontier is voice recognition? Beyond that, maybe thought recognition? Or, is it possible the next Google is being developed right now in the form of a better mathematical matching algorithm that will render Google obsolete over time—the digital equivalent of a better mousetrap displacing the current unassailable force in the marketplace?

One thing is certain. How Google will choreograph its own accelerated destruction will be one of the most-watched events in the business and consumer universe.

As we've stated, ubiquitous technology doesn't need to mean forced obsolescence unless a company or business owner decides to stand still. For example, people like to go to the movies because they like the idea of going out, having some popcorn and getting the big-screen experience. Yet today with so many entertainment alternatives such as DVDs, TiVo and movie downloading, movie theaters are under pressure to go digital, eliminating the projection of film entirely. Many have worried that the conversion to digital will put exhibitors out of business because they can't afford first-generation digital projection. But as we already know, technology always gets cheaper as it matures and a digital philosophy could conceivably take exhibitors in unforeseen new directions.

Already, exhibitor-sponsored businesses like Fandango provide valuable data that goes beyond filling seats. Increasingly, exhibitors know exactly who's filling those seats, what they want to see and what they're willing to spend. Yet they've only begun to harness the potential of that technology for themselves.

We're obviously not in the entertainment industry, but why couldn't conversion to digital projection and efforts at improved audience tracking—right down to what they're buying in the snack line and when they're likeliest to catch a show—lead to more inventive programming that draws even more customers? For instance, digital feeds of classic movies on certain screens could turn a section of a multiplex into a revival house at key segments of the week when exhibitors know target audiences will show up. How will they know? They'll let their audiences tell them exactly what classic movies they'll support and what they're willing to pay to see them.

Customer-permitted exhibitor data could eventually be used for marketing purposes to other types of businesses—nearby restaurants, retailers and other businesses with a direct interest in what demographics are walking to and from that theater at various points in the day.

In the late 1970s and early 1980s, Hollywood shrieked that the videocassette recorder would kill its movie business. In fact, this example of ubiquity had the opposite effect. It opened up a revenue stream that's now essential to the industry. A June 2007 *Variety* report on the movie rental industry stated that studios typically expect a 15 to 20 percent return on each consumer dollar spent in the rental business, but will now capture 60 to 70 percent when films are more efficiently delivered over home cable systems.[12]

The lesson here? When companies sense an initial threat to their business from digital technology, they need to consider all the possible ways they can benefit from such adoption and how interlocking industries can benefit as well. In my opinion, movie theater owners need not fear the move to digital movie distribution in the home. People will always want to get out of the house every once in awhile for the experience of seeing a movie on the big screen. The question is how movie theater owners will use developing technology to find arbitrage and manage disruption in all segments of their operation.

Finding that tipping point

Ubiquitous computing (UC) is a term that describes an acceptance of computing in all its current and future forms. Today, we are nowhere near complete acceptance and usage of the Internet.

In our businesses, we are actively planning for the day when computing is not elective, but instinctive. A look at international figures of Internet usage shows the potential for global markets over time.

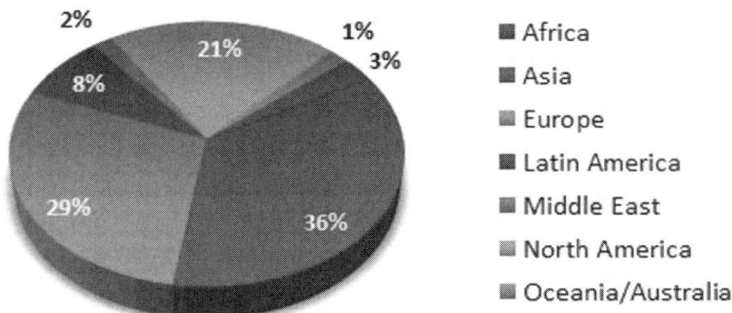

Fig. 2.5: Where Internet usage stands in 2007.

Gates puts it this way:

> In the digital age, "connectivity" takes on a broader meaning than simply putting two or more people in touch. The Internet creates a new universal space for information sharing, collaboration and commerce. It provides a new medium that takes the immediacy and spontaneity of technologies such as the TV and the phone and combines them with the depth and breadth inherent in paper communications. In addition, the ability to find information and match people with common interests is completely new. [13]

What ubiquitous technology really means

Experts consider ubiquitous computing the "third wave" of computing. The first wave consisted of mainframes, the room-sized computers that started the industry. The second wave was the personal computing era that began 30 years ago and then came the stage that Mark Weiser and John Seely Brown of the Xerox PARC laboratory called the "transitional" stage of the Internet[14] and distributed computing that has gotten people used to the idea of computerized power as a readily accessible tool no matter where they are.

Today, we're in the early stages of the era of ubiquitous computing or the age of *calm technology or third paradigm computing,* as some have called it. This stage represents technology that recedes into the background of our lives but is actually infinitely more powerful. "Calm" essentially means computers that are subtle, located every few inches, nearly invisible and yet omnipresent. As two PARC scientists wrote:

> Two harbingers of the coming UC era are found in the imbedded microprocessor and the Internet...They will be found in the alarm clocks, the microwave oven, the TV remote controls, the stereo and TV system, the kids' toys, etc. These do not yet qualify as UC for two reasons: they are mostly used one at a time and they are still masquerading as old-style devices like toasters and clocks. But network them together and they are an enabling technology for UC. Tie them to the Internet and now you have connected together millions of information sources with hundreds of information delivery systems in your house. Clocks that find out the correct time after a power failure, microwave ovens that download new recipes, kids' toys that are constantly updated with new software and vocabularies, paint that cleans off dust and notifies you of intruders, walls that selectively dampen sounds—these are just a few possibilities. [15]

When we look at our own businesses and the potential for future models we might create, this is the kind of change we're wrestling with. We need to go beyond the solutions current technology can bring about in today's fragmented marketplaces and see how those solutions will be delivered by next-generation technology.

We foresee the need to create technology solutions that not only respond but anticipate. The computers of the future will clearly give us more information, but in ways that are helpful, not intrusive. We think a day will come when, for example, InnerWorkings won't have to wait for a customer to instigate an order—they'll know when their supplies are running out or that some new printing option that's been devised can help them or that market forces have changed in such a way that their clients should react. At MediaBank, we'll be able to align a real-time media plan to instantaneous changes in consumer preferences and adjust our buys on a daily basis in ways that marketers can only dream about today. And at Echo we'll know where every truck in the U.S. is at every moment and be able to optimize supply in ways that are impossible today.

Does this mean human beings become secondary, overrun by machines that do all their thinking for them? Quite the opposite—human beings will be freed to do the planning, forecasting and innovating that they have little time for right now. And the scope of that thinking will increase parallel to the exponential power of the technology beneath them.

These are indeed exponential times.

Summary:

> *Markets are being disrupted at a pace that is unparalleled in our history. Even so, too many businesses find themselves trapped in an ever-expanding web of social and digital change and they are too paralyzed to adapt to the changing climate because the rate of change is so dramatic. Only with the aid of technology can a business both manage and manipulate these conditions. Those businesses that embrace the ubiquitous computing world that's now in its infancy should thrive in the coming years. Those that don't will find themselves disrupted and potentially obsolete.*

NEXT CHAPTER: The Law of Need explores our very human response to the difficulty of getting what we want. Sometimes consumers aren't consciously aware of this difficulty or pain, as we'll call it. But if a competitor is able to discover this pressure point before you do and a way to correct it, it could mean the end of your business.

Chapter 3

The Law of Need

Pain exists in almost every industry

At the turn of the twentieth century, IBM had developed "punched" card technology into a powerful tool for business data-processing. By 1950, the use of punch cards had become commonplace in industry and government, but this new process was incomprehensible to most of the public.

Yet the computer age had arrived, and there was an increasing need for instruction. Soon, computer science classes that involved punch cards became a major bane to science and engineering students in universities across the globe.

To set up a program, a student had to know how to produce and process a series of long manilla cards with holes punched in various locations in order to submit their programming assignments to the local campus computer center in the form of a stack of cards—one card per program line. Then they would have to wait for the program to go through the stages of processing, compilation and execution ("edit-file-run cycle"). In due course a printout of the results, marked with the submitter's identification, would be placed in an output tray outside the computer center. In many cases these results would be comprised solely of a printout of error messages regarding program syntax and a host of other problems, necessitating at least one, maybe several attempts to complete the cycle.

Physical factors also played a role in failures to successfully complete the cycle. Punch cards were sometimes entered in the wrong order, cards were missing, folded and mutilated and couldn't go through the computer. A familiar sight on many college campuses in the 1960s and '70s—especially on windy days—was a desperate student chasing down his or her punch cards as they swirled through the air out of reach.

This process was riddled with frustration and pain. Something had to be done.

Enter the microchip, which, combined with computers and software, has allowed virtually anyone to create or customize a program without so much as leaving the comfort of their own home.

Welcome to the Law of Need—when a process is so painful, it creates a world of opportunity to reduce the pain.

Tom Kuczmarski, a Chicago-based new products consultant, often gets credit for introducing the word "pain" into the product- and business-development lexicon.

Kuczmarski's concept of pain has to do with the environment in which new products are forced to evolve. Pain is something no one wants in any form and in the business world pain translates into inconvenience, added cost, missed opportunity and of course, obsolescence.

Pain is a bit like oxygen. It is hard to quantify, nearly invisible and yet essential to support growth and change. Without pain, there is nothing to disrupt. Just as there is no happy without sad, no good without evil, no dark without light—you need the contrast of dissatisfaction as a necessary catalyst to force change.

To alleviate pain in life, one looks for solutions. To alleviate pain in business, one has to look for solutions others might have missed or never searched for in the first place.

In a 2003 client survey, Kuczmarski reported that 85 percent of CEO respondents said conducting customer problem/need identification research prior to ideation is the most important driver of new product/service success in their organizations.

Without pain, there would be no real innovation. No one would be forced to deal with the misery that often accompanies the unknown. In fact, it is precisely this delicate balance of current pain versus reluctance to change that must be overcome in order for a business model to be truly disruptive, which we will cover in greater detail when we discuss the Law of Adoption in Chapter 7.

Spotting pain in existing industries

Our businesses wouldn't exist without pain. It is the first thing we look for when we seek to launch a new idea. It is the one essential ingredient for which there can be no compromise. Without pain, we do not proceed further. Again, we've focused on printing, transportation and media buying—all industries that have been around for quite a while. In fact, transportation and printing are two of the world's oldest industries, respectively dating back to the horse and buggy and Gutenberg's printing of the Bible.

The primary source of pain in these three industries is as follows:

InnerWorkings (Printing)

Back in 2001, the problem in the printing industry—as we saw it—was that buying print in the open market seemed incredibly inefficient. We started doing some research and we heard over and over again: "Typically I have three printers that I have been buying from for a while and every year I do my catalog and I give it to Bob or Sue and they send it out to these three printers and we get back bids and we've been using XYZ printing company for the last seven years and they do a great job and we love them and our catalog is so unique and specialized that we can't imagine ever using someone else."

You might ask, "Why mess with a service when customers are telling you point-blank they're happy with it?"

The answer lies in the identification of pain that comes with a closer examination of the force that underlies this process. While all of these customers said they were happy with the service they were receiving, they had hand-selected their printers so this was to be expected. As we dug deeper, it became clear to us, however, that many people higher up in the organization than those we initially spoke with were not happy at all and felt that they were overpaying for print. Among this group, absolutely no one told us, "I love my service and I don't care how much it costs." In fact, these people said, "I don't care who does my printing, I just know that we are spending tons of money on printing and I'm sure we can save money if we buy it more efficiently." In other words, the buyers were experiencing limited or no pain, but their bosses were experiencing significant pain.

Corporate America is always interested in ways of reducing costs and increasing profits as long as you offer it a process that's transparent, verifiable and easy to understand and adopt. In our research of the market, we found that customer satisfaction in the printing industry was based on a labor-intensive process that was not terribly well informed or automated.

We knew that most printing relationships were built on a single salesperson doing traditional face-to-face calls on a daily basis. On the other end sat a relatively inexperienced buyer who just wanted to get this job off his or her to-do list so they could move on to the next task or put out the next fire.

We smelled pain and inefficiency in that scenario and with experience you learn how to exploit it. In fact, pain can be transformed into pure potential for any company that masters its exploitation.

Given our past life in the promotional products and licensed apparel business, we knew there were lots of printers and a huge amount of excess supply when their presses weren't running. Printers don't like it when their presses aren't running—it means they're losing opportunity.

We believe that the printing industry is more commoditized today than at any moment in the past—there's much less art in it than there used to be. InnerWorkings' current chairman is John Walter, the former Chairman of RR Donnelley, the world's largest printer. John often points out that virtually anyone can buy a highly automated press, plug it in and begin printing with high quality nearly on the spot. Modern printing press technology has made just about anyone with commercial space and an electric outlet a potential printer. This, along with banks' increasing willingness to fund printing presses, has created excess supply in the market as there are now almost 40,000 printers in the United States alone.

Excess supply, fragmented buying, inefficient processes—these are the building blocks of pain. They are exactly the elements one should look for when trying to find a marketplace to re-engineer.

What our team didn't know when it launched InnerWorkings was whether or not we could produce the arbitrage we've been discussing. The existence of arbitrage lets you know that your solution is truly working and disrupting the existing paradigm. We didn't have that knowledge at the start, but we had a strong suspicion we'd confirm our expectations.

Any time that you are attempting to do something better, you can break your definition of "better" into lots of sub-categories. What does better truly mean? Better could mean faster. Better could mean more reliable. Better could mean more available. Better could mean cheaper. The easy one is cheaper because it's simple to measure and not as esoteric in nature.

As we developed InnerWorkings, we looked at the existing market and the technology available to us and asked a critical question: "If people were buying print for a dollar, could we buy it for 80¢ or 70¢ or 60¢ and actually provide an identical product, in every way, to the product they were currently getting from their existing suppliers?"

That spread, which may or may not exist in your concept, is arbitrage. Without it, you can't make money. What's made InnerWorkings so successful is that the arbitrage has actually turned out to be more like 30 or 40 percent. This has allowed InnerWorkings' clients to save more than 10 percent off their printing costs. Meanwhile, InnerWorkings can still generate healthy gross margins in the 20+ percent range. Which means two things: One, the market was far more inefficient that we had ever imagined and two, the deployment of InnerWorkings' total solution was far better than we had ever hoped.

Creating the solution

To deal with the pain we had identified in the printing industry, we needed a different approach. Technology alone was not going to solve this problem. After the Internet bubble burst in 2000, we realized that we needed to focus on businesses that were truly hybrids, relying on both people and technology to deliver value to the market. Neither can exist alone—they're completely co-dependent on each other.

In the case of InnerWorkings, the technology solution utilized a dynamic relational database combined with a modular order management system. This, combined with talented print buyers, allowed the company to serve multiple clients with a virtually limitless range of printing needs through differentiated front-end applications or order management tools and a universal back engine that captured and stored equipment profile data and pricing data across more than 6,000 print suppliers worldwide.

The primary backbone of InnerWorkings' custom-designed system is the result of years of proprietary printing knowledge embedded in its code. The team that built InnerWorkings' system had thought through and built custom order management applications to service nearly every conceivable permutation of print from pens to brochures, from golf balls to books, from point of sales products to direct mail, from commercial print to forms and labels and so on.

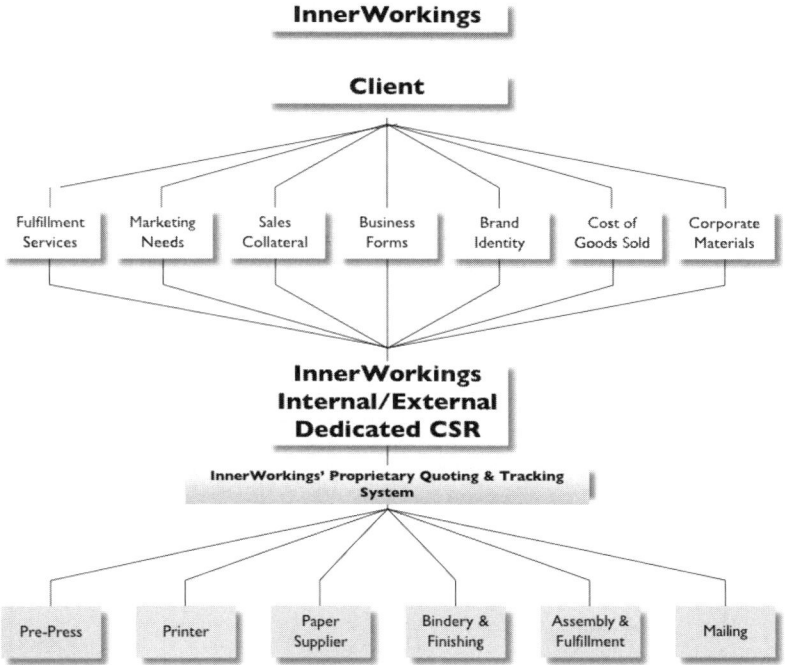

Fig. 3.1: Diagram showing InnerWorkings' relational approach to procurement

The above graphic shows how InnerWorkings matches customer demand to solutions in the marketplace.

But to make the technology work you need experienced print buyers who can analyze and manipulate the data that is collected to find the optimal supplier to produce a given job; hence the hybrid (half technology, half people) nature of the system.

InnerWorkings offered its customers the following:

- ✔ Dramatically reduced costs (between 10-20 percent off their current printing spend)
- ✔ Dedicated personnel that managed their print production
- ✔ An expansive vendor base and supplier network that increased their capabilities

- ✔ Systems and technology that streamlined the entire process
- ✔ Reporting and audit functions

These attributes are only made possible given the success of InnerWorkings' model and the arbitrage it created in the market. There is no other printer or print broker that I know of that offers the breadth of value and services that InnerWorkings is capable of offering given its technological and human advantage. How is that possible? It's the end result of a truly disruptive solution that has been accelerated through proprietary data, scale and operation leverage.

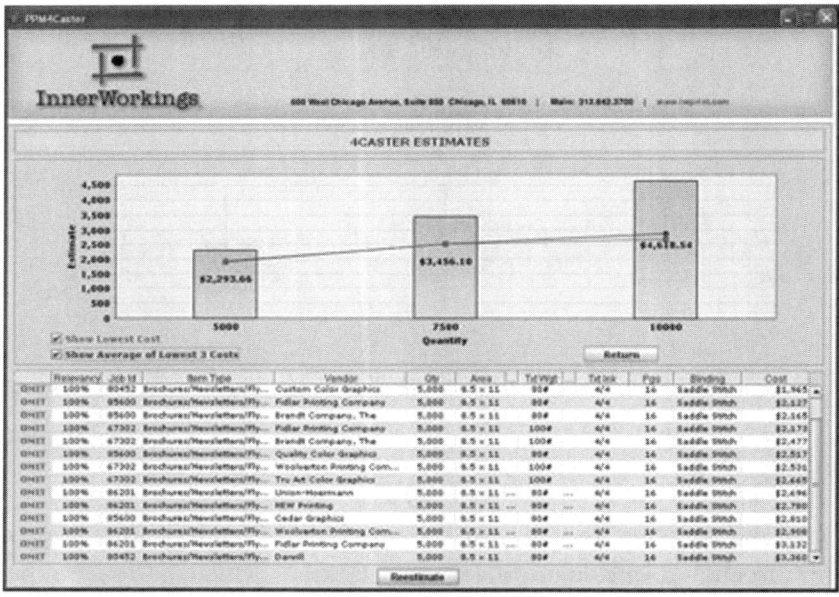

Fig. 3.2: A historic version of InnerWorkings 4caster application whereby specs of a job can be entered in and matched to historic pricing trends

The value of people in a world driven by technology

One of the advantages of InnerWorkings is that they now buy so much print that they have hundreds of people on- and off-site gathering market intelligence from thousands of print providers worldwide. This group of print buyers (or customer service reps as they are often called in printing) is among the largest group of print buyers working for any one company in the United States. With an average of eight years of experience, these print buyers use the technology application as a tool to help them buy printing as well as it can be bought, in my opinion.

In the case of Starbelly.com, our first technology company, we relied (as did most people in 1999) too heavily on technology and not enough on people.

When you are using technology to sell products that people react to viscerally (printing, fashion, etc.), you need people to bridge the inherent gap that exists between the physical world and the digital world. You need people to show products to customers and translate their concerns or needs. You need people to make critical decisions when data alone cannot manage the process. You need people to manage complex production issues that require countless hours of human interaction to resolve.

Here's the bottom line. In the year 2007—in spite of the technology wave that we are just beginning to ride—you still need people.

Echo Global Logistics (Transportation logistics)

InnerWorkings looks for excess capacity in the printing industry. Echo looks for those same opportunities in the transportation industry and then it brokers that valuable information through its proprietary technology.

The pain in logistics is similar to that in printing, with some specific nuances. In logistics, like printing, supply and demand are rarely in a state of equilibrium. At times, there are too few trucks available and at times far too many. In addition, based on weather, seasons, market conditions and holidays, supply and demand can fluctuate dramatically. For example, it's near impossible to get a truck out of Florida during orange season, when every truck inside the state can command a premium to start its engine. They can always find a shipment of fresh oranges to move.

Fig. 3.3: Echo's technology and business model allows it consolidate and aggregate carrier capacity and offer a unified solution to the market.

Likewise, capacity on trucks is much tougher to find before Christmas than it is after New Year's Day.

As we mentioned, about a year after Brad Keywell had the idea to launch a technology-enabled transportation company, we started thinking about building a logistics company to meet our shipping needs. InnerWorkings was dealing with a Midwestern printer that had a large job coming late off the press and was in a panic to get the catalogs picked up and shipped to the client. The problem? InnerWorkings needed to ship those catalogs during the Christmas holidays and it couldn't find a truck no matter how much it offered to pay. At the time, the company only knew a select number of trucking companies and as a result, it couldn't access the full supply of the market.

What we did know was that we could apply technology to help us identify who had open capacity. The problem was that InnerWorkings' technology solution was built for the printing market and InnerWorkings was growing at 100 percent or more a year. A transportation solution was necessary and someone needed to build it from scratch. Given that Brad was thinking about starting a logistics company, the stars were aligned and Echo Global Logistics was born. We had to start from the very beginning. All new technology had to be built, an expert staff found and a full-scale model had to come to life to attack the market inefficiencies that existed in transportation.

Echo is a third-party logistics provider (3PL) that brokers freight for a living. It uses technology to find optimal capacity in the market. What does optimal mean? The challenge in freight brokerage is to find the right truck moving in the right direction at the right time. If you can find that truck among the more then two million trucks that are moving about daily in the United States, you should be able to procure that truck at a discount because every transportation company wants its trucks full. That desire on the part of your supplier creates the opportunity for arbitrage you need to make a profit.

So two years ago, Echo started building a network of highly qualified brokers, carriers, specialists and logistics experts because as InnerWorkings discovered with the printing industry, there was arbitrage not only in dead-headed trucks (those that are returning from a destination empty), but half-filled trucks headed the customers' way. Today, Echo's network stands at 16,000 carriers. The company is buying space and time on thousands of trucks every day and capturing price data from each and every shipment that it procures. That data, along with its general capacity information, is used by Echo's clients and procurement team to make sure that they are buying freight more efficiently than anyone else in the market.

And because Echo is gathering so much data, it built a system that provides customers a variety of information tools they are unable get anywhere else—not just truck postings but interactive load maps, daily updates and alerts, comparative and market analysis, trending data and even real-time average fuel and accessorial prices that always affect the cost of getting a shipment from Point A to Point B. Echo also posts internal capacity, average historic prices and recommended routes, lanes and carriers for its expanding customer roster.

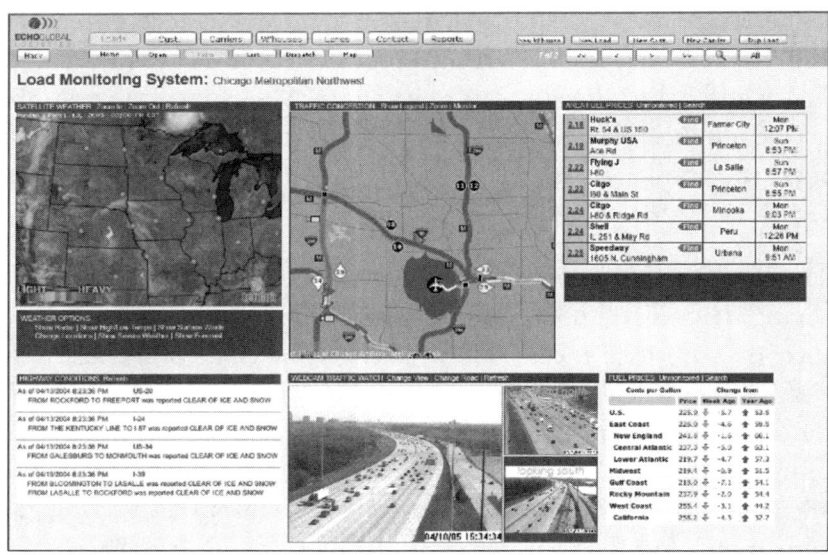

Fig. 3.4: Reporting and tracking functions that can be integrated into Echo's system.

It is tough to believe that after centuries of transporting goods, nobody has thought of a solution quite like Echo's. But again, it was not until technology had evolved to the point where you could collect and store vast farms of data and where you could query that data in real time at a cost that was manageable, that this solution became viable. Until now, the data would have been too hard and too costly to collect, store, retrieve and mine.

MediaBank (Media buying)

In the case of media buying, the pain was less evident at first. People buying advertising space don't normally say, "I hate buying that 30-second commercial spot on NBC." Why? Because they don't really hate it; there is nothing to hate.

To find the pain it was necessary to peel back the onion.

When the MediaBank team began looking at media, all it knew was that the space was enormous—north of $200 billion annually in advertising in North America alone. It also became apparent that it was a people-driven industry with no state-of-the-art technology serving as its backbone. Advertising sales reps from *Time* magazine, NBC or Clear Channel would call on media planners and buyers and provide them lists of available inventory—literally lists of inventory. Planners would collect demographic information about which audiences were likely to view which advertisements. Once a plan was laid out and accepted by the client, media buyers would go and negotiate, often in a one-off manner, for the media they had to buy to complete the plan.

There was no universally accepted electronic exchange, no common platform, no automated tool—just tens of thousands of smart people working very hard to place the buys, all just to re-invent the wheel over and over again at the end of each buy cycle. In their world, that process sounds like "the way it's done." In our world—it sounds like "pain."

Media buying is yet another haven for excess capacity and inconsistent pricing. Back in April 2006, the MediaBank team started thinking about television, newspaper, radio and magazine businesses and how there was no transparent way to see what the best options in media were at any given moment.

The space has always been devoid of good technology or a common exchange that lets buyers know what media properties are available and at what price. That fact, along with the sweeping changes that are affecting the advertising industry as more and more media is migrating from traditional forms such as TV, radio and newspapers, to the digital frontier of Internet, wireless and mobile, has created a landscape riddled with pain.

To put this pain in perspective, below we've listed some—certainly not all—of the existing problems with the legacy systems that many advertising agencies and media buyers use:

- ✔ Data is manually entered into multiple systems
- ✔ Data is often stored in disparate systems such as Excel and Access
- ✔ Analytics are fragmented and require significant human involvement
- ✔ Change is not easily supported within legacy framework
- ✔ Client customization is not supported within existing platform
- ✔ Inventory cannot be allocated among clients with tiered pricing logic
- ✔ Cash application is manual
- ✔ Credits cannot be easily posted, which forces manual reconciliation of Accounts Receivable
- ✔ Campaign profitability is not reconciled at the buy level
- ✔ Modules are not integrated, which prohibits reporting and optimization across media types
- ✔ Limited flexibility to modify or enhance system based on client needs
- ✔ System times out when idle too long
- ✔ Individual users must maintain multiple logins
- ✔ Language is archaic, forcing time-consuming training and inefficient use

- ✔ Information is stored in silos and cannot be leveraged
- ✔ Manual reconciliation consumes significant man-hours
- ✔ Client reporting is typically a manual process
- ✔ Buy iterations or revisions are not supported
- ✔ Routine transactions require significant paperwork
- ✔ New forms of media cannot be readily adopted into current systems or workflow
- ✔ Routine vendor communications are manual
- ✔ EDI process is fraught with errors and unreliable

Given all of these problems, the question was, "How do you stay on top of all these issues, much less track pricing and availability in real time, so that you can offer your clients real value?"

The result was the construction of an information highway where customers could manage their buys and obtain real-time pricing and availability for advertising space. In the most theoretical sense, if you had a product and you hired an advertising agency and said: "I want to spend a million dollars to market my product," the agency might come back and say, "Let's make a 30-second television spot. We'll fly to Australia and we'll produce the commercial and then we are going to buy a bunch of television time on *Desperate Housewives* or *Lost* because we are convinced that the most effective way on a cost-per-thousand basis for you to reach your target audience is national network television."

The problem with that conclusion is that if someone told you in the next sentence that every billboard in the United States was available for a penny, a media planner would immediately say: "The thing I just told you a minute ago about flying to Australia to make a commercial was completely wrong. You ought to buy every billboard in the country for a penny." The challenge, as you can imagine, is that media planners and buyers don't know what is available at any given moment in time because the market is not automated or transparent. Instead, planners and buyers rely on advertising sales executives who provide them information about what inventory they have for sale in a given block of time—this week, this month or this time slot on Super Bowl Sunday.

The current process is riddled with pain as buyers and planners spend their lives manually reconciling the inefficiencies of the market. There are literally dozens of legacy system problems that divide the entire advertising marketplace. Analytics are fragmented, data is manually entered into many redundant systems and client customization is largely a myth.

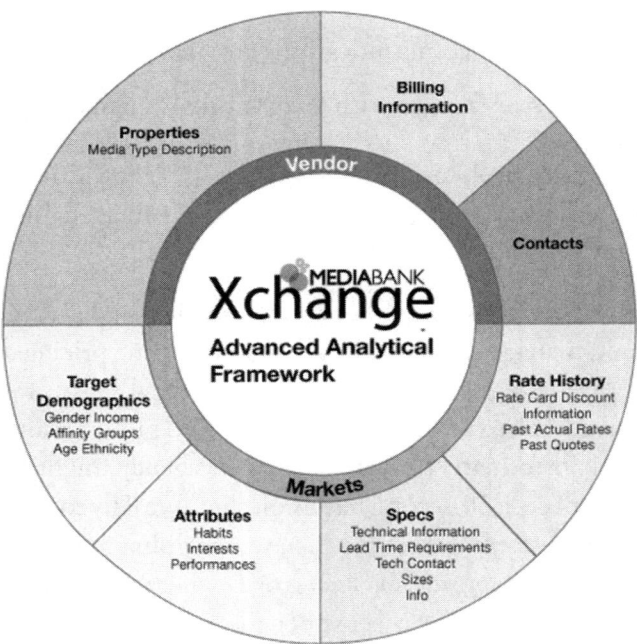

Fig. 3.5: MediaBank's Exchange Framework: demonstrating how the various components of information are aggregated into one central repository of data.

Because MediaBank has created a system using 2007 technology building blocks, it creates a modern, level playing field for advertising suppliers and clients to access from any point, anywhere. They no longer have to assemble data using cobbled-together homegrown systems that are obsolete practically from the moment they are created.

Pain and the point of commonality

In whatever business you hope to disrupt, revolutionize or reinvent, there must be pain. Pain can often hide itself and so at times you have to dig a bit deeper into the industry dynamics to uncover if pain is truly prevalent. Here are some questions we ask to make this determination:

- ✔ Does this industry have a supply/demand imbalance?
- ✔ Does it have thousands of suppliers of all sizes?
- ✔ Does it have a decentralized system of market and pricing data?
- ✔ Is there significant price elasticity?
- ✔ Are the manufacturing/production margins relatively high?
- ✔ Do you have options in terms of whom you buy from?
- ✔ Are the largest companies still relatively small in terms of the entire market?
- ✔ How many steps are involved from the inception of an order to completion?
- ✔ How automated is the process?
- ✔ How reliant on expertise and people are customers?

Depending on the answers to many of these questions, you might have a primary indicator of industry pain and a reason to look closer for the business opportunities beneath. For example, if an industry has thousands of suppliers, the odds are that it is difficult for a customer to figure out who to buy product from. That's pain. If the largest two or three companies control the bulk of an industry—autos, for example—the odds are that pricing is less negotiable. That's pain. If the process to place an order is manual with many steps from inception to order completion—that's pain, too.

SUMMARY:

Business pain leads to business opportunity, but finding that pain requires intense analysis of customer inconvenience. Once you find it and find the right technological solution to deal with it, you can disrupt a process and remake an industry.

NEXT CHAPTER: Industry disruption requires unique conviction unfettered by conventional ideas. Sometimes the best disruptive thinking comes from people who have never worked in that industry before. In the next chapter we will examine ways to step back and evaluate an industry that may be ripe for disruption—or not.

Chapter 4

The Law of Convention

Do not accept norms—rethink old problems

Why would anyone pay to watch TV? After all, from the start, it was free.

Cable TV began as a way to solve a TV reception problem in a mountainous little Pennsylvania town. In 1948, an appliance store owner named John Walson couldn't sell any TV sets in his Mahanoy City store because the few local residents who had televisions couldn't get a clear picture from the Philadelphia stations 90 miles away.

So he took matters—and a wire cutter—into his own hands. Mr. Walson put a TV antenna on a utility pole on top of the nearby mountain and signals were beamed over twin lead antenna wires down to his store where the picture was now crystal clear. But he knew he had to get a similar signal to his customers if they were going to buy, so he started hooking up the individual homes by transmitting over coaxial cable to homemade "boosters"—the early-day version of the cable set-top box. Around the country in small towns and rural areas, the Walson solution became common.

Moving ahead, by 1965, Charles Dolan got permission to lay underground cable for a TV system in lower Manhattan that would broadcast programming clearly without skyscraper interference. Originally called Sterling Manhattan Cable, Time-Life Inc. bought 20 percent of the company within its first year of operations. Then Dolan got another idea—launching pay programming over satellite.

Time-Life bit again and Home Box Office (HBO) was born in 1972 with the broadcast of a New York Rangers/Vancouver Canucks game. After adding first-run movies, HBO produced its first made-for-pay-TV movie in 1983, The Terry Fox Story, *and then a light bulb really went off. With the ability to program and produce, cable stations could offer the first real competition against the established networks (CBS, NBC and ABC). The 1984 Cable Act cleared the way for investment in cable systems and today, more than 80 percent of American households get their TV signal through cable.*

The Law of Convention states that the status quo opposed to your idea just might be the best thing for it.

When we launch a business, we want industry insiders to hate it. We want them to immediately tell anyone who will listen, "They've got it all wrong! It doesn't work that way!"

If an industry insider thinks our idea is spot on, it generally means two things: first, our idea is not revolutionary enough and second, there are most likely hundreds of other companies thinking about or doing the same thing. We want our ideas to feel "uncomfortable." They should border on shocking—someone who's spent his or her entire life in an industry should react by saying, "This will never work, these guys will go out of business within a year!"

There definitely are business ideas that have little more than passion going for them. But we believe that solid research and clear analysis can accompany passion to create a business that truly disrupts the norm. That process is the focus of this chapter.

When we invited John Walter, the former CEO of historic Chicago printing giant RR Donnelley to join our board at InnerWorkings, he spent a great deal of time investigating the merit of our business model.

He started by visiting a longtime business associate of his who said that InnerWorkings was just another run-of-the-mill broker and that the company's idea to use technology to find open capacity and maximize our customers' print buys was just a pipe dream.

In essence, his associate hated InnerWorkings' model, as we suspected he would.

Finding a fissure for revolution

We have found that truly revolutionary models can succeed if we've identified a rift in conventional thinking that proves out after research and testing. As you might imagine, it's essential to research and test before you try and exploit your idea.

A rift can be found in the smallest corners of the most specialized category within an established industry or in a development that revolutionizes centuries of business practice. Take eBay. Before, the only demographic groups who regularly used auctions were farmers, rich art dealers and foreclosure specialists. With the creation of eBay, ordinary consumers not only cleaned out their attics, but started businesses based on bid-and-ask transactions conducted with parties they'd never meet face to face.

On the more subtle side, a good example is Nintendo's popular Wii video game that revolutionized home gaming practically overnight. Prior to that, game companies were investing their innovation dollars in better onscreen graphics, greater memory and more complex storylines. Nintendo completely shifted gears and put its emphasis into the physical experience of getting up and playing the game. In doing so, it was able to win over both kids and senior citizens.

Both businesses had to overcome conventional wisdom in order to break into new markets and exploit new solutions.

There's a place for conventional thinking, even in our process. We view it as the protective layer as a new, budding business takes form. Conventional wisdom buys the innovator time to innovate.

Is experience overrated?

If you're using experience to justify the status quo, it's not only overrated, it can be potentially lethal. Entrepreneurs with a lack of experience in a particular business but who have a significant amount of passion for a novel solution are the reason behind some of the most successful businesses of the last half a century. For example:

- ✔ **Herb Kelleher** was an attorney who scribbled a doodle of his idea for a profitable air carrier system on a cocktail napkin in a Texas bar. Throwing out the traditional hub-and-spoke system of connecting flights, Kelleher went back to the old-fashioned point-to-point system of short hops with few connecting flights. The idea became Southwest Airlines, which continues a pattern of small but effective innovations aimed at keeping customers in the fold—everything from online boarding passes to a market-savvy fuel buying system that's kept its fares low.

- ✔ **Michael Dell** was a high school sophomore when he took an Apple II computer apart and put it back together just to see if he could. By 19, he had dropped out of pre-med at the University of Texas to start a PC firm that specialized in selling directly to the customer. Today, Dell Inc. is a $57 billion computer company based on that principle.

- ✔ **Sam Walton** was a store manager at Ben Franklin while he was planning to buy a department store. A variety store became available first and there he began an aggressive strategy to stock shelves with the lowest-price merchandise and deal only with suppliers who would drive those prices even lower. For years, Wal-Mart operated under the radar screen of such discount giants as Kmart and Kresge until the late 1980s, when the chain began nipping at the heels of Sears, Roebuck and Co., then the world's largest retailer. Today, Wal-Mart is not only the world's largest retailer but also the world's largest company.

What's significant is that the people who created those models weren't necessarily strained by or locked into the prevailing wisdom of how a market worked. If so, Southwest Airlines would have stayed away from short routes without frills in favor of the conventional wisdom of the time. It would have stuck to long hauls and barely edible meals in-flight. Would it still be around today? Who knows?

If Michael Dell had followed IBM's playbook, he would have stayed away from the idea of selling inexpensive private-labeled PCs to customers through a direct channel in favor of major retail outlets supported by national branding campaigns.

And at Wal-Mart, Sam Walton would have avoided opening large discount supercenters in rural communities with low populations at a time when conventional discounters were flocking to crowded urban intersections where their competitors were already doing business.

When you are about to launch a business and someone says it can't be done, that's not the way it is done or it shouldn't be done that way, you need to start investigating the marketplace from a neutral and objective standpoint. It's not that conventional experience and wisdom are necessarily wrong. It's just that in a technologically driven society where change can be measured in nanoseconds, what was true about an industry yesterday may be radically different tomorrow. The best entrepreneurs and managers hardwire that fact into their everyday thinking.

Conventional insight travels through a historic lens. It can only see and reflect on what is or what was. Technological insight, however, moves through a forward-looking lens. It creates possibilities that don't exist today but can exist tomorrow if the technology advancement is deployed to the current process.

Looking for blue ocean

W. Chan Kim and Renee Mauborgne, two professors at the European business school ISEAD, came up with the concept of describing business models and markets as either red ocean or blue ocean in orientation. Red ocean refers to the bloody waters where competitors battle in established markets. Blue ocean represents unpopulated markets where new ideas can form and flourish without the constraints of existing competition.

Blue oceans denote all the industries and ideas not in existence today. It is literally new market space, but not always in completely uncharted waters. According to the authors:

> Although some blue oceans are created well beyond existing industry boundaries, most are created from within red oceans by expanding existing industry boundaries…in blue oceans, competition is irrelevant because the rules of the game are waiting to be set.[16]

If you were to go back to 1987 and ask yourself what companies would be the top 50 in 2007, you would not have predicted the economic models of probably 50 percent of the group, let alone the names. If we had the ability to see the future and the list of the top 50 companies in the year 2027, that same dynamic would probably hold true—we'd recognize only about half of the list.

Just as disruptive business models are being accelerated by the rapid advancement of technology, the oceans will become increasingly red for current leaders in their marketplaces and they'll either sink or find a way to keep swimming. Indeed, today's Wal-Mart might be a very good example of a major company struggling to match past performance in what has become a very red ocean.

How do you know you're still thinking red ocean when you should be thinking blue? Kim and Mauborgne lay out the following traps: [17]

- ✔ You've defined your industry just as your competitors have and you seek to be the best within it.
- ✔ You look at your industry through the lens of generally accepted strategic groups (luxury automobiles/economy cars/family vehicles) and strive to stand out in that particular group with no movement or expansion outside that boundary.

✔ You keep looking at the same buyers: the purchaser, the user or the influencer.

✔ You define the scope of your products and services by the present standards of a single industry.

✔ You accept that industry's functional or emotional orientation.

✔ You always focus on the same point in time—and current competitive threats—in your efforts to formulate strategy.

InnerWorkings, Echo and MediaBank are three examples of blue ocean models that were created within red ocean marketplaces. We've taken existing products and existing solutions and re-engineered them just enough to build entirely new marketplaces.

We tell people all of the time that one of the challenges we face when we launch a new business is that we're typically so innovative in our approach to solve an old problem that we have to spend much of our time convincing people there's a need for our solution. From day one, we often have no direct competitors.

If we had a dozen competitors doing the exact same thing we were doing, at least the market would know there's a need and we could compete on the merits of our offering relative to our competitors. When you take a new solution to a market, you first have to overcome the conventional thinking that dooms you to fail or conform.

During the early days of InnerWorkings, we were going to prospective customers and telling them they should not have an internal print buyer. We were advising them that they should outsource that function to us and that we would put somebody onsite who would act as their buyer allowing them to reduce or redeploy staff without reducing service.

How big was the market we were walking into? Nearly 40,000 printers and 15,000 print brokers. But at that time, none of our competitors, at least none that I know of, were going to their clients and saying they shouldn't be buying what they'd been buying for years.

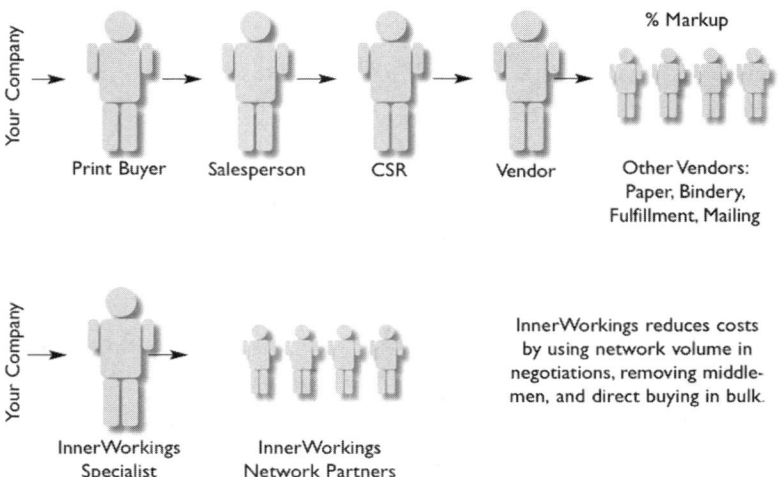

Fig. 4.1: Diagram of InnerWorkings' model

The following chart represents changes we brought to the print buying process.

Current process of buying print	InnerWorkings' way
Print originates at any point in the organization (Sales, HR, operations, etc.) without a central gatekeeper	Identified where print demand generates within an organization so inefficiencies can be eliminated
Fiefdoms resistant to give up their control of that area of the budget	Moved all printing decisions within an organization to a central point of contact
Responsibility for the print buy is assigned to someone within the organization who really doesn't understand the business	Named a customer service representative (CSR) with experience in the print industry to oversee your organization's entire print buy
Traditional print brokers call on clients and position themselves as cost-effective pseudo-manufacturers of print	Built a wall between print demand and historic print supply. Our CSRs matched the job to the lowest-cost quality provider

Current process of buying print	InnerWorkings' way
Print brokers or sales reps go to printers and work through their internal sales departments with CSRs and/or sales reps who generally earn commission on each order	Deal directly with printers as house accounts and the printer pays little or no commission to his staff, which leads to further savings
Paper distributors mark up their paper between 5-15% and printers then add their own paper markup of 5-15%	Often purchase paper directly from the mills or merchants and arranged for shipments to the printer avoiding unnecessary markups
Many printers outsource special finishing with an additional 10-20% markup	Choose printers based on in-house capabilities that were stored in our database. Avoid markups by selecting the right printer with the right equipment
By delivery, between 30-60% of direct costs have been marked up along the way.	Procurement is so efficient that even with markup, InnerWorkings is still below the competition's pricing.
Client thinks he's part of a seamless process because he gets the entire job done through a broker or salesperson	Quality control processes and order tracking are built into management systems that control costs as jobs move through the back office.

InnerWorkings came up against serious resistance in the marketplace at first. In the early days, the majority of the customers we called on were not only disinterested in our model but they were offended by the idea that we were not physically printing their order. It was not until years later, as more and more conventional companies began to copy our solution that the idea became more mainstream.

Today, business process outsourcing within the print industry is a growing and accepted trend and one that InnerWorkings is fortunately the leader in.

In the case of Echo, we decided early on that we were going to build part of our back office operation in India so that we could use inexpensive global labor to find trucks, negotiate rates and manage our dispatch functions. Experts in the industry told us repeatedly that "only Americans" could buy freight in the domestic U.S. market. They felt that certain truck drivers would be unwilling to negotiate with people with an Indian accent. It was not until we had fully tested and deployed our India-based solution with overwhelmingly positive results that the doubters began to believe.

In the case of MediaBank, industry veterans told us repeatedly that the advertising industry is a relationship-based marketplace and there is no way technology can ever replace the value and expertise that marketers bring to the table. They told us that advertising is not a commodity—in other words, a billboard is not a billboard, a TV spot is not a TV spot, a banner ad is not a banner ad but something more ethereal. They told us that marketing experience, not advanced technology, is the magic ingredient to guide which media outlets should be purchased. We were skeptical of that viewpoint at first, but gradually accepted that talented people with experience could not be replaced. However, technology could dramatically enhance their ability to buy, especially as the number of available properties was growing by the minute at an unprecedented rate. It was not until we landed some of the largest media-buying agencies in the world as clients that the critics began to understand exactly what we were trying to accomplish.

In each business there have always been early doubters who relied too heavily on conventional wisdom and not enough on the prevailing force of technological change. We've learned how to listen to them, but not be guided by them.

Great blue ocean innovators

Apple. This company straddles the line between deploying truly revolutionary business models and being a company that simply breaks out innovative products on a more consistent basis than anyone on the planet.

The Macintosh delivered personal computing in a fundamentally different way than ever before. Apple invented the user interface, created the mouse, made navigation point-and-click instead of endless typing of code. It is often credited with "inventing" the personal computer and in doing so, ushered in new markets, new industries and a new culture.

With the iPod, Apple re-engineered a nearly century-old business process—the way music is bought and sold. While the iPod is only one of several devices where consumers can download music, Apple created a delivery system for digital music that became an industry standard and put a big dent in piracy of online tunes. When its music site iTunes came along, Apple built a music library large enough and cheap enough to get listeners to turn honest and pay for their music.

Today, there have been 100 million iPods sold worldwide and Apple's next step is its much-anticipated foray into the wireless phone business.

A lot of people are saying that Apple doesn't belong in the business of selling cell phones—which is probably just what the company wants to hear.

CNN. Today, the cable news field is crowded. But for nearly 20 years, Cable News Network in Atlanta held the monopoly on a 24-hour news channel that would span the globe. Back in 1980, the conventional networks nicknamed Ted Turner's fledgling enterprise "Chicken Noodle Network." But without CNN, there would be no CNBC, no FOX and no MSNBC. CNN forever changed the landscape of news by going against the grain of conventional wisdom about when and how a news channel should deliver the news to obtain advertising revenue.

eBay. Its online auction system has transformed the online marketplace and created an entirely new universe for buyers and sellers who previously could not reach each other to conduct business. In its wake, entirely new markets have been born and items which previously collected dust in the attic are now creating significant value for their owners.

The Home Depot. No one had ever attempted to bring the discount store experience to the hardware, lumber and building products industry, which was fiercely dominated by independent retailers and wholesalers. But in 1979, founders Bernie Marcus and Arthur Blank forever changed the home improvement industry when they opened the first The Home Depot store in Atlanta, Georgia. Today, it is the No. 1 building products retailer with over 2,000 stores nationwide.

Summary:

Listening to conventional wisdom is worthwhile in the early stages of business development where you need to truly evaluate your competition and gauge potential customer resistance. But view it for what it often is—a negative force against development of truly unique efforts to conquer a market and a force that is almost always blind to technology.

Next Chapter: Giving up a dream isn't easy. So when do you pull the plug? Every business idea needs a system of reality checks to clear a new concept to the next level of development. The Law of Objectivity states that not every idea is worthy and suggests how you can tell the difference.

CHAPTER 5

The Law of Objectivity

Not every idea is worthy

By June 1812, virtually all of continental Europe was under Napoleon's control, except for Russia. So Napoleon invaded Russia in the summer of 1812 in an attempt to force Tsar Alexander I to submit to the terms of a treaty that France had imposed upon him four years earlier.

Having gathered nearly half a million soldiers from France as well as all of the vassal states of Europe, Napoleon entered Russia at the head of the largest army ever assembled at the time. The Russians decided to fight the French army with a defensive campaign of strategic retreat, destroying the vegetation on the land as they fell back. As the summer wore on, Napoleon's massive supply lines were stretched ever thinner and his then-dissipated force began to decline in effectiveness.

By September, without having engaged in a single pitched battle, the French Army had been reduced by more than two-thirds from fatigue, hunger, desertion and raids by Russian forces. Nevertheless, a major battle was needed to end the affair and get the French forces out of Russia. With winter approaching, the two armies met in September in a massive battle, taking the lives of over 100,000 men.

Napoleon's remaining troops faced death from hunger and exposure, so he ordered his troops to begin the march home. Because the route south from Moscow was blocked, the French had to retrace the entire 500-mile route of the invasion while temperatures in the frozen Russian landscape dropped to well below zero and the barren land turned into an arctic dessert.

By the end, only 10,000 French troops survived. The campaign ensured Napoleon's downfall and Russia's status as a leading power in post-Napoleonic Europe.

If Napoleon had only understood the true obstacles that the Russian landscape and weather posed to his army, he might have chosen a different strategy and saved more lives.

Such is the Law of Objectivity—taking your idea off the blackboard and into the field to see if your solution really has merit. Failing to do so can be catastrophic.

Innovators are a dedicated breed. It takes conviction to have ideas that may not be completely revolutionary but sustain a belief that you can do something better, improve an existing process and sustain that effort with a combination of will, determination and intentional ignorance of all that has happened before.

The best innovators are true believers long after the crowd has told them that their ideas are off-target, unworkable or downright silly. These are the individuals who break through the Law of Convention—the process of applying analysis and solid research to a passionate belief to prove that the conventional wisdom about a product, a business or an industry must be wrong.

However, in this chapter we're talking about the skill to realize when an idea on paper doesn't have the potential to disrupt an industry in practice. This chapter is about the essential balancing act that every successful entrepreneur or business leader must achieve—getting an idea past that critical stage of impartial review we'll call the Law of Objectivity.

In simplest terms, this is the stage in which you take the business off paper, put it on the road for its first few critical miles and see if it truly functions as a disruptive force in an industry. The Law of Objectivity requires that you go beyond research to solidly test your concept in the real world before you proceed or turn back.

During this stage, you are attempting to prove that your beloved idea is essentially worthless.

Moving from idea to industry-destructive model—or not

The genesis of InnerWorkings was our singular hatred of the way we had to buy printed materials for our businesses. When we were at Starbelly.com, even though we essentially *ran* a screenprinting and embroidery business, we had terrible experiences every time we went out to purchase paper-printed items like brochures, catalogs and other forms of marketing collateral. We felt frustrated by nearly every aspect of the process. We questioned the lack of pricing availability and service comparability across a wide range of providers. We wondered why it cost $500 to print a brochure at one printer and $1,500 at another. We questioned the people-intensive aspect of the business—why everything had to go through a single salesperson or rep and not through technology where processes could be automated and tracked at every stage of production.

A vast majority of the printing marketplace, in our minds, operated like a closed mom-and-pop cottage industry no matter how big or small the players were. We wanted transparency. Enter the Law of Need, which we covered in Chapter 3.

We didn't wander into the business, however, solely based on our own displeasure with the industry. As with life, an element of chance is always present. A few years after Starbelly, one of my partners, Rich Heise, was playing golf with a print broker, Brian McCormack, who had an interesting business model. His office was located right inside the office of his largest client, which happened to be a local advertising agency in Chicago. We were impressed by how high his margins were and how satisfied his client seemed to be with his performance. Having spent tens of millions on technology to try and automate the promotional products industry years earlier with limited success—and we'll get to more about that below—a light bulb went off.

Maybe we had had the right idea in the wrong industry.

Once we started doing our initial research, we were deep in the Law of Convention, which we covered in the last chapter. We heard from other print buyers in the printing community that an effort to create a technology-driven model to harness real-time capacity to optimize pricing would never work. There were simply too many players guarding their turf, nobody would share that level of information with us and customers would never break from a printer that met their budget and gave them great service.

We ignored all of this and confident in our thesis, we went after the most difficult vertical we could find in the printing industry—the book business. In our research, we identified a variety of printers in the book business that could serve a variety of needs. Then we went looking for publishers—companies that needed to buy printing services to get their books into bookstores. We made proposals to a handful of publishers we thought were open to new ideas: "We can save you 10 percent or more on your printing bills. In return, you allow us to procure all of your printing for you."

We got some key early adopters to accept this offer. And there appeared the first crack in the Law of Convention—these companies took a chance on us. We were doing the heavy lifting their buyers could have been doing. We were doing it at no cost to them and we were promising them at least a 10 percent reduction in the cost of each printing job.

Did we know we could definitely save them 10 percent? When we made the claim, it was impossible to know for sure. We suspected we could and if we couldn't, we would have made up the difference as a cost of our research.

They didn't know they were doing our R&D for us. With these companies essentially opening their books and records in exchange for our sweat equity, we found something startling when we began matching their needs against our growing list of pricing and equipment data from the printers we had contacted.

We realized that in most cases we could cut their average price not by 10 percent, but by over 30 percent.

So we delivered their promised 10 percent savings, which made them happy, and we captured 20 percent in gross profit, which made us happy. We had found arbitrage—the first critical hurdle necessary for making it through the Law of Objectivity. The second, as we'll discuss in a minute, is *Value*.

Testing for value

When you actually launch a disruptive business, your mood needs to change from passionate to objective. This means you need to distance yourself a bit from your love of the concept. Your primary concern at this stage should be: Does this idea have value and can I make money at it?

There are two specific tests that we apply to any business we have launched to determine if it should make it through the Law of Objectivity.

EBITDA neutrality. EBITDA (Earning before interest taxes and depreciation) is a key measurement in determining whether a business is working and whether or not there is arbitrage. In simple terms, EBITDA neutrality means that your operating income (revenues less expenses) is equal to or greater than zero. We pull out certain items from this test (interest, taxes and depreciation) because they are non-operational in nature. For example, you might pay a lot of interest to a bank, but if you make money over time and retire your bank debt, that component will disappear. Hence it's not related to the core operations of the business.

If you can't achieve EBITDA neutrality within 12 months, that's a signal that you're doing something wrong and you should either shut the doors or make a radical change. We believe that if you can't get to breakeven in a year, don't desperately look for solutions; the odds are your business is broken. While this is not always true (i.e. Google reportedly lost money for more than a year, as did Genentech—two of the most valuable companies in the world), most of the time this philosophy is accurate.

Winning customers. This key test is obviously much simpler and far more decisive. In simple terms, if you can't win customers you don't offer value. If you take a product to market and you can't get your key audience to respond in six months or so, you might also want to consider closing up shop. Again, while this is not always true (some businesses purposely don't solicit customers for a longer period of time and they have solid economic reasons for it), it is usually spot on. Certainly once you begin selling your product, if people aren't buying within six months, it means something is wrong. It could be your sales approach or salespeople, but in our experience it often has deeper implications regarding the viability of your model.

Even a bad salesperson can usually sell bottles of water to someone who is dying of thirst in the middle of the desert.

When great ideas fail—for the right reasons

As we've explained, Starbelly.com was one of those local Internet-era legends where at the time what mattered most was the idea. In the last waning days of the 1990s Internet boom, we presented an idea to bring the traditional process of selling promotional items—mugs, shirts, pens and pencils—online. The business model appeared to be brilliant and all of the stars were aligned for us to execute on the model. The space was large ($15 billion annually). The process was devoid of technology and we had experience in decorating products, which gave us all the comfort we and our investors needed to proceed.

Our model created the possibility that technology could replace salespeople who typically received 15 percent of each dollar of revenue generated by a promotional products distributor. We had experience in a connected industry (licensed apparel). We had great venture capital backing from Chase Capital Partners and Flatiron, two of the leading venture capital firms at the time. All of the stars for Starbelly were aligned.

But in hindsight, we were destined to fail.

If you know anything about the promotional products business or have somehow landed on dozens of their mailing lists, you'll know from the stacks of catalogs cluttering your desk that the promotional products business is all about plentiful inventory and seemingly endless choices and options. It is a business with millions of SKUs (stock-keeping units, a single piece of inventory in retail lingo), with endless colors, styles and features of items you can buy with your individual or company name. We thought automating the process of buying these items via the Internet would be a big task, but not insurmountable.

But as our model matured, we found that the sheer number of items, descriptions, choices and infrastructure necessary to match the traditional catalog selection to a customer's need exponentially added to the complexity of the lean business model we had forecast. To match the effectiveness of the old-industry model online, we had to build a technology behemoth.

It's not the first mistake we made in business and I doubt it will be our, or my, last.

We were blinded by the euphoria of the Internet boom, which kept us focused on the Law of Convention—we were nowhere near the Law of Objectivity in our thinking process at Starbelly, nor was anyone pushing us to be.

Our idea was scooped up and flooded with millions of dollars of capital at extremely high valuations even though we had only sold our solution to a handful of clients. As we were building custom interfaces for our clients and loading the images we thought they would want to buy into our data warehouse, the items continued to grow, the exceptions continued to grow, the SKUs continued to grow. Just as we thought we had a handle on it, the customers demanded more and more customization.

And our old-industry competitors who were not confined by the limits of technology were happy to fulfill any client requirement, no matter how specialized, as long as the client was willing to pay the standard market price, which included standard commissions for the sales representative on the account. We were traveling into a technology vacuum with no end in sight and our competition, still living in the dark ages, was making money hand over fist.

Once the Internet bubble burst, so did our sources of funding. There went the big idea, abandoned before it even left the launch pad.

Famous flameouts

Starbelly was just one name in a graveyard full of technology-driven business models that burst in the spring of 2000. Some memorable ones from that period of time include:

EToys.com. This site can still be found online, but in its late 1990s heyday, it was seen as the successor to Toys R Us. By 2001, KB Toys, one of the smaller national independent chains in the toy business, had bought the name at a bankruptcy sale and used it to liquidate its after-holiday merchandise.

Pets.com. Remember the sock puppet? Pets.com was literally the last major dot-com IPO before the bust. It sold accessories and supplies direct to consumers over the Internet with a huge marketing budget that made its sock-puppet dog mascot a household image. It launched in August of 1998 and went from IPO on the NASDAQ to liquidation in nine months. At its peak, the company had 320 employees, of which 250 worked in a group of warehouses across the country. Petsmart had made a bargain-basement offer to buy the company, which Pets.com's investors turned down, but eventually its domain and some remaining assets did end up with Petsmart at a fire sale.

Webvan. While Peapod has emerged as a survivor in the Internet-based grocery business, it seemed poised for extinction with the appearance of Webvan. Webvan was founded by Louis Borders, who also co-founded the Borders bookstore in 1971, with original investors including Yahoo!, which made the disastrous move of encouraging Webvan to rapidly build its own infrastructure to deliver groceries in a number of cities. (Peapod, meanwhile, has always worked in partnership with established grocery chains to gather, buy and deliver food and merchandise—it never had to build that giant piece of the puzzle.) Webvan even paid top dollar to recruit the head of Andersen Consulting (now Accenture) to run the operation. When the company's post-mortems were written after its 2001 bankruptcy filings, it was noted by some that the company's senior management didn't have any direct experience in the grocery business.

Flooz.com. Based on a Persian slang term for money, Flooz was an Internet-based pioneer in the so-called e-cash movement. Starting in 1998, it offered customers cards hooked up to Internet accounts that would store purchase credits that could be used at various merchants. Flooz.com was started by former iVillage co-founder Ted Levitan and also notably used Whoopi Goldberg in a series of TV commercials before the company collapsed on August 26, 2001.

Kozmo.com. Started in 1998, Kozmo.com allowed you to order a wide variety of products—from snack food to movies—and get them delivered for free within an hour. The company didn't anticipate the cost of timely delivery in the seven cities it entered and it shut down in March 2001. Though it never had an IPO (one was planned), Kozmo raised about $280 million and even secured a $150 million promotional deal with Starbucks.

GovWorks.com. GovWorks.com was intended to help citizens get in better contact with their local governments while allowing them to renew drivers' licenses and pay fees through the Internet in addition to other tasks taxpayers commonly stand in line to accomplish. Its efforts and failures were chronicled in the documentary "Startup.com." The business closed its doors in 2000.

These businesses failed because they, like Starbelly, did not fully face the often dark and pessimistic realities needed to pass through the Law of Objectivity. It's doubtful there will ever be another business era quite like the late 1990s. The Internet bubble took down hundreds of companies and cost the domestic equity markets nearly $7 trillion before all of the smoke cleared. When it comes to investor exuberance and sudden rushes of capital, memories are startlingly short. Some say the rising valuations of real estate and hedge funds feel a lot like the late 1990s. Only time will tell.

Learning to say no

Another example which didn't make it through the Law of Objectivity is a business we almost started in the banking industry. Between the launch of Echo in February of 2005 and MediaBank in April of 2006, we looked at an idea that we thought would revolutionize the commercial banking industry for small businesses.

We even formed a company that we were ready to launch.

In the midst of the post-9/11 recession, we were always hearing about great business ideas that couldn't get funded. These, of course, were companies that would have had money thrown at them a few years earlier. We considered an Internet solution for the problem: "Why don't we build a website where small businesses will post their business plans and financials and allow individuals looking to invest to review those proposals and make loans over the Internet?" The small businesses could propose their own financing terms, say 2 percent over prime instead of high-risk banking rates which might be 5 percent over prime, and the marketplace of lenders would review the business and its prospects and bite or pass on each deal.

Why would this business attract us? It wasn't simply the people-helping-people aspect of matching lender to borrower, though we thought at the time we could help some talented people while making money at it. We saw the familiar pattern that draws us to all of the businesses we've launched—a chance to replace a slow, people-heavy process with technology. Loan officers used to have significant utility when their skills were critical to the process of finding and making loans. Their ability to personally judge the creditworthiness of a borrower rested on their training and experience in reviewing a potential borrower's character and financial strength. It was all about the individual back then.

Today, computer-based lending models and credit scores have taken over much of that process. Banks still have loan officers sitting at their desks with a smile waiting to greet you—many will even travel to a particular territory if they think they can drum up some business. But both loan officers and their loan committees are now subservient to giant credit committees, statistical models and overarching regulations.

So why not streamline the model while keeping the most important tools of the process intact? By allowing individual investors across the world to review each loan and decide whether or not to invest a few thousand dollars at a time, we would diffuse the risk that a bank normally takes on and get the experience of thousands of individual investors, not just one single loan officer.

While this idea made it through the Law of Convention, it stopped at the Law of Objectivity. We found several Internet-based companies that were already doing some form of this. Several of them, including Prosper.com, seemed very far along. The space was crowded and the competition was fierce. It was no time to get in.

Significant competition with established business models close to our idea was a very obvious signal to us not to stick our toe in this red ocean. While we loved the idea, we just felt it wasn't worth the effort, given the marketplace. By the time we built our website, tweaked our model and fully launched our business, we would have forever been trying to catch up to the companies that already enjoyed a healthy first-mover advantage. Your signs may not be as evident, but you have to try and be both detailed and impartial as you test your concept before you take it wide.

And don't be afraid to pull the plug if you need to.

There are great innovators and great innovations. If your particular business idea is a once-in-a-lifetime breakthrough concept, then you should align yourself with it and hold on for life. If, on the other hand, you have the necessary skills to create new businesses, launch new ideas, think of new products or solutions that might be disruptive in nature, then you shouldn't grow too attached to any one business, any one idea or any one innovation. Too often people think of their businesses as their children and as a result, they can't let go—whether it's early in the process, as we have described in this chapter or later in the process when a business is failing and no one can seem to muster up the objectivity to put it out of its misery.

The discipline of objectivity is actually the same in both instances.

For example, just out of law school, my partner and I bought a business in Wisconsin that manufactured children's licensed apparel. It was 1994, and licensed apparel was a growing industry, at that time $10 billion in size. In addition, the hippest entertainers of the era were frequently seen wearing oversized NBA jerseys and the like on MTV. Our business was in the sweet spot of that fashion trend.

The company operated two plants in Wisconsin. One was a cutting and embroidery facility and one was an old-fashioned sewing plant. In total, the company had roughly 100 employees and produced about $3 million worth of children's licensed apparel annually as a licensee of the NBA, NFL and NHL.

Over the next five years, the company had two hurdles it needed to overcome. The first was that the manufacturing of children's apparel, which for centuries was domestically produced, was moving overseas at a daunting pace. Today, it is hard to find children's apparel that isn't imported from overseas. To overcome this hurdle and to offer our products at a competitive price, we had to develop an importing division and as a result our inventories (and debt) ballooned to nearly $10 million.

The second hurdle was that just as our inventories were growing so that we could service our clients, fashion trends shifted dramatically. Kids wanted to wear grunge, not sports logos, so retailers starting cutting back on their orders and the industry began to contract. To make matters worse, the professional sports leagues, in an effort to capture more revenue, began exploring master licenses with fewer companies (like Reebok and Nike) who could afford to pay huge sums of money upfront to reduce competition.

The bottom line is that we found ourselves caught in the perfect storm—our financial condition was deteriorating rapidly and we couldn't sell our way back to health.

The challenge for us, like many companies, was not that our business was failing. Businesses fail. Our challenge was that we held on too long. Blinded by ego and inexperience and our genuine desire to succeed, we kept trying to "make it work" until the very end when the bank finally pulled the plug.

Summary:

There's a point when a business idea reaches a critical stage beyond the passion and excitement of its inception. The Law of Objectivity represents the first real chance you have to test your idea objectively in the marketplace and it requires solid research, execution and non-negotiable metrics to establish whether you should go forward or not. Most important, you have to be prepared to let the idea go if it's not meeting those benchmarks.

NEXT CHAPTER: The Law of Informational Advantage states that how a company begins to collect, analyze and manage its information is among the most important strategic decisions it will make. In the simplest of terms, if you can enter an industry with an informational advantage, you can disrupt that industry.

Chapter 6

The Law of Informational Advantage

Data is your most critical asset

Navajo was an extremely complex language that was never written down until Philip Johnston, the son of a former missionary raised on a Navajo reservation, suggested to the U.S. Marine Corps that written or spoken phonetically, it might be unbreakable as a military code. The language had no alphabet or symbols and it was estimated that less than three dozen non-Navajos—none of them Japanese—could even understand the language at the start of World War II.

Johnston, a civilian born in 1892, remembered that Comanches were used as code talkers with U.S. Army units during World War I. When his proposal to develop a Navajo code was accepted by the Marines, Johnston worked with Marine camp and cryptographic officers to recruit Navajo civilians and servicemen to the secret project, first organized at Camp Elliott in San Diego.

Johnston thought that conversational Navajo would be enough, but the Navajos refined the idea by choosing specific word and letter substitutions to represent the exact words the military wanted coded. Words were tested, chosen or thrown out, translated into English and back again.

The project was a huge success. Navajo code talkers took part in every assault the Marines conducted in the Pacific from 1942 to 1945. They served in all six Marine divisions, Marine Raider battalions and Marine parachute units, transmitting messages by telephone and radio in their native language—a code that the Japanese never broke.

The Law of Informational Advantage states that information is often your most coveted asset and so gathering, analyzing and protecting key business data has to be at the center of any destructive idea and innovative business model.

The value of information

Over the last 40 years, virtually every successful destructive business model has succeeded on the back of leading-edge information technology. Wal-Mart would not be the world's largest retailer in 2007 unless Sam Walton started gathering customer purchase data as far back as the 1960s, which he would shrewdly use to negotiate for better pricing from his suppliers.

At our companies, we are relentless gatherers of information that we use as leverage for better industry understanding, better service and most important, better pricing that not only wins us customers but also assures that we make money. With each passing day, there are advances in computing power and analytical technology that help us do this in an increasingly efficient manner.

Finding a destructive solution means cutting through the complexity of business practices that dominate an industry. We have found that creating a successful disruptive business model means running through four predictable stages:

- ✔ Determine a business goal;
- ✔ Find the highest-leverage approach to meet that goal;
- ✔ Research the ideal technology;
- ✔ Deploy the smartest application of that technology to collect data.

In June 2007, Bill Gates gave the commencement address at Harvard University, thirty years after what would have been his graduation day if he hadn't dropped out to start Microsoft. While the majority of his address was devoted to applying "creative capitalism" to the most serious problems in the world, he also spent a moment on how low-cost computers have made the world "smaller, more open, more visible, less distant," and what that means to the world as a whole:

> The magical thing about this network is not just that it collapses distance and makes everyone your neighbor. It also dramatically increases the number of brilliant minds we can have working together on the same problem—and that scales up the rate of innovation to a staggering degree.[18]

The potential for informational advantage grows with every gain in microprocessor power and with every new wrinkle in software design. We understand this as a key driver of our current and future businesses.

More than 2,200 years ago, the Chinese military strategist Sun-Tzu wrote that "intelligence is of the essence in warfare—it is what the armies depend upon in their every move." He added that victory belongs to the commander who gets the right information in a timely way:

> Complex systems such as battle conditions are rich in information—information that must be acquired immediately. The commander's wisdom must be funded by direct access to persons who serve him as eyes on the site-specific conditions and who enable him to anticipate the outcome. To be reliable, information must be firsthand…There is thus an important relationship between intelligence and timing.[19]

In this chapter, we'll focus on the technology strategy we've used in each of our models to boost our informational advantage. By way of context, our companies focus their energies on markets open to Business Process Outsourcing (BPO)—business processes that are not core functions of an organization. Printing, transportation and media buying are good fits for BPO for these reasons:

- ✔ Each of these industries is made up of a large and fragmented number of service providers with pricing and services all over the map.

- ✓ Technology has advanced to the point where we can find open capacity for our customers that fits their economic needs at the exact moment they need the service.

- ✓ These are typically not core services to any company that buys them, so they're an ideal choice for outsourcing.

InnerWorkings

InnerWorkings is a fully integrated BPO solution to manage all of a client's printing needs. It targets the Fortune 1000 and it has attracted business through recruitment of brokers or sales reps with existing client relationships.

InnerWorkings' technology allows its buyers to purchase many of the components for a print job directly from the primary sources and then monitors the finished product toward completion at the printer. I gave some details on how the process works in Chapter 5, but here's how InnerWorkings' people and the technology work together (or at least how they worked when I was involved with the company on a day-to-day basis).

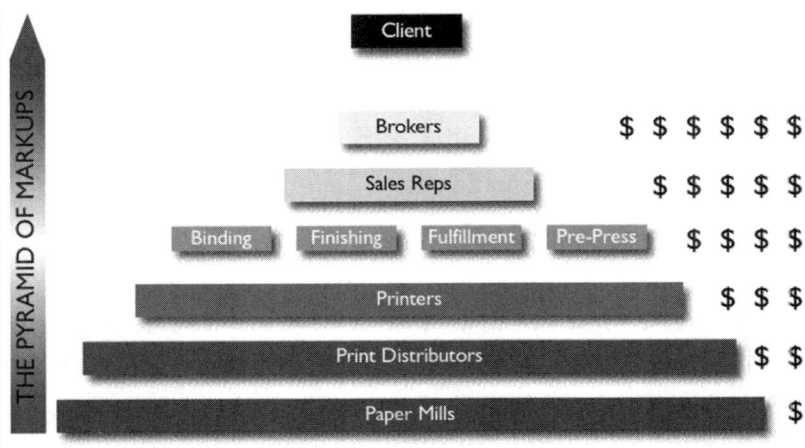

Fig. 6.1: The InnerWorkings process

Once InnerWorkings' print production manager gets an assignment from a customer, he or she acts as a magnet for all print demand inside that organization, aggregating the jobs and funneling them into PPM4™, InnerWorkings' technology application. Each job is turned into a quote within the system within 24 hours or so after receipt of the project request. The internal quoting database allows InnerWorkings to analyze the cost structure of the job and allocate that job to multiple suppliers for bidding. Since it already has capacities, capabilities and volume-specific data loaded into its system, this allows InnerWorkings to maximize its margins by feeding work to those printers who have open capacity or at least have been the most aggressive bidding on projects that match the specifications that are now being quoted out. How does InnerWorkings know this? Because its technology captures data from its network of printers who communicate their excess capacity to InnerWorkings, either in the aggregate or through the prices they provide.

InnerWorkings' focus is on putting as much information in front of its customers as possible. Here are some of the various facets of the system in use or used in the past to maximize the efficiency of its print buyers:

- ✔ *PPM4Caster.* InnerWorkings' proprietary database provides real-time cost estimates for potential print jobs within their major product categories. These estimates can be used by InnerWorkings' account executives during the sales process and by procurement managers to compare bids and negotiate favorable pricing. They can also be used by their clients at times to prepare budgets and run "what if" scenarios.

- ✔ *Customized order management.* Its technology automatically generates customized data entry screens based on product type and guides the procurement manager to enter the required job specifications. For example, if a procurement manager selects "envelope" in the product field, the job specification screen will automatically adapt so that the procurement manager is guided to specify the correct size, paper type, window size, placement and display style.

- ✓ *Cost management.* InnerWorkings' technology's CMS module stores and reconciles supplier invoices to executed print orders to ensure the supplier adhered to the pricing and other terms contained in the print order. In addition, it includes checks and balances that allow InnerWorkings to monitor important indicators relating to a print order.

- ✓ *Standardized reporting.* Its technology generates transaction reports that contain quote, supplier capability, price and customer service information regarding the print jobs the client has completed. The reports can be customized, sorted and searched based on a specified time period or the type of printed product, price or supplier. In addition, the reports give clients insight into their print spend for each individual print job and on an enterprise-wide basis, which allows the client to track the amounts it spends on paper, print and logistics.

- ✓ *Historical price baseline.* Several of its larger clients have provided InnerWorkings with pricing data for print jobs they completed before they began to use its services. For these clients, PPM4™ can automatically compare InnerWorkings' current price for a print job to the price obtained by the client for a comparable historical job, which allows InnerWorkings to demonstrate, on a job-by-job basis in real time, the cost savings it has achieved for the client.

At times, InnerWorkings used all of the valuable information it collected to help its client create something called IW Stores. InnerWorkings has created customized Internet-based stores for certain clients that allow them to order pre-selected products, such as personalized business stationery, marketing brochures and promotional products, through an automated ordering process with viewable and variable PDF capabilities. Their historical buying patterns help guide this product selection and allow for the appropriate levels of inventory to be built based on past buying patterns. These stores are highly automated, as they are the end product of using information to guide the procurement of a known commodity.

Chapter 6: The Law of Informational Advantage

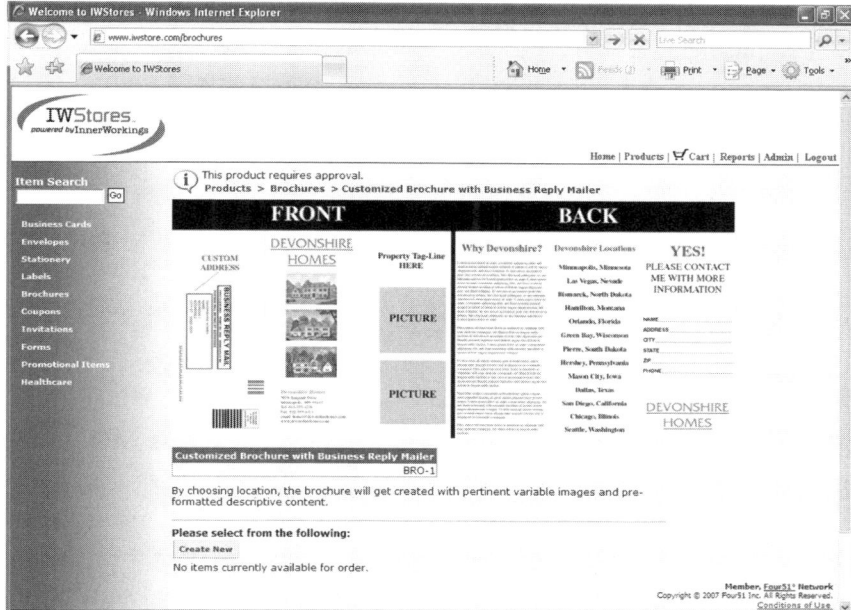

Fig. 6.2: IWStores' window demonstrates how a customer can select products and have them placed in their own custom estore.

While technology in the printing world can never fully automate the process of buying print (for example, someone could always say what would it cost me to buy this one item that may be so unique that there is no good history in terms of how much it should cost and who should produce it), InnerWorkings has gone about as far as you can go, in my opinion, in terms of collecting data and maximizing the value of that data to more efficiently procure printed items.

Echo Global Logistics

Echo Global Logistics uses proprietary technology to find excess capacity on truck, rail, air and other forms of commercial transportation. Due to our poor experience finding transportation options at InnerWorkings, we believed that the traditional carrier/dispatch side of the freight business was ripe for a systematic, technology-based platform in which experienced transportation professionals could support data gathering and rate regulation using state-of-the-art tools. Our various technology solutions offer a series of advances that enables our clients to better manage the following:

- ✓ Truckload visibility and direct and ancillary cost management
- ✓ Automated search for lowest-cost providers across a vast network
- ✓ Integrated small parcel pricing, audit and tracking
- ✓ Integrated intermodal, expedited and international freight management
- ✓ Access to thousands of carriers and optimization of shipments
- ✓ Integrated track-and-trace and dispatch functions
- ✓ Analytics for current and historic shipments

MediaBank

What's made our work with MediaBank so exciting is that we're in an industry that's not only opaque from a pricing standpoint; it's also in the midst of cataclysmic change. Media and the delivery of media are rapidly going digital and that's widened the possibilities we can offer the marketplace. Not long ago, the main advertising media consisted of print, radio, television and billboard. Today, the choices are much more varied and constantly growing:

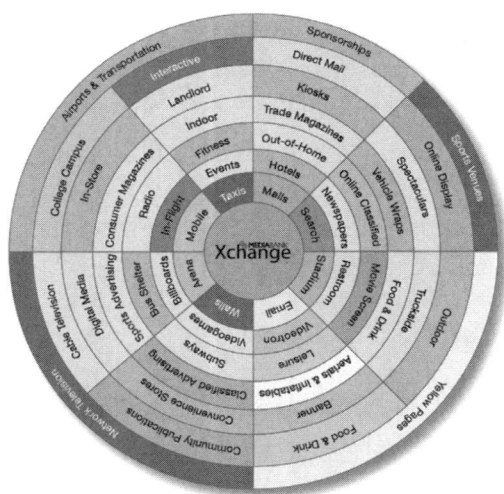

Fig. 6.3: MediaBank industry diagram

The chart above shows the many markets where MediaBank is collecting data to better serve its clients.

According to a June 2007 report in *Advertising Age*, the top 100 U.S. advertisers last year increased ad spending by a modest 3.1 percent to a record $104.8 billion.[20] But most of that growth came from "unmeasured disciplines," such as direct marketing, sales promotions and digital communications, including unmeasured forms of Internet media such as paid search.

In fact, one of the greatest areas of growth in 2006 advertising spending was the Internet (measured and unmeasured media), up 25 percent.

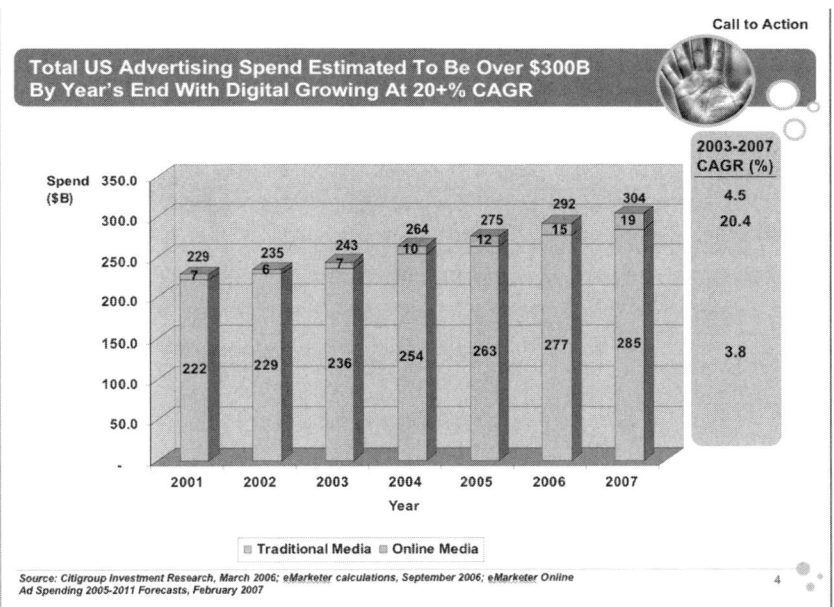

Fig. 6.4: Advertising Industry Data

This may not bode well for older, slowing media options, but it bodes well for MediaBank because we focus on digital media and its impact on the market. Our role is to serve as intermediary between old and new advertising media and the advertisers who want a skillful, state-of-the-art way to harness vast farms of data in real time.

At the heart of our solution is the MediaBank order management and analytics suite (MBOX and MBIQ), our scalable procurement platform that provides advertising agencies and advertisers a holistic view of their digital and analog media spending. With an emphasis on all media—including emerging technologies—we offer advertiser-focused tools that streamline the management of complex multimedia campaigns for global advertisers.

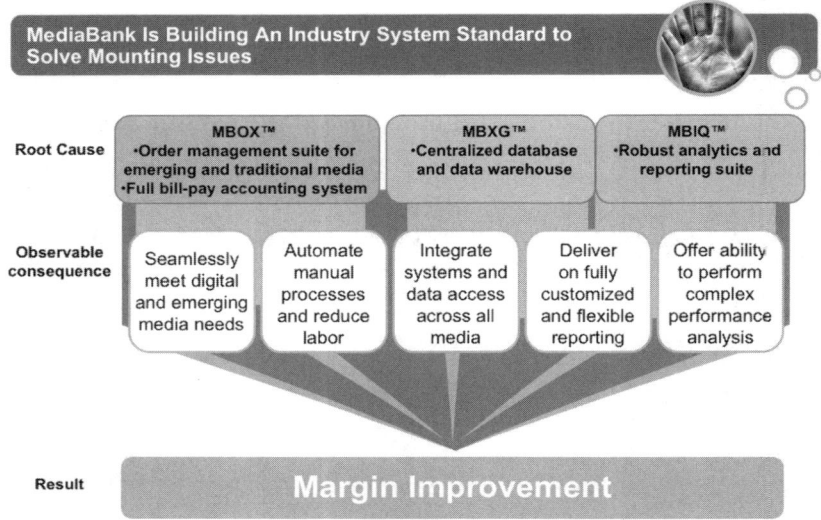

Fig. 6.5: *MediaBank's historic product offering by product suite*

We also deliver value through the MediaBank Xchange (MBXG™), our internal database of thousands of available media opportunities, amassed by consolidating available and proprietary data sources and complex searching and analytical tools that are embedded within its code.

MediaBank provides a secure forum that allows media buyers to access data on nearly every conceivable form of media available on the market—from publications to direct mail, from online advertising to newspaper FSIs, from transit advertising to sponsorships, from place-based advertising to traditional outdoor. Through this unique offering, MediaBank provides an electronic exchange whereby advertisers are aligned to the most appropriate media in the market to achieve optimal buying.

In addition, we have constructed a revolutionary order management tool with full-scale planning integration, automated end-to-end order management, full bill-pay functionality and an integrated digital module. This software is unique in that it represents a quarter-century leap forward, bringing cutting-edge technology and automation to the process by which large media-buying agencies buy media. The software was constructed over a yearlong period by a team of nearly one hundred talented folks working hand-in-hand with one of the largest buyers of media in the world. Together the combined team mapped out the requirements and functional specifications that gave rise to this disruptive technology solution.

Building the system has not been easy. We did face major challenges in this process:

- ✔ In mid-2007, we were still going through the learning curve to define the characteristics of various ad media in a single electronic format. Capturing this data has been complex and arduous, not only because it's developing and morphing so quickly, but also because it exists in disparate states.

- ✔ Our order management system had to accommodate both the digital and analog world. Building a single platform for both the old and new universes of advertising was a challenge.

- ✔ Creating a database that captured pricing, performance and other key comparisons of disparate media (billboards vs. 30-second radio spots) was problematic and required numerous iterations before we got it right.

- ✔ Refreshing and keeping data accurate when rates change by the minute is a constant effort—one that improves with each passing day as our technology evolves.

- ✔ Building a product set and making sure it stays ahead of the industry when you have such a large and diverse landscape is the stuff case studies are made of.

These challenges exist because the market is fragmented and devoid of technology standards and automation. Even within the same type of media, there are no standards in terms of definitions, specifications or products. The lexicon changes based upon the vendor you are using or the client you are serving. Pricing is not consistent, sizing is not consistent, availability is not consistent and so on. The industry has been so specialized, so customized and so influenced by creative forces that long-established supply chain and procurement norms do not exist.

Solving the mystery of ad spend

The department store magnate John Wanamaker once said, "Half the money I spend on advertising is wasted. The trouble is I don't know which half."

It seems foolish with the technology tools we have available to us today to continue making major media decisions on the basis of trust. The historic problem is that traditional media planners work hand-in-hand with media buyers who use out-of-date tools that have no true measurement of the inventory available in the ad market. You're relying on what one professional knows based on the quality of their in-house systems to recommend the resources *they know about at any given point in time.*

Even the best media buyers and planners in the world are crippled when their data is old, limited and nearly impossible to manage.

We wondered what would happen if we created a database that helped clients design media plans in real time and matched them up against inventory that was available at that precise moment. Our technology allows us to match a client's target audience with tens of thousands of available media properties whose attributes reside within our common database platform. By identifying and tagging each media property with common attributes such as demographics, price, frequency and more, we are able to compare various media properties that span across all major categories of advertising within minutes so that our clients can compare and contrast which forms of media are the most appropriate, most available and most effective given their budget. This ability does not exist in the marketplace as far as we know and allows us to achieve two significant milestones in the industry:

Chapter 6: The Law of Informational Advantage

✔ Our database application helps redirect a company's media spend to new properties previously unknown.

✔ Our database application opens up the world of media to thousands of smaller corporations who until now have lacked the required advertising budgets necessary to engage a large media-buying firm. MBXG allows us, with a more precise method, to do in minutes what currently takes days, weeks or months.

For example, assume a customer contacts us and wonders what it would cost at this exact moment to buy a billboard in a specific market and how that billboard compares in terms of reach and frequency with a radio spot or a bus wrap in that same market reaching that same demographic. The request pings our database and results are displayed back to the media buyer.

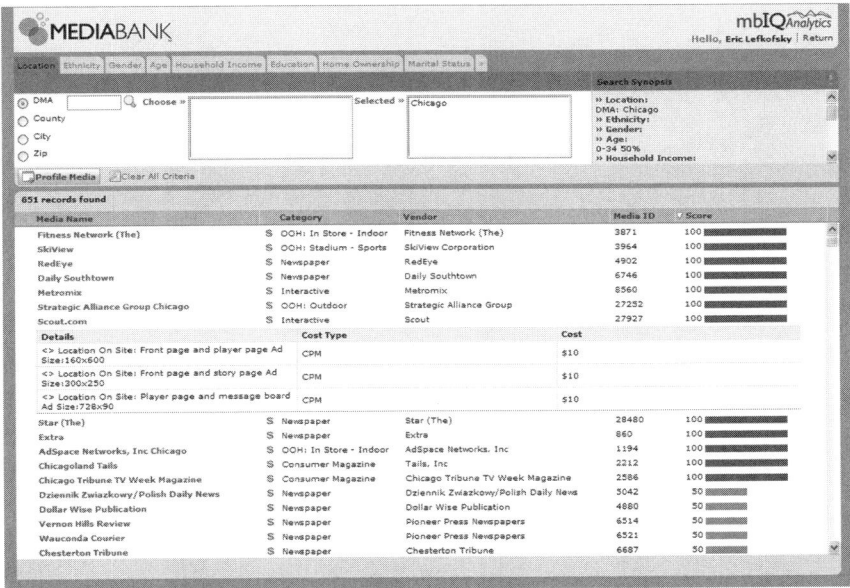

Fig. 6.6: A historic version of MBIQ (an analytics tool)

MBIQ provides a clear picture of how data can be collected, stored, managed, manipulated, sorted and analyzed to produce an outcome that was "unknown" prior to the process. In the case of MediaBank we are literally creating potential advertising cocktails that we believe are only available through our technology. And prior to the collection of data, the media cocktails could not have been created because there was no clear picture as to what could be bought across all media categories and at what optimal price at a specific moment in time.

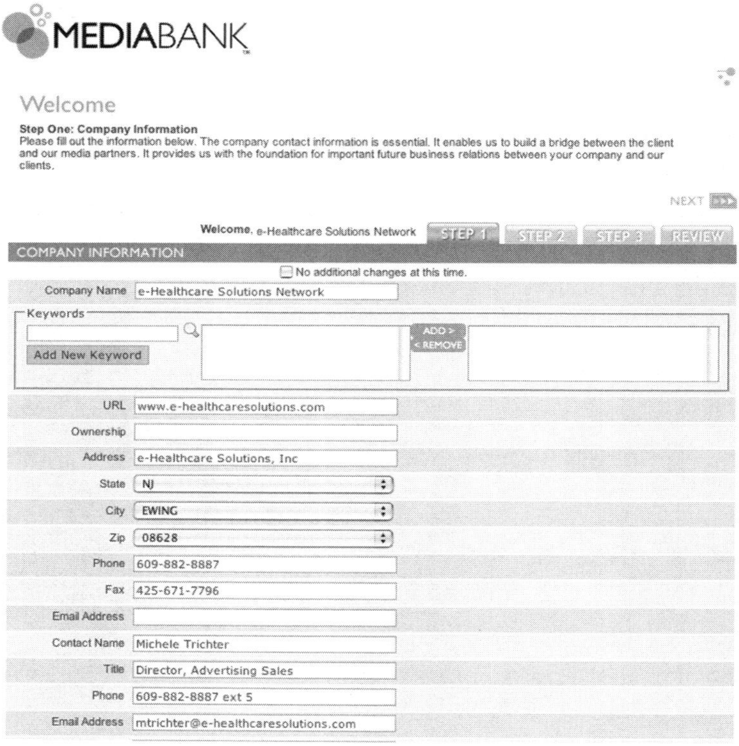

Fig. 6.7: A historic version of MediaInfo (an automated data collection tool)

Our solution, once fully developed, represents the pinnacle of using information to create value and arbitrage in a market that before MediaBank was devoid of accessible, clean and manageable data. In the simplest of terms, the media cocktails we take to market only exist through the mining and manipulation of data. Without the data, the product does not exist.

Information gains clarity over time

Information is the byproduct of data. The way you gather data is not a tangential part of your business. It is your business.

Gates points out that the Law of Informational Advantage starts with developing an ideal picture of the information you need to run your business while understanding your markets and your competitors. "Think hard about the facts that are actionable for your company. Develop a list of the questions to which the answers would change your actions. Then demand that your information systems provide those answers."[21]

What we can do with information and data today was impossible to even imagine a decade ago. Not only are we able to collect data faster than ever before in history, we are also able to store data at costs that are fractional to their historic rates.

Today, data can be manipulated, molded, and utilized in ways that historically we could only dream of. You can extract data at the most micro or macro of levels—drilling up or down to gain perspective. You can pivot data for dimensional insight. You can instantly add or remove variables to determine the key value drivers of the data you have just collected. You can exchange data in real time with just about every living person on the planet. Data can be integrated, mixed, incorporated, combined, assimilated, sorted, arranged, split, parceled, divided, extrapolated, generalized, normalized, rationalized and just about every other "ized" you can possibly think of.

And yet despite all we can do with data, the Internet does not allow us to fully utilize the possibilities of data mining. A recent *Business 2.0* article states:

> For all the wonders that today's Web can deliver to your fingertips—the Norwegian word for ice cream, a seat on the next flight to Paris, the best price for a Clash CD—it has a fundamental flaw. It's basically a compendium of billions of text documents designed to be read by humans. You can search it for keywords, but the results aren't much use until

you sort through them to find the page that has the info you want. To take the Web to the next level—to move from Web 2.0 to Web 3.0—the information in the those documents will have to be turned into data that a machine can read and evaluate on its own.²²

Imagine the possibilities, the solutions, the innovations—the businesses—that can't exist today but will become possible as the Web becomes smarter and data becomes more addressable and intuitive in its very nature. This new reality is at the epicenter of the Law of Informational Advantage.

SUMMARY:

The Law of Informational Advantage is about the value of information as an essential element driving businesses forward in the twenty-first century. Envisioning the data your clients need is one thing; the real challenge is harnessing data in a way that will create future value for your organization by opening up markets, finding arbitrage that no one knew existed and ultimately disrupting an entire marketplace.

NEXT CHAPTER: In the next chapter, we'll discuss the critical leap businesses must take from pain to adoption. In our expanding technology-driven economy, there are limitless opportunities for businesses to attack painful processes. But it takes more than just a solution to get clients to adopt—you need an enduring answer to a problem that triggers a permanent change in customer behavior.

CHAPTER 7

The Law of Adoption

Value > Pain = Adoption

Thirty years ago, the average American's idea of bottled water was a dusty dispenser in the corner of an office with an empty Dixie Cup holder. Then, in 1976, a little green glass bottle started turning up in chi-chi restaurants and at the upscale groceries that existed at the time—Perrier. The French beverage was fizzy, exclusive and, well…water.

Bottled water was almost a joke at first. People scrunched up their noses as they saw this strange, 12-oz. green bottle start appearing next to the distilled water at the grocery store selling for more than a can of Coca-Cola. The idea of paying for something that came naturally and freely out of every faucet was not only foreign to most consumers at the time, it was absurd.

But despite the jokes made as consumers passed up these bottles at first, another spring water import showed up a year or two later also from France—Evian. It wasn't bubbly like Perrier, but it came in a handy plastic bottle that could be carried on a walk or run, allowing consumers to take the bottles of water virtually anywhere. Right about this time, as we entered the early 1980s, this once comical product began to take off and the American consumer started chugging water.

What was the tipping point? Maybe it was a perfect storm of Yuppie culture where spending meant status or the growing health food movement from California that pushed Americans away from meat and gravy and toward healthier meals. Or it could have been the early health club boom where Spandex and bottled water became fashionable almost overnight.

Today, Perrier, Evian and at least 30 other brands are responsible for a $16 billion U.S. business and lots of empty bottles in the recycling bin. If you ask practically any bottled water drinker, they'll tell you that they don't touch tap water because bottled water is so much safer. They're largely wrong of course—most city water systems produce water that's perfectly safe to drink. But they'll tell you they don't want to take a chance or they simply prefer the taste of bottled water to tap water. To them, bottled water has value and they're not going back, no matter how heavy those bottles are or how much they cost.

Welcome to the Law of Adoption—when your customer discovers that the value of your product or service is greater than the cost of switching.

We've already talked about the concept of pain—that initial trigger that gets people to start thinking about changing an ingrained habit or developing an entirely new one. We're going to talk a bit more in this chapter about developing the value proposition that creates the actual catalyst for customers to make profound—and hopefully permanent—changes in their behavior. That decision, which we'll refer to as adoption, fuels disruptive businesses within any industry.

When new value arrives into a market that is greater than the pain associated with changing existing practices, you have an environment that is ripe for adoption. It may take months or years for a marketplace to migrate to a valuable new solution, but once the tipping point has been achieved, migration happens and it's up to you to nurture customers with both the value of your model and consistent improvements in your technology to keep them loyal over time.

Value starts with knowing your customer

How well do you really know the person, business or organization you are trying to sell?

This isn't a book about marketing, but to understand adoption you need to first understand the concept of one-to-one marketing and what it's meant to most industries. Customer Relationship Management (CRM) dictates that consistently creating something of unique value to customers will award you their trust for a lifetime—as long as you can renew that value promise again and again. There is nothing static or simple about this relationship and unless it's nurtured, it can be lost in a heartbeat.

There is a great deal of uncertainty around the topic of CRM. Diamond-Cluster, a Chicago technology consulting firm, says the following:

> There remains a great bit of confusion around the definition of CRM. It is neither software nor something that begins in the IT department. CRM is a way of thinking, a business approach that begins and ends with the customer.
>
> CRM is a functionally integrated, customer-centric way of doing business manifested through a set of operational capabilities enabling a company to maximize the value of its customer base while simultaneously providing optimal utility to the consumer.[23]

The goal of customer-centric strategies is to create *learning relationships* with customers in order to better understand their unique wants and needs. These learning relationships allow customers to participate in all aspects of the business, exerting influence on the products and services that are made available to them.

We want to spend a few minutes here discussing CRM as a backdrop to the larger issue. In order to understand adoption, you have to understand your customers.

Global business consulting firm Bain & Co. defines CRM this way:

> Customer Relationship Management (CRM) is a process companies use to understand their customer groups and respond quickly—and at times, instantly—to shifting customer desires. CRM technology allows firms to collect

and manage large amounts of customer data and then carry out strategies based on that information. Data collected through focused CRM initiatives help firms solve specific problems throughout their customer relationship cycle—the chain of activities from the initial targeting of customers to efforts to win them back for more. CRM data also provide companies with important new insights into customers' needs and behaviors, allowing them to tailor products to targeted customer segments. Information gathered through CRM programs often generates solutions to problems outside a company's marketing functions, such as supply chain management and new product development.[24]

In other words, CRM is a discipline in which you capture and react to your customer's needs and you allow those needs to dictate the products and services you ultimately take to market.

The Law of Adoption takes place after you have moved through the stages we've described in the previous chapters to create a business concept of real value. In this cycle, you are soliciting customers to adopt your idea at the expense of other solutions in the market.

Technology accelerates the Law of Adoption

Because our proprietary technology is constantly measuring the behavior and decision-making of our customers and suppliers, we're in a position to know what they value at any given moment. We don't assume it will be the same thing they will value six months or even six weeks from now. Adoption is a living, breathing instrument that must be nurtured.

If shipping customers are thinking about turning the way they buy freight upside down, we don't wait for them to tell us. *Our technology tells us.* Our systems are continually built to pick up cues—changes in usage requirements, order patterns and other behavioral data that allow us to analyze, suggest and develop solutions that evolve as customer needs evolve. Customer service shouldn't be based on response—it should be based on anticipation.

We're living in exponential times, but we're also living in increasingly customer-centric times. Your customer base—consumers, businesses, governments and virtually every person and institution in between—is growing increasingly impatient. They don't want to have to live with pain for very long before a solution appears to take that pain away.

They also want solutions that are customized to their specific needs. For example, at InnerWorkings, when we used to visit print buyers it was nearly impossible for us to finish a meeting without them saying at some point, "No one else has the same problems or requirements that we have. Our situation is completely unique." While this is a uniform convention, it is completely inaccurate. Everyone shares the same problems. They just feel different. Everything is always in a rush, everything is last minute, everything constantly changes and costs are always a concern at some level of the organization. That was and is the nature of printing. Our challenge was to convince the clients that our solution was specific to their needs because it was virtually impossible to convince them that others shared their needs.

These forces (pain, fear, speed and customization) are in a constant state of conflict. On the one hand, consumers are impatient and they want relief quickly. On the other hand, they want the relief tailored to them even if it costs them time. And finally, regardless of their pain or their lack of patience, they are resistant to change. Adoption is the result of successfully bringing relief and harmony to these conflicting forces in an effort to win clients.

To get adoption you need to blend art and science. Science allows you to view ordering and usage patterns with an eye toward revolutionizing process and disrupting an entire industry. Art is all about the ability to see through conditioned, almost Pavlovian responses to old-industry questions in an effort to uncover opportunities to build value. For example:

- ✔ "We like our printer—we've used him for years."
- ✔ "We trust our media buyer. We know they understand the market and we don't have to think about it."

- ✔ "We work the phones until we find the most economical transportation solution in our area."
- ✔ "We buy print as well as it can be bought."
- ✔ "What we buy is not a commodity."
- ✔ "You don't understand our business."

The staff of InnerWorkings, Echo and MediaBank has to listen for a particular element in the voices of potential customers. They listen for that phrasing, that tone of voice that suggests *resignation*—a non-verbal throwing up of hands. In general, I love resignation because it suggests the customer is conflicted—which creates opportunity. He or she has both a desire to change out of frustration and a resistance to change out of fear. Fear of what? The risk inherent in trying something new.

Conflict is your window of opportunity. If you can get a potential customer to take a leap of faith and try a new solution, odds are you will produce remarkable results. In most cases, reluctance to change has kept customers from taking advantage of new technologies or new methodologies to deal with problems they face every day. They won't say it, they might not even know it, but at some level they're scared. In order to win them over, you will have to put them at ease.

The Law of Adoption focuses on how well you introduce your customers to the opportunities and benefits they'd obtain by accepting change and following you in a whole new direction.

In Kim and Mauborgne's *Blue Ocean Strategy*, adoption is the last stage in the sequence of determining a commercially viable blue ocean idea:[25] Identifying and eliminating hurdles to adoption is the critical last step in determining "the successful actualization of your idea." We know all about adoption hurdles. In the companies we've started, the biggest selling challenge has been to simply get entrenched customers and suppliers to consider a different way of doing business. Again, Kim and Mauborgne:

> Even an unbeatable business model may not be enough to guarantee the commercial success of a blue ocean idea.

Almost by definition, it threatens the status quo and for that reason, it may provoke fear and resistance among a company's three main stakeholders: its employees, its business partners and the general public. Before plowing forward and investing in the new idea, the company must overcome such fears by educating the fearful.[26]

Making adoption happen

There are many elements that go into adoption of a business concept. Fortunately for us, we had several helpful factors that acted as a catalyst, moving customers in our direction. First, the progression of software solutions over the last 30 years gave us the raw material to develop customized solutions that have allowed us to redefine the printing, transportation and media-buying industries. Second, the Internet predisposes customers in those industries to be open to faster and more advanced solutions to their problems and that made it easier to put our solution on their desktops.

In every industry where you try to launch a brave new idea, there will be early adopters and you should resolve to treat them like gold. They are not only your first revenue stream. They are your R&D department.

As we've said, the evolution of technology, the Internet and the expanding wireless universe have created an opportunity to build systems that will fundamentally change the basic mechanics of many service-oriented business models. From insurance to banking to health care to brokerage and so on, we are witnessing the convergence of two powerful and often opposing business concepts—service and efficiency.

By building and/or adopting technology solutions that are designed to re-engineer the back-end delivery function of a service business, the framework of the service itself can be revolutionized, creating both price arbitrage that will allow the business to scale at a greater rate than the rest of the marketplace and operational efficiency that can be used as a tool to attract and retain clients.

Here are some companies that got the mix right—they had the right idea, the right technology and the right service to foster rapid adoption of their products:

optionsXpress: In seven years, Chicago-based optionsXpress has become one of the nation's largest online options and stocks discount brokerages by focusing on the retail investor. Through its public online brokerage subsidiary optionsXpress and brokersXpress, an online trading and reporting platform for independent investment professionals, the company offers a wide range of educational and proprietary investor tools and competitive commissions.

The success of optionsXpress is notable because it has gathered more than 225,000 individual customers with its low-cost, high-feature model despite the collapse of the stock market in 2001, which nearly wiped out the day-trading movement.

The company has eliminated pain in a number of ways. It has a simple user interface that allows new customers to fund their accounts in a day, its learning tools are easy to use and its trades are often cheaper compared to the competition.

Its site is constantly ranked among the best on the Internet for ease of use and navigation and that's fueled its accelerated adoption in the market. This is a classic example of how technology, when applied in a new manner to an old problem, can sweep through an industry and create disruption.

Expedia.com: Founded as a division of Microsoft in October 1996, Expedia is now an independent Internet-based travel company that includes the following Web-based businesses under its name: Expedia, Expedia Corporate Travel, TripAdvisor, Classic Vacations, eLong, Hotels.com and Hotwire.com. Though it opened the same year as its archrival Travelocity.com, it has taken the lead in redefining the travel agency business. Once the site gained a reputation for accurate sales of flights, hotels, tours and car rentals, its cost and efficiency advantage turned the traditional travel agency business upside down. Today, Expedia competes with dedicated sites at airlines, tour companies and rental car companies for business, but Expedia's growth and adoption have been admirable. Expedia received more than 29 million visitors in July 2007, generated over $2 billion in revenue in 2006 and had a market cap of over $10 billion as of October 2007.

Barnes & Noble: Who would ever have envisioned the neighborhood bookstore as coffeehouse, singles club, music store, catalyst for gentrifying neighborhoods and, last but not least, Internet powerhouse? Barnes & Noble (B&N) got its start in Wheaton, Illinois, in 1873 as a book printing business and opened its first bookstore in New York City in 1917 on Fifth Avenue and 18th Street, which it still considers its flagship location. After current chairman Leonard Riggio bought that location and the B&N name in the early 1970s, he began to consolidate retail ownership of some of the major names in the bookstore business—B. Dalton, Doubleday and notably, BookStop, a Texas-based discount bookstore acquired in 1989 that would give Riggio the killer weapon that would pile up the corpses of dozens of local and regional book chains around the country—discounting on best sellers. B&N would migrate its mail-order catalog online for the first time in the late 1980s with an early venture that Sears, Roebuck and Co. and IBM started called Trintex. It moved its online bookstore to CompuServe, then to America Online and then started its own independent site, www.barnesandnoble.com, in 1997. It's an amazing story in that B&N managed to disrupt not one, but several industries—the traditional book business, retail development and Internet retailing. It remains an innovator in a very tough business in these key ways:

- ✔ It saved the bookstore business by turning the bookstore into a gathering place—literally a community center.

- ✔ By creating a global system of discounted inventory both in-store and online, it retains the same customer loyalty and attention span across both platforms.

- ✔ As the traditional record store industry has consolidated, B&N has captured what's left of that market as a destination area in its stores.

- As Wal-Mart turned the tables on its suppliers by forcing them to kowtow on price and selection to reach its extensive customer base, B&N did the same with the entire publishing industry. Now, book producers large and small have to fight for shelf space in B&N and Borders, the nation's two largest book chains.

Netflix: The trip to the local video store had become something of a common activity in most American neighborhoods—families piled in the car or wandered down the block and spent anywhere from a few minutes to an hour walking up and down the aisles, staring at the empty video boxes, wondering what to take home for the night. Once home, there was the pressure to watch the video and then put it by the door so someone would remember to drop it off to avoid paying late fees.

Nobody was talking about renting DVDs on the Internet back in 1998 when Reed Hastings founded Netflix. In fact, the now-ubiquitous DVD video format wouldn't outrun the long-dominant VHS tape as the primary medium for movie rental until 2003. Today, Netflix is the world's largest online movie rental service, offering nearly 6.8 million subscribers access to 80,000 titles. It disrupted the 20-year-old video industry as follows:

- It eliminated the need for customers to go to their bricks-and-mortar video rental retailer with an online ordering system and home delivery service based entirely on the U.S. Mail.

- It eliminated the annoying industrywide late fee by charging customers a monthly fee for a specific number of DVDs delivered to their home with no deadline for return.

- It developed a proprietary algorithm that used historical buying patterns based on customer choices to predict future video selections that customers might be interested in.

- It allowed customers a freedom of choice and the ability to queue up their movies without the "staring at the shelves" phenomenon of the traditional video store.

- It is currently testing direct-to-customer digital movie delivery that may someday usurp its groundbreaking DVD model.

These businesses all started with pain and the entrepreneurs behind those businesses never took their eye off creating solutions that relieved that pain. For example, Netflix is looking at digital distribution because it realizes that someday its loyal audience which was once too busy to go to the video store might be too busy to go to the mailbox.

Functionality is everything

To achieve adoption your solution has to work. It has to be spot on. Good technology cannot take a bad business model or a bad solution and make it work. That said, assuming you have actually thought through a solution to an existing problem and your solution solves, technology's role is instrumental. As we have discussed previously, technology may be the backbone of what you actually deliver, as is the case with many of our companies. Or technology may be less critical to your solution but it may still serve as a catalyst, either on your end or your customer's end, to foster more rapid adoption. For example, in Expedia's case, technology serves both as a fundamental element of the business itself (it's an e-commerce website) and as technology has spread (more users on the Internet) its revenues have gone up proportionately as it uses the Internet, which is growing organically, as its primary distribution channel.

Technology's influence on the rate of adoption should not be overlooked. For example, Eric Schmidt, the CEO of Google, spoke recently at a conference I attended about a small company that made plastic food which had purchased certain key words on Google like "fake food" and "faux food" etc. The business grew something like 1,000 percent in the last few years based upon visitors who found it for the first time on Google and without Google would have had a hard time finding it in the first place. In this case, the company does not rely on technology to deliver its products (at least not that I know of given that it manufactures plastic food), but technology had served as the most influential force in the growth and adoption of that particular company's products in the market. In other words, without Google, this company would not thrive in the manner it does today.

Send in the clowns

It is one thing to disrupt an industry. It is completely another to sustain a business that continually disrupts a marketplace when others crowd in.

We've been fortunate to be disruptive pioneers in most of the industries that we have entered. This was particularly true for MediaBank, where we realized that most media buyers—representing some of the most influential and creative thinkers on the planet—were using legacy systems that were based on technology that was 20 years or more old.

The advertising industry, like the media industry as a whole, is undergoing massive change. The traditional roots of analog media are being overtaken by a tidal wave of digitization. Whole segments of the industry are either going away or being reinvented at this moment. Ten years ago, the dominant players in the media industry would have made it virtually impossible for us to walk in with our solution and take significant market share away from them. Today however, technology has advanced to the point where no individual, no matter how much hands-on experience he or she has, can operate efficiently without a dedicated technology solution to help do some part of the job at the speed the industry requires. Given the effects of digital media, human experience and automated tools are more inseparable than ever and those who won't adopt will fall behind.

Our next adoption challenge

As I'm writing this chapter, we're in the midst of launching a new company called ThePoint.com, a revolutionary concept in the burgeoning activism space. ThePoint is an online collaborative network of people working together to solve problems. By leveraging the collective intelligence and contributions of hundreds of millions of Internet users, we're building a one-stop hub to facilitate the transition from a loose collection of words and opinions into highly coordinated action among hundreds, thousands and who knows, millions of people.

Chapter 7: The Law of Adoption

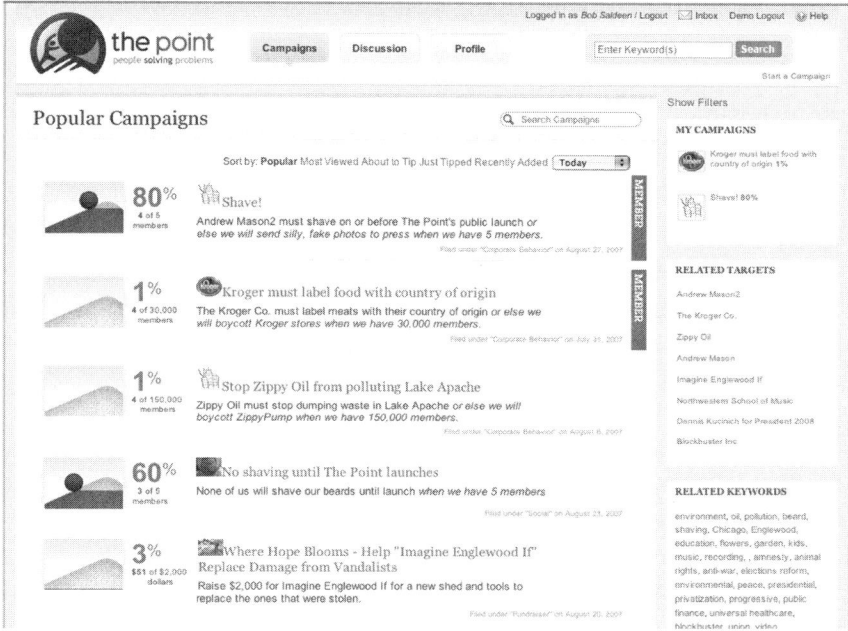

Fig. 7.1: A historic version of the ThePoint.com's home page

ThePoint is a place where people can solve the problems they share but can't solve alone. Building off of the Web's proven effectiveness at aggregating knowledge and building networks of like-minded people, The Point introduces the Tipping Action Model, a framework which allows people to commit to take an action that will solve a problem, but not actually take the action until enough people join together to guarantee success. From consumer rights to activism to organizing labor to fundraising, ThePoint brings unprecedented simplicity to solving countless problems that, until now, seemed unsolvable. With ThePoint, every action makes a difference.

We see ThePoint.com accomplishing the following:

- ✔ Connecting people to others with similar problems
- ✔ Providing an outlet for people who are frustrated and thereby motivated to achieve results no matter what the issue or subject is
- ✔ Minimizing the effort required to participate

✔ Maximizing the impact of each individual contribution

ThePoint organizes the grievances of our users into action-oriented groups (campaigns) that are created on the fly to solve a specific problem that is shared by the group members. Users are guided by their concern into one of our main sectors: employment, consumer, political or social, where they find and congregate with like-minded users who are also seeking resolution. Together, as they reach critical mass, they have enough aggregate power to either synchronously carry out the desired resolution or force the party that has wronged them to take corrective action or suffer the collective consequence.

ThePoint leverages the Internet's enormous interest-driven communities to organize groups that were traditionally dispersed and poorly represented. We hope users will gravitate to ThePoint to resolve issues, such as:

Example Issue Type	
Economic	I want to take action against someone who sold me something
Economic	I want a big conglomerate to treat me fairly
Economic	I am seeking to buy something that requires a large body of people
Political	I want to join others in communicating a message
Political	I want to tell my legislators that I and others want him or her to vote a certain wcy
Employment	I have a grievance and I want to form an alliance and seek a resolution
Employment	I want to negotiate as a unified group
Social	I have a problem or issue and I want to discuss it with others
Social	I want to form or join a community of people that share something in common with me
Public	I want to discuss a local problem or find others that might have a similar experience
Corporate	I am a small company and want to find other small companies that have the same problem I have

Adoption occurs through a significant effort to personally convert one user at a time or more virally as the application is thrown into the marketplace and people, over time, gravitate towards it. This latter phenomenon has fueled sites like Wikipedia, YouTube and MySpace and we hope to follow in their path with ThePoint.com.

Let's take a minute to consider Wikipedia. You launch a topic and people with various interests and expertise gravitate to that topic and work on it like a quilt—adding detail, applying facts and scrubbing it for accuracy and depth. People don't have to be *told* to do this—they just show up and do it. There is a famous story about a college student who put his term paper on Wikipedia and within 24 hours the entire paper had been corrected, edited, rewritten and accredited. Whether this story is true or not, it certainly highlights the collective force that is fueling the open source and collaborative movement on the Internet today.

The new phenomenon of sites like Wikipedia opens up a world of possibilities. The idea that people congregate online is one thing. Plenty of people congregate online for all sorts of reasons. But after the first 15 years of common use of the Internet by people from all walks of life, we notice that users are willing to use their personal expertise, their own curiosity and the tools they bring to bear in the offline world to solve problems online and move information ahead. We sense a growing sophistication and sense of purpose in the online community that we believe is still relatively untapped. This new pool of natural resources represents a cataclysmic shift in how products can and will come to market. Instead of one person, one team or one set of developers, you now have access to the universe of talent that exists in the market.

Our primary business attraction to ThePoint.com is the opportunity to build meaningful and lasting traffic. But we believe customer adoption will create a new system of conflict management and a call to action that can create future revenue opportunities as these communities develop.

> ### *Hypothetical Example*
>
> 1. MADD (Mothers Against Drunk Driving) learns of a chain of bar/restaurants (e.g. TGIF) that offers 2-for-1 specials at "Happy Hour."
>
> 2. The MADD representative puts the concern on **ThePoint**. She sets the action requested as "I will not patronize TGIF until they stop encouraging drunk driving with inexpensive drink specials."
>
> 3. With some additional user input, the system calculates the number of "points" needed to reach the tipping point. In this case, we might consider the size of the restaurant chain and the average bill (800 restaurants and $35).
>
> 4. The system calculates a running total of the effect of this action. Each user represents (as an example) one visit per restaurant per month. 1,000,000 users = $35,000,000 in lost revenue per month.
>
> 5. The link for this action goes on the MADD website ("Click here to do something about TGIF's alcohol policies.") Additionally, an e-mail with ThePoint link goes to MADD membership and affiliates.
>
> 6. Users click on the link, register their grievance by "Pointing" and contributing to the tipping point calculated for the restaurant to take action.
>
> 7. Ultimately, TGIF recognizes the magnitude of damage the campaign could potentially inflict, and concedes to its demands.

We haven't fully decided how to monetize the traffic if it shows up, but we clearly understand the value of traffic, as evidenced by today's climate where YouTube was purchased for over $1 billion without meaningful revenue or profits. Why? Because traffic is valuable especially when it's predicable and visible. It's no different than people habitually reading the morning newspaper. If an advertiser knows that his or her demographic is going to show up like clockwork and look at something—then there is value to the advertiser and accordingly to the site owner.

SUMMARY:

Getting your potential customer from "Why?" to "Why not?" is the essence of adoption. The Law of Adoption is closely related to the Law of Objectivity—without a cold, hard look at the possibilities for customer and supplier adoption of your business idea, it shouldn't leave the launch pad. When it comes to technological solutions that can accelerate, support or supplant the human model that dominated before, it's essential to have a solution that's transparent, easy to use and most important, painless.

NEXT CHAPTER: You've got a revolutionary idea that you're sure is going to disrupt the market it's in. But you have to ask yourself how big that market really is. The Law of Space requires that you choose to innovate in a large enough industry so you can carve a niche quietly away from your competitors who are playing in the crowded section of the pool.

CHAPTER 8

The Law of Space

*Make sure you pick a big enough
industry to sustain growth*

The year was 1975 and Sony Corp. had captured the burgeoning U.S. market for upscale consumer appliances with its Trinitron color TVs. Sony was in the vanguard of postwar Japanese companies that took over the American market in electronics, automobiles and other products that benefited from a far superior Asian manufacturing process.

That year, Sony introduced the Betamax, the first home videocassette player, paving the way for home recording of TV broadcasts of shows and movies. The problem, however, was that Betamax was built on a closed operating system—Sony created proprietary technology that worked only with videotapes that operated on their equipment. To get adoption in the market, other manufacturers would have to license the Betamax format as an industry standard. Sony didn't see this as a limitation, because in the 70s, whatever Sony produced, the world wanted.

Within a year, JVC—a subsidiary of Sony rival Matsushita—introduced its own proprietary home video recording technology, VHS. Unlike Betamax, VHS was much friendlier to others looking to license its technology and had several manufacturing advantages, including two hours of recording time instead of the one hour offered by Sony—that meant a consumer could get a whole movie recorded on VHS. By 1984, 40 companies signed on with the VHS format, far outpacing Betamax's reach at the time. By then, the home video sale and rental business had emerged and studios found that the plethora of VHS-format recorders naturally required that they produce more films in VHS format than Beta. By 1988, Sony had to concede the battle—that year, it began producing VHS recorders.

The lesson that Sony painfully learned is that you can't design a disruptive product and then fence it in with all sorts of proprietary restrictions. You end up stifling your idea before it has a chance to grow.

Welcome to the Law of Space.

When I was a freshman in college, a high school buddy of mine, Noah Siegel, had a father in the carpet business. One of his constant problems was what to do with remnants, those sections of carpet left behind after a room with wall-to-wall carpet was finished or an area rug cut off a bolt left behind weird sizes that no one wanted. And of course, there was that leftover green shag in the corner of the warehouse that no one had touched since 1973…

One summer, my friend's father casually suggested that we load up those remnants in a van and try to sell some of them at school during move-in days as a way to earn some beer and pizza money.

At the time, we had no clue how good that idea was. We thought this was going to be a one-time thing, but by the end of our first year we were selling out our inventory at my alma mater, the University of Michigan, and we knew we were on to something bigger. Swarms of students and parents were lined up to purchase our carpets because the idea of walking on that icy-cold floor every day was unbearable and the only alternative was a carpet store miles away. What they needed was available now, sitting in our truck.

We had to navigate a few issues. We had to figure out how to sell carpets when there were city restrictions and permits needed. We also had to find out how to get a constant supply of remnants since we had long since solved my friend's father's problem of having excess remnants in his store. By my senior year, we had five schools under contract (Purdue, Michigan, Notre Dame, Ohio State and Wisconsin) and we were selling thousands of remnants every summer. The business had actually become real—real employees, trucks, revenues and happily, real profits.

We started thinking about further expansion. And that's when the light bulb flickered off.

We sat down and realized that even if we had 100 percent market share, which meant we would have had contracts with over 100 major universities, we might be able to achieve annual sales of $10 million. While that was a lot of revenue for a couple of college kids managing a business part-time, it was finite. In other words, our grand slam was relatively small. In addition, we knew we could never hope to achieve 100 percent market share and so our prospects were even dimmer.

It was my first introduction to being in a market that was literally too small to disrupt.

Find the ocean, not the lake

Our discussion of blue ocean businesses in previous chapters introduced the concept of wide open spaces in the business environment—industries with little evidence of consolidation, standard pricing or service. Fetuses need space to grow—the same is true for a business with a truly revolutionary idea. The larger the industry you target, the less likely you'll be noticed or distracted while you workshop your idea. In the Sony example that started this chapter, it's true Sony started with a revolutionary idea, but it literally drew its own boundaries too tight while challengers galloped ahead.

Let's look again at the industries we've entered:

- ✔ InnerWorkings is part of the $175 billion print industry.
- ✔ Echo Global plays in the $900 billion transportation industry.
- ✔ MediaBank is just one company in the $300 billion advertising industry.

Even at $280 million in forecasted 2007 revenue, InnerWorkings' share is a tiny fraction of the printing industry. Despite its rapid growth, InnerWorkings' size has given it the cloak of secrecy—or competitor disbelief—that made it possible to grow at the rate it has accomplished today. Now that InnerWorkings has scale, it would be too costly, in my opinion, for those same competitors to inhibit it and it would require some 6,000 suppliers all acting together in concert to do so.

It's good to be the small fish innovating in a big pond because you're hidden from your potential competition—you have chosen the most conducive surroundings for growth.

In addition, disruption can be very costly and you may need to fund the business for a time and make strategic corrections. The larger the industry, the larger the growth potential and ultimately the higher the value people will place on your future revenue stream. So it's nice to stay under the radar as you work through many of these issues.

A common mistake we see among new entrepreneurs is that they're attacking spaces that are too small, going after problems that are not relevant enough, big enough, meaningful enough or ultimately valuable enough.

The markets we've attacked

InnerWorkings: According to the 2000 U.S. Census, the printing industry alone accounted for $175 billion of gross revenue in 2002. By print demand, the highest users of print were at that time:

- ✔ Advertising (44.8%)
- ✔ Wholesalers (9.3%)
- ✔ Non-profit organizations (9.2%)
- ✔ Periodical publishers (3.5%)
- ✔ Commercial industrial (3.5%)
- ✔ Technology (2.6%)
- ✔ Business services (2.0%)

- ✔ Insurance (2.0%)
- ✔ Book publishers (2.0%)
- ✔ Social services (2.0%)

When we launched InnerWorkings, we saw the U.S. printing industry, one of the oldest and most established industries in the United States, riddled with layers of inefficiency and mark-up. Since the advent of the Internet, we knew the old way of doing business was both impractical and unsustainable.

InnerWorkings' model provided clients with the best of both worlds—human interaction, contact and experience combined with state-of-the-art technology, systems and processes. Prior to going public, InnerWorkings had identified less than a handful of companies throughout the United States that were approaching this industry from a new and different perspective. None of these companies had adopted the InnerWorkings model at that time. By being first to market, InnerWorkings gained substantial market share and identifiable brand recognition. Given the size of the industry ($175 billion of print with over $9 billion in the company's headquarters state of Illinois) and the cost and expense reduction opportunities that InnerWorkings provided to its clients, the company experienced dramatic growth.

Echo Global Logistics: The third-party freight logistics market in the United States is growing at nearly 15 percent per year; it is expected to reach over $130 billion by the end of 2007. In addition, it's an expanding segment of the $900 billion transportation and logistics industry. The driving force tends to be outsourcing of this function; most companies consider it a non-core activity. According to a 1998 Forrester Research report, 78 percent of industrial suppliers and buyers outsourced all or part of their transportation operations.

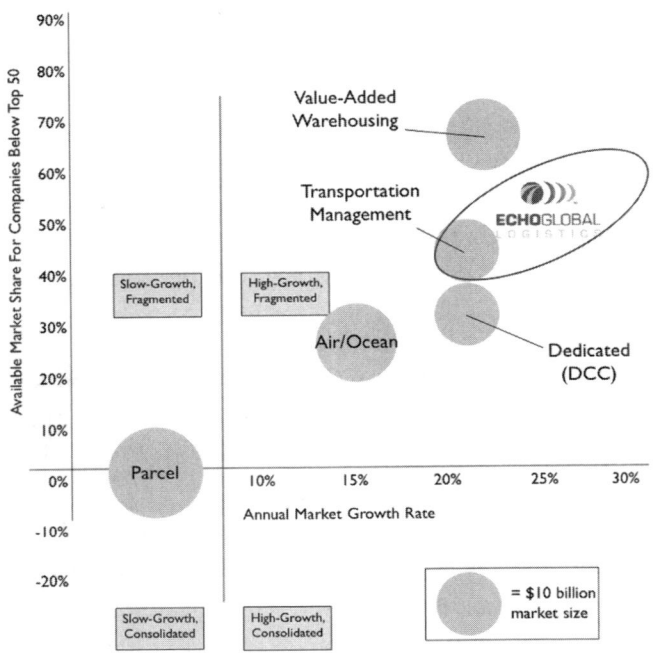

Fig. 8.1: The segment of the transporation industry where Echo resides

Centralized or offshore manufacturing is increasing, as is centralized warehousing, as you can see in the chart above. Both indicate increased shipping in addition to natural growth of economy and population. Third-party logistics is highly fragmented, generating over $113 billion in revenues in 2006 and an estimated $130 billion in revenues in 2007 in the United States with more than 1,000 participants. CH Robinson, the largest surface-oriented, non-asset-based third-party logistics provider in the country, has less than 6 percent of the total market. The majority of companies have fewer than five employees. Each segment of the 3PL industry is marked by extreme fragmentation and disparate service offerings and value propositions.

Our research showed that the industry had low fixed costs, low capital expenditures and consistent demand. Better still, gross margins tended to remain stable or widen in economic downturns. In times of tight capacity, the need for available trucks is greater and the prices shippers are willing to pay are at a premium. Echo passes changes in fuel costs and other related costs on to the customer, thus the margin for the transportation intermediary actually increases in times of tight supply.

Traditional freight brokers have been impaired by weak technology and limited scale. For example, only 4 percent of freight brokers have staffs in excess of 100 people. These brokers are not taking advantage of new and emerging technologies in global mapping, advanced analytics for route intelligence or rate predictive tools and applications.

Furthermore, centralized services for carrier relations and dispatch are very limited. Many of the largest players have every one of their offices competing against each other for loads and carriers, which results in a maze of rules and restrictions. Each office or branch is, essentially, an independent business.

This type of industry-wide fragmentation and enormous scale is exactly what we look for when thinking about a new marketplace. If you made a list of the top 10 characteristics you would like an industry to have, transportation has just about all of them.

MediaBank: The old media-buying model is undergoing significant stress. The traditional approach of looking first to television and then to radio no longer covers what will be an evolving digital media market as it expands. Strategy and planning on one side and procurement on the other need to be separated and yet fully integrated. Doing so allows the cost of media to become more transparent to and controllable by procurement professionals and financial experts.

No longer should media buying exist in a vacuum, blanketed by marketers and outside the scope of modern economic control.

Hundreds of thousands of new billboards have been built since December of 1995. According to Netcraft Web Server Survey (Netcraft.com), as of March 2007, there were 146.3 million users of the Internet in the United States and over 108 million unique websites, each with an opportunity to advertise. In addition, with the growth of cable TV across thousands of markets on both terrestrial cable and home-based satellite networks, non-Internet advertising media is exploding as well. And if satellite digital radio ever goes commercial, that might also provide hundreds of new stations to support national and regional advertising. The bottom line is that the number of new advertising mediums is expanding by the minute.

The dramatic rise of new media over the past decade has created a market opportunity that MediaBank is ideally positioned to capture. The challenge in navigating the current landscape is not a marketing challenge or an advertising challenge or a media planning challenge—it is an informational challenge. The problem is that there is too much media with too many consumer variables and there is no automated mechanism today for a media buyer to effectively understand where and when to buy media.

The advertising industry has experienced modest growth over the past few years, fueled primarily by online forms of advertising.

Total U.S. advertising spending is expected to increase 1.7 percent in 2007 to $152.3 billion, according to the full-year forecast released in June 2007 by TNS Media Intelligence.[27]

2007 Advertising Growth Estimates by Medium (Ranked By Growth Rate)

	% CHANGE vs. 2006
Internet[1]	16.00%
Cable Network TV	5.90%
Outdoor	4.60%
Consumer & Sunday Magazines	4.50%
Spanish Language Media[2]	3.70%
Network Television	1.30%
Syndication TV	1.20%
Radio[3]	-0.30%
Business-To-Business Magazines	-1.50%
Newspapers[4]	-2.90%
Spot TV[5]	-5.50%

Source: TNS Media Intelligence

NOTES:
[1] Internet display advertising only
[2] Spanish Language Media consists of Hispanic Network TV; Hispanic Spot TV; Hispanic Magazines; and Hispanic Newspapers
[3] Radio consists of Local Radio; National Spot Radio; and Network Radio
[4] Newspapers consists of Local Newspapers and National Newspapers
[5] Spot TV estimates do not include Hispanic Spot TV

Although companies have dramatically increased their marketing budgets over the past decade, the impact of this spending has failed to keep pace. Now, as we enter into a potentially extended period of slower economic growth, it is imperative that organizations restructure their marketing spend by adopting a do-more-with-less approach. This will require the management of marketing dollars as both a cost and an investment, manipulating market opportunities as never before.

As you can see, every industry we chose to focus on is quite large. The way to think about size is simple. If your business grows at 50 percent a year for 10 years, what percent of the market would you capture? If the answer is 20 percent, the industry is too small, in my opinion. If the answer is 2 percent, the industry is big enough and exciting enough for you to focus on.

How scalable is your idea?

If you have a truly innovative business concept, it's almost destined to fail in a very small space. Consider that you have a great idea for selling rubber hats with personalized names on them for people who want to wear rubber hats on their heads. After designing the most attractive rubber hat possible, you immediately sell to the 2,000 people in the United States who represent a 100 percent market share. A monopoly might be a nice fantasy, but in this space, you're doing $9,000 annually with no chance of achieving higher revenue.

There are some basic questions you should ask yourself at this stage, even if they seem elementary. Does this business actually solve a specific problem in a large market? What's the value proposition? Do I think that many people need to buy this thing? Once we build it, how scalable is it? Can I see this thing going from one client to a thousand clients, from $100,000 in revenue to $100 million in revenue and beyond? And finally, *how big is the marketplace?*

Space and scale are interconnected. To scale you need space, as scalability involves a couple of factors:

✔ As your business grows, the cost of each incremental dollar in revenue must go down.

✔ The business needs to become attractive to the largest possible mass of suppliers and customers.

Space is the only frontier

We feel the prospects for the businesses we've founded are limited only by our imagination and our execution. We've chosen to flood very wide spaces with outsourced technology solutions that connect to established providers in the various industries we're in with an incentive to fill trucks, sell print or buy media. These are giant industries with no efficient means of doing what we're doing.

Again, you're looking for large industries with plenty of players and plenty of pain.

Here are a few interesting cases to think about, all focusing on large fragmented industries with wide open space to build disruptive models:

Skymeter Corp.: (www.skymetercorp.com) Skymeter is a satellite-based system for toll collection, traffic congestion management and pay-as-you-drive insurance ratings.

Tolling is a business as old as the roads. Today, several state governments have sold sections of toll roads to private owners. The Indiana Toll Road was leased by the state of Indiana several years ago to an Australian-Spanish partnership for $3.8 billion for the next 75 years, but critics have asserted that with increases, the private partnership will collect $133 billion as tolls rise over time—not a bad deal for those who own the road.

Skymeter's approach aims to destroy the traditional tollbooth, the parking meter and the assessment model insurers use to set premiums for drivers.

The system is based on global navigation satellite systems like GPS and Galileo and the company believes that it can open up all sorts of new possibilities in these ancient spaces, from congestion management on the roads to pay-as-you-go parking and variable insurance based on your specific driving history that's collected from above as you drive.

The more aggressive tolling being done in cities like London to cut back their serious urban traffic problems is a natural for satellite-based providers who can give drivers incentives to use alternate routes by lowering fees for driving or parking based on congestion. Safer, less-frequent drivers would save the most money on insurance based on their accident-free time and schedule on the roads, at least in principle.

In summer 2007, this company was preparing its product for multi-industry field trials by road authorities, parking authorities, insurance companies and traffic system integrators. Skymeter was planning to set up "data-sharing programs so that each participant may examine the data from other industries or other cities, yielding considerably more value for each participant."

Salesforce.com: With over 30,000 customers since its founding in 1999, Salesforce.com is now the No. 1 customer relationship management (CRM) software solution in the world. Salesforce.com's Internet-based program has forced consolidation in the out-of-the-box side of the CRM software industry—including the purchase of Siebel Systems by Oracle in 2005—as the company launched the AppExchange so software developers could build their own Web-based enterprise applications atop Salesforce.com's infrastructure. The capabilities of this group-engineered software are approaching products made by leaders like Microsoft and Oracle.

A July 22, 2007 *USAToday* piece said "there is little debate over Salesforce's imprint on the software industry. Robert Desisto, vice president of research at Gartner, who in 2005 issued a grave report about Salesforce's sales prospects, now deems it a leader in the $2 billion software market for salespeople. By 2011, one-fourth of new business software will be delivered via services such as Salesforce, he says."

The Exception to the Rule

The one exception to always looking for large industries is to find smaller industries that are in the midst of rapid expansion. Take for example the following:

Nextmedium.com: As consumers continue to leave the room or change the channel as traditional advertising comes on, advertisers are constantly looking to streamline the way they get their message in front of the right eyeballs. Los Angeles-based Nextmedium.com automates and standardizes the process of product placement in TV shows, movies and videogames. Today, product placement is estimated as a relatively small space, about $2 billion in total revenue, but most deals are being done on the fly without any standardized pricing or measurement. Nextmedium is also working with Nielsen Media Research to start measuring placement, which extends their products into the much larger rating and research segment of the market.

Today, Hollywood. Tomorrow, your cell phone? Depending on how well this company executes and how communication technology evolves, its market space could get a whole lot larger in the near future.

SUMMARY:

> *The Law of Space asks a very simple question—how much real estate can your idea cover? It's a critical question for the future of your business because as technology and consumer needs evolve, you don't want a product or solution that serves only a limited audience—you want to be behind an idea that can morph and grow without physical restriction.*

NEXT CHAPTER: Whoever said there are no stupid questions was a prophet years ahead of his time. The Law of Ignorance discusses the proper management of the learning curve in every stage of your business cycle—planning, testing, roll-out and beyond. And it all starts with simple questions.

Chapter 9

The Law of Ignorance

Don't be afraid to ask the stupid questions

Depending on which biography you read, Albert Einstein didn't utter a word until he was either three or five years old. After that point, he used the power of words and thought to question elements of our physical world that no one until his time even dreamed existed.

Einstein once said, "The important thing is not to stop questioning. Curiosity has its own reason for existing. One cannot help but be in awe when he contemplates the mysteries of eternity, of life, of the marvelous structure of reality. It is enough if one tries merely to comprehend a little of this mystery every day. Never lose a holy curiosity."

Einstein never failed to indulge his own curiosity, asking questions of anyone he met. He was a regular sparring partner with his teachers, other scientists and political leaders. He promoted his ideas at their earliest stage, always aware that if he made a mistake, there was time to go back to the drawing board and get it right.

According to a 2004 story in Discover *magazine, "In 1911 Einstein predicted how much the sun's gravity would deflect nearby starlight and got it wrong by half. He rigged the equations of general relativity to explain why the cosmos was standing still when in fact it wasn't. Beginning in the mid-1920s, he churned out faulty unified field theories at a prodigious rate. American physicist Wolfgang Pauli complained that Einstein's "tenacious energy guarantee[s] us on the average one theory per annum, each of which is usually considered by its author to be [the] 'definitive solution.' "*[28] *For a while, Einstein even denied that black holes existed.*

Einstein's insatiable quest for knowledge, however, and his ability to accept that there was a world of knowledge to which he was ignorant, allowed him to weed through every wrong solution until he finally stumbled upon the right one. When the poet Paul Valery once asked Einstein if he kept a notebook to record his ideas, Einstein looked at him with mild but genuine surprise. "Oh, that's not necessary," he replied, "It's so seldom I have one."[29]

And yet his most famous equation, $E=mc^2$, is widely considered one of the highest intellectual achievements of humanity.

Question, try, succeed, fail, question again. Business may not tolerate as many mistakes as Einstein made in the early years of his work in physics, but the minute an entrepreneur or business leader stops asking questions or assumes his or her model is perfect, trouble ensues.

Welcome to the Law of Ignorance—when knowing nothing may actually help you learn everything.

In established companies, particularly the largest ones, the process of researching a new idea can take months, even years. There's a structure for it, specific staff dedicated to it, an actual corporate culture built up around the concept of innovation.

Take the Post-it Note, truly a disruptive product at the time.

In the 1970s, Arthur L. Fry and Spencer F. Silver of 3M—Fry a new products developer, Spencer an adhesives specialist—met at a seminar Silver hosted on a particular reusable adhesive he created. Fry sang in a choir and he was always trying to find a bookmark that wouldn't slip out of his hymnal onto the floor.

Once Fry saw Silver demonstrate his adhesive on paper, Fry wrote up his idea to create a reliable, reusable bookmark and handed it in to his bosses. According to MIT,

Management initially worried that the product would seem wasteful; but the staff could not get enough of the samples Fry was passing around. Soon, 3M gave the invention its full support. It took another five years to perfect the specifications and design machines to manufacture the product, but in 1980 Post-it Notes were introduced nationwide.[30]

Do you think it would have taken five years for a smaller company to get the Post-it Note to market?

The great challenge for large corporations is that they are often paralyzed by the weight of their own infrastructure. In order for them to muster resources, they need to gain consensus among many people and navigate vast internal politics. While this phenomenon has historically not impaired larger corporations from being innovative (i.e. Apple's iPod, Toyota's Prius, etc.), the pace of technology change will make it increasingly more difficult for larger companies to compete if they cannot accelerate the speed with which they bring new inventions or products to market. Quite simply, technology will morph the environment around them in a manner that could render the innovation obsolete by the time it's released.

A five-year or even a five-month process doesn't work for disruptive businesses in today's technologically charged environment. The thought process is simple; the tools, basic; the speed, fast. Really fast—maybe a week or two. Relentless curiosity, a phone and an Internet hookup should do it.

We'll learn more about getting ideas to market fast in Chapter 13.

But getting back to Post-it Notes, if someone gave you this book to read, it probably had that person's Post-it on it, not a sheet of paper from a notepad. A destructive idea that's lasted 27 years? That's a feat to be admired.

But all good ideas have to start somewhere and somewhere is always the beginning.

Ignorance is the first step

As Anthony Jay once said, "The uncreative mind can spot wrong answers, but it takes a very creative mind to spot wrong questions."

When you're interested in a particular business and you don't know much about it, don't think you're out in the cold. You're actually in the right place. You are at the starting line, the beginning. The Law of Ignorance states that anyone with little or no knowledge of an industry actually has a better chance of spotting a rift in a business that can be exploited.

As we've said, we started InnerWorkings, Echo and MediaBank out of pure frustration. We couldn't buy print quickly or affordably, we couldn't find trucks at the right times and prices we needed and we wondered why much of our media-buying experience was so obtuse.

We understood our problems, our irritation with them and our nagging suspicion there might be an incredible business opportunity in finding solutions to the pain we were experiencing.

What we didn't know were the industries we were frustrated with. So we started asking questions—hundreds of stupid questions. But as it turned out, they were the kind of stupid questions Anthony Jay would have approved of. Here's how we made a seemingly random investigative process effective.

Finding the "soft middle"

Our very first test project at InnerWorkings was books, a challenging vertical if there ever was one. We had a couple of books we wanted to produce for our first client, but our real purpose was to learn about the industry. If you've ever looked at a book closely, you can identify the separate processes that need to come together to successfully produce the book you hold in your hand:

1. People need to write, edit and lay out the manuscript on pages that fit a particular size and length. (Part human/part digital)

2. Photos, drawings and charts need to be designed and dropped into the manuscript clearly and accurately with proper notations. (Digital)

3. Someone needs to design the cover and dust jacket of the book to make it attractive to buyers. (Part human/part digital)

4. Press time must be contracted to print and bind the interior pages as well as the cover and back cover of the book if it's paperback or the book jacket if it's hardcover. (Human/digital) Within this stage, you need to weed through a great deal of complexity. You're forced to learn the steps and jargon that go into the process very quickly:

   - Prepress requirements and how they relate to ripping and trapping files;

   - How plates are made for the press;

   - How you need to configure your printed signatures to maximize the speed at which paper goes through a printing press;

   - Ink requirements, coating, gathering your printed signatures into folded sections to be bound;

   - Bindery options such as spiral, perfect, notch, case and so on. These and many more details go into the process of manufacturing a book. If you don't understand all the terminology just stated, don't worry—we didn't either. It was something we had to learn.

5. Transportation must be contracted to deliver books to bookstores and other clients (Part human/part digital)

Why did we label each of these points digital or human? Because we started wondering how much an infusion of technology could revolutionize each step of this antiquated, uneven process. Our basic conclusion was that with better use of technology that creates better-informed and more efficient buyers, you could procure books more inexpensively and get them to market in a more efficient manner.

We had our thesis. Then came the process of learning so we could prove or disprove that thesis.

Our strategy was to find a bunch of print suppliers in the book industry. We went in with the fact that we wanted to print two books for which we had a full set of manufacturing specifications (size, color, pages, quantity and other details) and at that point, we didn't reveal much more than that. We just got quotes on how much they would charge us. We received about twenty quotes back. We sat down with that list and drew lines through the top five and bottom five printers price-wise. Then we were left with the ten in the middle.

These ten became our new best friends.

Over the next four or five days, we had a number of conversations with this group of suppliers stuck in the middle of the pack. We knew we were not likely to do business with these guys, but we needed them to be our teachers, to educate us on all of the elements of the business that we did not understand. You see, the bottom five were the suppliers that we were most likely to actually work with due to their attractive pricing. We didn't want to call the five highest-priced printers because we sensed that they might be inefficient or uncompetitive and we couldn't learn as much from them as we could from the others. The middle group was unlikely to get an order, but they were close and we assured them that we still might do business with them down the road so they could see that offering their counsel wasn't futile.

We had identified a group of suppliers that had the knowledge we needed. Like an Oreo cookie, we had found the soft middle.

Of course, based on whatever industry you're in, the competition might already know that you're out there. Keep this February 2007 comment from Microsoft CEO Steve Ballmer in mind. When someone in the audience at a Merrill Lynch investor conference asked him if there was any particular company he was afraid of, Ballmer responded that he was far more worried about being blindsided by a disruptive business idea than any one company in particular:

I think about new business models more than I think of individual companies…Having a competitor that is nominally close to free is always a challenge…That is a set of pricing pressure that nobody should ignore.[31]

Even though your suppliers might eventually be afraid of you or your model, they are still one of your best sources of information as you're developing it. You have to find a way to enlist their help and gain their insights.

Think like an eight-year-old

Someday my son may read this and cringe, but the way a typical eight-year-old kid finds out about the world is a great example for how you investigate an industry for disruption. "How is a baseball bat made?" is a question that veers off in a multitude of directions until it satisfies his curiosity. I start with the response, "Well, you begin with a piece of wood from a tree…"

"How do you chop down the tree?" he asks.

"Well, it takes a big gasoline-powered saw that cuts through the tree," I counter.

He doesn't miss a beat. "Then what happens?"

"They take all the trees they cut down to a factory where it's made into bats," I counter.

"What kind of machine makes it into bats?" he asks again.

"It's a huge machine that the trees get fed into and it cuts them into boards and that wood is ultimately used to make the bat."

"What about aluminum bats?"

"They don't come from trees. Aluminum is metal, something man-made. It doesn't grow in the ground," I respond.

"Do baseball mitts grow in the ground?" he jokes.

"No, they come from leather, but that's a whole different topic," I say, subtly cutting off the discussion.

At some point, the questions have moved outside the realm of relevancy. You see, it appears as if this process is just that of an eight-year-old starting out curious and then getting silly. But what the eight-year-old is really doing is building walls and boxes around an issue that was free of form and shape at the start. When my son started his questioning, he had no idea (literally no idea) how a baseball bat was made. He didn't understand how lumber from a tree can become a product. He didn't understand the labor involved or the aluminum alternative that also can become a similar object. While kids get smarter every day, they don't understand process and their base of knowledge in a new category is quite often non-existent.

What's important here is to know that at the outset of questioning, both my son's baseball bat example and my printing process example are roughly the same. Our thinking is devoid of boundaries and we need to ultimately understand the things we don't understand—we need to build walls around that which is without form or structure.

Those walls my son was building around his baseball bat query? Once he had enough walls to at least understand the topic or know what was relevant to the topic, he could move on. As they learn and develop, kids build mental boxes to contain all the answers and information they collect. And because they start with a clean slate, they tend to learn quickly and understand completely, because their investigation is not limited by what they already know or the preconceptions that they already bring to the table.

Like most parents, there's a point at which I run out of answers. And that's a lesson in itself because most of the people you will be talking with will eventually run out of answers as well. Knowing when you hit this point is a signal that you either need to go in a different direction or seek a new source of information.

As we were investigating InnerWorkings, that's exactly what we did. "How does a book go to press?" led to our understanding of how many towers were on various presses and how they worked, the general choreography for assembling a completed book, how the book was bound, how a cover was printed, the various options for lamination and bindery and all the other steps in between.

Learn how to listen

As these companies thought they were soliciting our business, they were willing to talk to us. They were and still are willing to trade their time for the possibility of business down the road. As someone who needs their help, you need to embrace this. Too often people are limited by their own egos (I'm certainly guilty of this at times) and they're hesitant to ask very basic questions that reflect their ignorance.

The idea is to make your ignorance work for you.

You start by asking every question on your mind about a company's business and you work it all the way back. With research we did online as well as on the phone, there was nothing we didn't ultimately understand or at least become knowledgeable about as it related to the process of printing our two books. In fact, we probably spent more time buying those first two books at InnerWorkings than we spent buying just about any product or service since.

So here we were in late 2001. We finally understood the roots of our pain regarding the printing process and we had the makings of a plan to address that pain. We knew that one of the main attributes of InnerWorkings' model had to be a system that reflected transparency of all printing and pricing data available in the market at any one time. If we could get the foundational information to start the business with a simple series of phone calls and online searches, we could leverage that foundation of simple questions and answers into a sophisticated proprietary database of information.

Today, that foundation now serves InnerWorkings' current network of more than 2,000 customers worldwide.

One of the cornerstones of InnerWorkings' technology was the custom-estimating function of its proprietary database. By 2002, InnerWorkings developed relationships with its top 10 printers and paper suppliers to offer price data that would enable the company to build algorithms that calculated estimated price "on the fly" for several of its major product categories. This was but another advantage that InnerWorkings was delivering to the market, using technology to boldly go where no print procurement agency had ever gone.

And it all started by asking questions like an eight-year-old.

Ten key questions to disrupt a business

In the early days, you're really trying to become a student of your suppliers' and competitors' businesses, because you have to disassemble those processes in order to rebuild them. Here are some general questions to frame the conversation, but because these questions relate specifically to procurement, you might want to tailor them based on the industry you're hoping to enter:

1. We're trying to do X and we're trying to learn a bit more about the business. What's your history and experience? (First you have to establish a basic relationship.)

2. What equipment do you use to produce X? (See how old their capital equipment is and how often they replace it.)

3. Has that process/raw material gotten more or less expensive in the last few years? (Check how close they are to their suppliers.)

4. Who do you directly compete against? (Always seek out as much as you can about the competition.)

5. What makes you better than them? (You need to understand advantage and disadvantage in the marketplace.)

6. For our next project, we might be increasing the quality/quantity of what we need to produce. What solution would you suggest for that? (This will give you an idea of the high-end product in this industry and what it costs to supply it.)

7. What are the busiest/slowest times for you? (This will help you predict capacity in the market that you can capitalize on.)

8. What are potential problems that could occur in getting my order/job/project filled? (This will tell you about various manufacturing breaking points that you need to be aware of.)

9. Are you investing in any new equipment to serve your business? (This gives you an idea of production equipment or technology that's average or cutting edge in the industry.)

10. Are you expecting any price increases in the next few months? (Understand the factors that go into their price adjustments to determine if you can find a way to overcome these price drivers in your business structure.)

Turning the Q&A around

In the case of InnerWorkings, we started learning from our suppliers. They helped us build our industry knowledge and frame our business model. But we were obviously not ready to launch.

It was time to apply the second half of the Law of Ignorance—having various constituencies turn the table around and ask pointed questions (like an eight-year-old) of our business team to help us understand where the holes in our knowledge were. Some of the people we invited to be part of that process are now key advisors and directors.

In the early years of InnerWorkings, we often heard from venture capital firms the following question: "Tell me why you don't think your business model will work." Now, for a company that was doing tens of millions of dollars in profitable business which was growing at triple-digit levels, it was often hard to imagine that someone would be asking another person to identify the flaws in our model, especially in light of how well it was performing.

But the more you think about it, this question actually had a specific purpose. The venture capitalists were trying to build walls around our business model—to understand how big it could be, what others thought of its strengths and weaknesses. Much like we advocate in this chapter, they were poking and prodding to "understand" the boundaries of our model.

I try to remember this proverb when I start investigating a business: "Ask a question and you're a fool for three minutes; do not ask a question and you're a fool for the rest of your life."

Summary:

> *Disruptive businesses call for quick discovery and it doesn't have to be an expensive or time-consuming process. It is critical, however, that you immerse yourself in an industry's workings in the most direct and uncomplicated manner possible—asking question after question until you fully understand the business you plan to disrupt, learning along the way, no different than a child learns.*

Next Chapter: When you're this far along in the development process of a disruptive business, it's easy to become oversold on the concept you've been living with. The Law of Awareness states that if everything feels like a go, you need to stay open to cues from customers, competitors and your own employees to the issues and elements that are both right and wrong with your model.

CHAPTER 10

The Law of Awareness

It's easy to fool yourself

Imagine yourself in the Defense Department in World War II Washington. The sexiest woman in Hollywood has just walked into your office and declared that she has a sweeping new solution to keep the U.S. military's radio-controlled missiles from getting shot out of the sky on the way to their targets. Do you listen to her idea or simply ask for an autograph?

This is the true story of actress Hedy Lamarr, who with partner George Anthell saw the government turn thumbs down on their revolutionary "spread spectrum" technology that would beget the cell phone industry 40 years later. In the 1930s, Lamarr was not only a European matinee idol but also the wife of a prosperous Austrian Nazi weapons manufacturer. As she grew to despise the Nazi regime and her husband, she started paying close attention to her husband's conversations about how easy it was for radio-guided missiles to be sent off course by a jammed signal sent from the ground.

By the time Lamarr escaped to Hollywood in 1940, she and avant-garde musician Anthell had translated Lamarr's idea—that communications could continue unhindered by "hopping" across various radio spectra—into a device that involved a player piano synchronized to a transmitter that would constantly change radio frequencies and thus avoid jamming. The government never bought the idea that Lamarr and Anthell had actually patented in 1942—they told Lamarr to go out and sell War Bonds instead.

Once the patent expired in the late 1950s, Sylvania grabbed the idea and sold the "Frequency Hopping Spread Spectrum" concept to the U.S. military before the Cuban Missile Crisis. And that early technology has morphed into the millions of cell phone towers we see across today's landscape.

One might wonder, however, whether the United States might have won the war a little sooner if the government had listened to a brilliant idea from an unusual source.

Welcome to the Law of Awareness—paying attention to all the forces in the marketplace is essential to success.

Businesses are formed in the wee hours after people finish up at the day jobs they're not so crazy about, in classrooms, on subways, in bathrooms, even inside companies they care about but know are marked for extinction because they don't understand the threat from smarter, nimbler competitors.

But conquering a new business idea can be a bit like David fighting Goliath. And technology, in that metaphor, is the slingshot that allowed David to defeat the mighty Philistine. That's why we believe any business idea is susceptible to disruption—including our own.

We've learned not to analyze our business prospects in a vacuum. Over the course of time, we've learned to listen to our employees, our customers and experts inside and outside our industries who question us rigorously on every aspect of our operation. Each constituency has given us unique perspective and kept us from making some big mistakes, as you'll see below.

The Law of Awareness states that to keep a business disruptive, you need to constantly analyze market data and solicit feedback, adjusting your model with each grain of insight you obtain. We all need input because humans are great rationalizers—often we can't recognize our own flaws, much less the flaws in our business arguments. Building a mechanism for constant, constructive criticism is critical to your business structure.

An old business joke says that if the railroads had understood that they were in the transportation business instead of the steel-rail business, we'd all be flying on Union Pacific Airlines.[32]

As you create an innovative business idea, you need to create a culture that keeps it innovative by empowering those around you to both see and react to the flaws and hidden benefits in everything you're doing.

At the companies we've launched, we believe in fostering a culture that honors logic. We are ruled by logic a bit like Mister Spock is on the TV show *Star Trek*. All things being equal, if you remove emotion from the equation, the vast majority of the time the logical approach is the right approach. Statistics don't lie. It's the reason that I get on a plane even though I hate flying and I still to this day can't possibly understand how the plane actually stays up in the air.

Learning from failure

When you look at people who've achieved business success, keep in mind that they've probably failed at least once. Not necessarily massive failures where the bank has taken the house or car, but they've probably found their idea was flawed and either ran out of money before a wide launch or ended up closing their doors after a period of time. My partners and I have had our share of these experiences and we've learned from each of them. I've been in business since I was 18 and in college—starting with that carpet business—and if there's one thing I've learned it's that every business failure contains valuable insight that can and must be reused throughout your career.

Let's go back to Starbelly, our promotional products e-commerce business. When we got the idea to start the company in 1999, it seemed foolproof. We were already in the decorated apparel business and it seemed like a no-brainer to extend our knowledge to promotional merchandise sold online. The early Internet retailing buzz, however, was in the consumer space and so, when we wrote the business plan our focus was business-to-consumer. But we changed our focus and adopted a business-to-business model within 60 days or so after completing the business plan. Almost as quickly as we had decided to serve consumers, we jumped to the other spectrum and focused our sights on the market for corporate golf shirts, labeled mugs and hundreds of other advertising specialties aimed at businesses.

This was a radical change in our business.

The business-to-consumer model was all about selling a dozen t-shirts to a soccer mom who wanted to get a gift for her team or selling a dozen hats so a dad could put the name of his newborn child on something to give to his friends and family. By switching our focus to businesses, we were leaving the consumer retail and affinity market we were familiar with and entering the world of corporate promotional products and premiums. This new space was different. It had its own industry association. It had its own traditions and practices. It had market leaders and history. In other words, this was a big change for us made possible only because our ears and minds were open. Had we been set in our ways, we never would have shifted our focus so dramatically so early; throughout all of the ups and downs with Starbelly, the one uncontested right move we made was to go after the business-to-business space.

That being said, the shift was still riddled with difficulties. The sheer number of items in various colors, sizes and quantities we needed to make the business work literally crippled our model—and the Internet collapse in 2000 did the rest.

So we know something about awareness because we learned it during the biggest reign of corporate hubris of our generation. We believed that moving fast to get our business online was the sole driver of its success and we were singularly focused on moving fast. In a period of weeks, we took the focus of our model from consumer to business without the rigorous due diligence we highlighted in Chapter 9. Even though the decision was right, our process to make the decision was wrong. We were heavy on Internet Kool-Aid and light on industry data. We needed to learn more from the players in the promotional products industry to determine how things really worked. We were too quick to assume that the existing model was antiquated and that a customer's desire for change would be our primary driver of success.

We had absolutely no doubt in our business model and absolutely no conclusive evidence to support our vanity.

We were living in a state of blinding Internet euphoria.

My partner Brad Keywell took a class at the University of Michigan when he was getting his business degree before law school. It was inspired by the legendary investor Sam Zell, who maintained at the time that entrepreneurship couldn't be taught. He sponsored a contest daring others to disprove his idea and he solicited business plans from professors around the country who would win if they debunked his thesis that entrepreneurship can't be taught in the schools.

The winning professor submitted a business plan for a class called Failure 101. The entire semester was devoted to the practice and study of failure. It was a wonderfully provocative class about how we humans hate to fail and how much knowledge we miss by avoiding failure. The professor went through a series of exercises where students were laughed at, ridiculed and simply ignored. He even had one exercise where students were told to make stuff out of Popsicle sticks to sell on the street—whoever made the most money won.

When you're put in a hopeless situation like that, it really does redefine your concept of failure. Students were out there selling while debunking their own self-perceptions as serious, shrewd businessmen and women. It must have been amazing to see who won and lost each week. But what was truly valuable about Brad's experience was how he and his classmates were flung out of their corporate context into a completely vulnerable environment, which is what entrepreneurs face every day on the job. When you're forced to test your earliest concepts of success and failure, something amazing happens. You're either defeated by failure or it becomes your greatest teacher. You can't truly become wise in business without failure.

As Thomas Edison once said, "Many of life's failures are people who did not realize how close they were to success when they gave up."

In the last half a decade, we've found that disrupting an industry often means lots of very rapid, very short-lived failures, finding out lots of things that don't work and then figuring out what does.

Failure has a regenerative quality. If you embrace it and learn from it, failure can be an agent of growth.

Learning from criticism

As we mentioned before, we now make it a practice to bring in great minds to investigate our businesses at all stages and we expect them to respond with both barrels blazing. By great minds, we mean business leaders we respect, many of whom we have had the privilege to work with as members of the various boards of the companies we have founded including:

- ✔ John Walter: Former Chairman and CEO of RR Donnelley and former President of AT&T
- ✔ Jack Greenberg: Former Chairman and CEO of McDonald's
- ✔ Linda Wolf: Former CEO of Leo Burnett
- ✔ Betsy Holden: Former CEO of Kraft
- ✔ Peter Barris: Managing Partner of New Enterprise Associates
- ✔ Lou Sussman: Vice Chairman, Citigroup
- ✔ Sam Skinner: Former Chief of Staff, former Secretary of Transportation, and former Chairman and CEO of USF Holland
- ✔ Dipak Jain: Dean of Kellogg School of Management, Northwestern University

We also listen to our employees, our customers, our suppliers and our competitors. To say the least, such reactions are not always easy to hear. We have a culture of openness and bluntness in our businesses. We want the cold hard facts and we want them without any mediation. We've also been fortunate that as we've developed a track record, it's made it easier to bring in a much more diverse group of business talent to rake our concepts over the coals.

There are many businessmen and women who have helped us by providing their insights, but I will highlight one as an example. Rick Kash is the founder and CEO of The Cambridge Group, based in Chicago. Kash's 30-year-old consulting firm has steered hundreds of businesses through their growth stages with an emphasis on understanding profitable demand and how and where it originates in the market. He sat down with us as we were developing our launch of MediaBank. We explained to him that MediaBank had the potential to upend the entire advertising business overnight. At the time, our approach was to sell our solution direct to the end advertisers themselves without going through an agency or media-buying firm.

Rick cut to the chase pretty quickly.

While he was fascinated with InnerWorkings and Echo and liked the businesses, he pointed out that both of those companies were essentially buying and selling commodities—printing and transportation. MediaBank, he said, was a completely different animal and we just didn't get it. In his opinion, creative media was not an easily priced commodity and therefore a particular form of expertise was required for its procurement. That expertise, according to Rick, was deeply rooted in the creative relationships between agencies and the largest advertisers in the world and we had little or no chance to break through those trusted relationships even if our idea was revolutionary.

Here we were, sitting proudly with a business model we were certain would revolutionize media buying, certain that we had the solution that would make every major advertiser in the nation switch overnight to our model. Kash highlighted the one great flaw in our hypothesis—that we completely ignored the creative process and the personalities that defined the advertising industry. He said media buying, besides having a clear need for automation, was a specialized business because of the chemistry between advertising agency and client, between media plan and media buy.

We were a little shocked at this reaction at first—we didn't think the creative side of the media-buying business would have any bearing on our technology-rich business model. We just thought that if we placed our solution in the hands of the Fortune 500, they would start making their own choices, allowing data to free them to optimize the market.

But the more we thought about it, we realized that client expertise, insight, research and thoughtfulness are much more significant factors in media buying than in transportation or printing. To this day, the advertising industry is dominated by giant advertising holding companies (WPP, IPG, Omnicom and Publicis) that have deep relationships with marketers at many of the Fortune 500. "You're never going to get into the middle of that relationship," Kash said. And I believe he was largely correct. The value they provide is significant and the resources at their disposal are virtually limitless.

In the beginning, we were quick to reject Kash's ideas. We had already heard the old song that media was not a commoditized business—we thought that he, like the others, was stuck in the Law of Convention. But as we looked closer, we realized he was right and we needed to embrace an alternative model. Eventually, we took his advice and that of others to redirect our solution by offering our software to the largest media-buying agencies as a partner, not a competitor. In other words, we didn't need to call on Microsoft; rather, we'd call on Interpublic Group, which was buying media for Microsoft.

In June 2007, MediaBank bought Datatech Software Corp., a leading provider of advertising software solutions for network, spot, print and direct response media, as well as integrated production and accounting functionality. They had the connections we didn't have to traditional media; we had the connections to digital media that they didn't.

In 2008, if we're successful, our solution will be servicing a large percentage of the Fortune 500 through our media-buying agency clients. Had we not changed direction, we would most likely still be trying to get our first Fortune 500 client to take a meeting with us.

Learning from listening

Great ideas often emerge from two groups—your employees or your customers. Why? Because both are intimately interacting with your product. But you have to create the kind of environment in which you get that feedback and use it constructively. As we've stressed throughout this chapter, disruptive companies are not formed without this kind of communication flowing throughout the organization.

As Hollywood mogul Steve Ross once said, "You can't operate a company by fear, because the way to eliminate fear is to avoid criticism. And the way to avoid criticism is to do nothing."

CEOs need to break through the walls in their organizations to reach ALL constituencies directly. Your technology can open the gates to this valuable information if you design it in such a way that data flows without restriction. In addition, you need to disrespect (that's right, disrespect) the traditional boundaries and walls that exist within most corporate hierarchies, which often create barriers to get through the weeds to the real information and the real root of the problem.

I have been accused at times of micromanaging. While I don't mind the description, I actually think it's inaccurate. I have grown too impatient to really spend the time that is required to be a good micromanager. Instead, my philosophy is to disrespect traditional organizational boundaries when I am actively engaged in a business. Just because someone works for someone who works for someone who might work for me or for whom I might be consulting, is irrelevant. I want and need to be free to go to anyone at any time and have a direct conversation. I don't want information to be filtered, mediated or translated. As they say, the devil is in the details and I believe you need to be in direct contact with the details. Not all the time, not even a majority of the time, but at least some of the time.

Without this connection, you are lost. As Gates says, "Genetic research, like science in general, progresses through a series of unexpected connections. The more information that scientists have about the work of other scientists, the more likely they are to fill in gaps of knowledge and connect the dots between seemingly unconnected data."[33]

Just like scientists who are forced to openly share information in order to find a cure, you need to build an environment where information flows without restriction and collaboration is encouraged without limitation.

But getting information from inside your organization is only half the battle. You need to construct the same type of open pathway for information to flow from your customers.

In a 2005 *Chief Executive* story entitled "The CEO's Role in Innovation," Clive Mendelow, chief operating officer at Philadelphia-based real estate giant Binswanger, said, "Innovation begins at the interface between the company and the customer…And this isn't just the cliché concept of listening to your customer. This is creating a culture of understanding the big picture in which your customer operates. It's not just understanding the customer; it's understanding the milieu, the environment."[34]

Brian Murray, operations group president for HarperCollins, described in that piece how Swiss jewelers became so focused on making incremental improvements to the tiny mechanical parts in their watches that they were blindsided by the emergence of quartz technology. The Japanese swooped in on their markets:

> If you listen to your existing customers, a disruptive innovation can come along, like something that's technology-based, which the customers are behind the curve on. They don't know what new markets could be coming down the road…So you need to have two sets of antennae out there: One listening to your customers, but the other looking at what is completely disruptive that even your customers may not be attuned to.

Once you have open channels between your employees and your customers, you should find ways to encourage not just open communication, but innovative communication. In other words, let them be part of determining how your disruptive solution will evolve over time. Emerson

Chairman Emeritus Charles L. Knight also commented in the *Chief Executive* piece that "While some innovation occurs in high-level planning discussions and management retreats," businesses need to push for more unpredictable channels of information. During his tenure, Knight said that as much as $20 million a year would be budgeted for employees "who had potentially lucrative, unproven concepts that needed an infusion of cash to get off the drawing board." Granted, that's a product-driven approach, but whether you're talking about specific products, systems or anything that resembles a disruptive idea, you need to build the right pathway for information to flow.

Learning from transparency

And how do you build this pathway? I believe there are two critical aspects that must be in place:

1. Information has to be honored as if it is holy—literally holy. You can't respect the data sometimes and ignore it others. Either you are going to allow information and data, if statistically clean and accurate, to govern your actions or you are just wasting your time in collecting it in the first place.

2. The highway upon which information travels in your organization must be kept pure—literally pure. You can't allow anyone to filter it, tamper with it or manipulate it. The data is what the data is. If it's clean, it's clean. If it's dirty, it's dirty. If it tells you your favorite product is no good, your favorite product is no good. If it tells you that you lose money every time you take an order less than $75, you lose money. Information doesn't lie, but it can be tampered with and if the pathway upon which information and data travels in your company requires human intervention and human manipulation—the process is tainted.

It is amazing to me how often we are engaged by high-level executives to conduct an audit of an internal procurement function and the process gets tainted due to someone's self-interest.

It typically goes something like this: We are engaged to perform an audit. We ask for 20 random invoices. The invoices are pulled by someone further down the food chain in that organization who for their own reasons doesn't want to work with us. They pull selected invoices that they believe represent abnormally low prices. We know this is happening, but we still conduct the audit because we're confident our price advantage should still allow us to deliver savings.

We come back with numbers that are dramatically lower than their historic prices. And boom—they tell us, "Oh, our mistake, we didn't provide you the right data, our price wasn't really X, it was Y, or that item had another component to it, or our price was only that high because we had a special rush that we forgot to tell you about...." In other words, the data was tainted. What's amazing to me is not that people want to protect their jobs or come across as if they buy something as well as it can be bought to protect their ego. We've found those are natural reactions to the idea of outsourcing. What's amazing to me is that their companies allow it to occur. And why? Because their organization does not, at its core, honor and respect the purity of data.

Adds Gates: "Numbers give you the factual basis for the direction in which you take your products. Numbers tell you in objective terms what customers like and don't like. Numbers help you identify your highest priorities so that you can take fast tactical and strategic action."[35]

In other words, without numbers—pure data—you are flying blind.

But getting back to Awareness, early in our days at InnerWorkings, we had the idea that we would approach our customers exclusively with an enterprise solution. We wouldn't take a job with Company X unless we could take *all* its printing work. Our plan was to place an individual onsite at their office acting as a sort of print traffic cop for the entire organization. Now, that idea certainly had merit as InnerWorkings still has that system in place at many of its largest customers even today. But as we discovered by really listening to our early customers, enterprise solutions weren't always going to get us through the door.

We discovered that organizations aren't always likely to say, "Hey, we just met, but you're welcome to take over my entire print spend and I'll outsource everything to you including the most critical elements of my marketing budget." In the beginning, customers were impressed by the potential of our solution, but at times they wanted to test drive us first. When we had that feedback returned to us over and over, we retreated from our enterprise-only salesforce model and developed a team of transactional sales representatives who would focus on serving a particular piece of business within an organization and use that as a stepping stone to an enterprise relationship down the road.

This is a critical point about listening. If you're going to listen for anything, listen for arrogance. Particularly your own.

Learning from adjustment

Test it, measure it, refine it. Repeat.

When we talk about adjustment within a business model, we're not talking about small tweaks and changes, though with success, a company gets to that point over time. Because we believe that awareness means an ability to recognize that nothing is sacred in a business idea, we have adjusted business models wholesale in their first months of operation.

Consider as another example our early days of Echo, when we thought that the way to obtain market share was to sign exclusive deals with particular truckers who would work for us on a contracted and committed basis. At the start, we thought there would be some advantage to us having our own trucking capacity—having our own captive fleet—so we formed a partnership with a small trucking company that had signed up owner-operated trucks throughout the Midwest. The idea was for us to build a huge fleet of trucks through which we could direct some of our brokered loads to maximize their capacity. Even though we felt strongly about the merits of the idea, we decided to test our concept with two trucks just to see how well the model would work.

We quickly determined we were better off being a truck broker than a trucking company—we didn't want to repair trucks, pay for their fuel, manage a fleet of drivers, worry about liability, etc. We wanted all of that management responsibility and additional cost in other hands—not ours.

For us, refinement isn't something you do once a year. It's much like a portrait where the artist goes back to the canvas several times to remove some shading here, add a drop of paint there. Constant refinement is confirmation of the Law of Awareness—that you are always looking for different market behaviors and are ready to steer change to your advantage.

Summary:

> *The Law of Awareness states that you can't lead only with your own instincts whether you're in your first year of business or your fifth. Every disruptive business needs to develop a superior listening and learning system that draws immediate feedback from every key constituency you have—customers, employees, suppliers, competitors and wise outsiders willing to give you an honest point of view.*

NEXT CHAPTER: The Law of Arbitrage is more than finding profit in a disruptive business idea. It's all about the ways to determine whether your disruptive idea actually works and how to keep it working.

Chapter 11

The Law of Arbitrage

How do you know if your solution actually solves?

Las Vegas and Wall Street are two vital American institutions built on a simple concept—spread. The difference between what goes into the slot machine and what comes out has created billions of dollars in wealth. In the case of Wall Street, that tiny commission on each trade, the fractional advantage that comes with size and scale on the trading floor, has fueled some of the most influential and valuable financial institutions in the world: names like Goldman Sachs, Morgan Stanley, Merrill Lynch and Bear Stearns.

The concept of arbitrage is similar to spread insofar as spread is the amount you can earn by trading on advantage. The dictionary defines arbitrage as the system of buying assets in one market and selling them in another to profit from unjustifiable price differences. We would argue that business arbitrage isn't just about profit—it's about value.

When Charles R. Schwab started his own brokerage house in San Francisco, few could have anticipated the decision this little company would make on May 1, 1975. As of that date, the Securities and Exchange Commission told the brokerage industry that it no longer could charge fixed commissions. While most brokerage chieftains rubbed their hands together and hiked their rates, Schwab cut his significantly, becoming the nation's first discount brokerage.

That critical decision was "all about creative destruction" of the rules that had been in place for generations, Schwab said. "The benefit for everybody now is extensive choice."[36]

Welcome to the Law of Arbitrage.

For us, arbitrage has never been about profit, though we believe a business cannot generate a profit without it. Arbitrage has been about identifying a new model that disrupts existing pricing and service standards long held as industry norm. It allows us to win customers and gain market share at disruptive rates.

For us, arbitrage is the end product of value. If your model delivers inherent value in a marketplace, you will be able to accomplish one of the following: Either you will be able to buy something better, sell something better or clients will be willing to pay you a premium for your goods or services. In each case, you have found a reason to exist. You have found arbitrage.

We believe arbitrage contains two elements: value and sustainable profits. As you might have guessed, the second flows naturally from the first.

Echo has created a business model that saves its clients in excess of 10 percent off of what they're already paying for transportation at their business. But if the value the company was creating was all about price, whatever success the company has enjoyed wouldn't have lasted this long. Why? Because a competitor would come in and undercut our price or offer a one-time savings if our clients agreed to switch. Echo has not only produced savings but transparency and efficiency in an industry that before had neither. It has also created a unique optimization of the supply chain that delivers value day in and day out in a manner that cannot be sustained by its competitors. We didn't invent freight brokerage. In fact, there is an entire industry segment known as third-party logistics that's dedicated in large part to the brokerage of transportation. We simply found a gateway to use technology and data to create exclusive pricing and service advantage in the marketplace. These unique offerings in the marketplace fit our definition of arbitrage.

Creating value that moves an industry forward

Arbitrage goes beyond profit. It's about the economic value of knowing that your solution works and hopefully works in a way that is unique in the market. A good solution not only works for the company, but for the customer and supplier and everyone that touches your model in between. The central question to ask is this: Is the market truly better off because of what you offer? Are you revolutionizing an industry or have you just copied someone else's model with a slightly different twist?

It's easy to say that price-driven models like Southwest Airlines or Wal-Mart haven't made their markets "better." They have just made them more price sensitive. But they've actually done so much more. The fact that Wal-Mart and Southwest deliver their products at a lower price than their competition has fueled their significant growth and awarded them high customer acquisition. But the real arbitrage they've created is a fundamental paradigm shift they've brought to their respective industries.

In Wal-Mart's case, it's inventory management, supply chain automation, vendor efficiency and other technology-aided measures that have elevated its model to No. 1 in the world. For Southwest, it's no-frills flying, lower wage structures, shorter routes, alternative terminals and customer relations that made it the No. 1 passenger carrier in the United States. These companies deliver great price and great value because they used technology to re-engineer the entire infrastructure of their business. They deliver great price because their models create significant arbitrage and they choose to pass a great deal of that arbitrage on to the customer in the form of savings.

Over the past 10 years, information has become far more available, pervasive and usable to create arbitrage. Information can be captured and utilized to create markets and products and to capitalize on opportunities in ways that never before existed.

When people think about a business, they don't spend enough time thinking about arbitrage. Too often they think about the end product of arbitrage. For example, one might say, "The way I'm going to break into the auto industry is to make a car that I can sell for $1,000. That way I could completely disrupt the auto industry." That might be true for an extremely short window of time, but it won't be long until people figure out that your $1,000 car (made for $800) isn't remotely close to the average quality of cars on the road today. Unless you can find the secret that makes your product a legitimate, lasting alternative in the marketplace, you haven't found arbitrage. You have simply found a price war.

Arbitrage is addiction

In *BusinessWeek's* 2007 list of most-innovative companies, many of the leaders were able to price their particular offerings not at a discount, but at a premium thanks to the distinctiveness of their products and services. Every single one is disruptive to the markets they serve— indeed, price is almost irrelevant as a component of the overall value they deliver in the market.

Fig. 11.1: The Apple iPhone

Apple Computer was *BusinessWeek's* **No. 1** choice for the third year in a row, saying "The iPod creator is a master of superb product, store and experience design." Apple's customers are fanatically loyal despite the significant price advantages in the PC world. Apple has found arbitrage in the new consumer markets it has single-handedly built in its own image through proprietary technology—Macintosh, iTunes and its most recent product, iPhone.

No. 2 company Google has its engineers spend 20 percent of their time on products of their own choosing, thus guaranteeing that innovation is a built-in component of virtually every employee's workday. While search is free to everyone, Google's development process is constantly finding arbitrage, developing new models for advertising and communication that link to revenue in ways unexplored on the Internet or in traditional media. Google has created an entire marketplace in which search is monetized through options built on words, images and sound.

No. 3 company Toyota single-handedly put gas/electric hybrids on the map with its market-leading Prius while becoming the envy of the industrial world with its continuous improvement process. Employees come up with process revisions on every area of production from paint (giving robots individual spray canisters instead of pouring paint into hoses that have to be flushed out between jobs), to sorting parts (putting selections of parts for the right car models into tote bags so line workers don't have to decide which parts are right). [37] The company has mastered the art of encouraging simple ideas that squeeze cost out of its operation.

Fig. 11.2: Michael Graves Teapots at Target

No. 15 company Target has reversed the emphasis on price that has always defined discount retailers. It's done so through the recruitment of upscale suppliers and designers (Isaac Mizrahi and Michael Graves) to fill its shelves. As Wal-Mart has stumbled with more upscale experiments (its George clothing line has been a disappointment) Target has continued to grow by setting its sights on customers who appreciate a little savings but don't live and die by discounts. Target's arbitrage stems from its ability to find and sell attractive fashionable merchandise in well-organized surroundings. It brings a hipness to discount pricing while maintaining a reliable customer experience.

Ideo, at No. 28, often gets mislabeled as a product design company, but in reality it's a product *experience* company. It examines closely what customers say and do in response to the company's current brand offerings and takes that data to improve current products and see what new offerings make sense and in what form.

According to *BusinessWeek*:

> As the economy shifts from the economics of scale to the economics of choice and as mass markets fragment and brand loyalty disappears, it's more important than ever for corporations to improve the "consumer experience." Yet after decades of market research and focus groups, corporations realize that they still don't really know their consumers—or how best to connect with them.[38]

Ideo has found innovation and arbitrage in its ability to build products that are fused with the very experience the product is designed to serve.

The above examples are well-known and focus mainly on consumers. But any business—even those like ours that are focused on business process outsourcing—have to develop a model that fuels customer addiction.

Real innovation results in real arbitrage

In John Todor's recent book *Addicted Customers: How to Get Them Hooked on Your Company,* he writes:

> Value no longer means a good product at a good price. The challenge for companies is to understand the new concept

of value. Most companies do not. The good news is that a number of highly successful companies have already cracked the new value code. The result for them is rapid growth, high profits and a core customer base that indicates that their business model is sustainable. [39]

Todor points out that there are two types of buying personalities—indifferent and engaged. The personality that emerges depends on the type of value sought by the customer and unfortunately, most businesses are oriented to sell to the indifferent via price. Engaged customers, meanwhile, may be buying goods and services that support basic needs or are otherwise commoditized, but actually value the buying experience more. This leads to the award of lifetime value and lifetime customer equity.

The greater the arbitrage you have found, the more your customers will gravitate toward your model or product. Arbitrage is the end result of discovery—the discovery of a way to provide real value for your customer no matter what your industry is. Whether you are in printing, transportation, media buying or virtually any other industry, an engaged customer who's addicted to your process is a customer who can be retained for life.

Arbitrage is (pleasant) surprise

In the world of business process outsourcing, you have to be able to walk into a customer's organization and present a complete solution that management didn't know existed, much less existed at a lower cost. In addition, the foundation of your disruptive model has to be intact and you have to be able to prove to the market that your model works. Here is the foundation and proof of the arbitrage we've established in the markets we've chosen to disrupt:

The foundation of InnerWorkings' arbitrage: InnerWorkings uses data which it collects in the open market to do two things:

1. Determine which suppliers are ideally situated to produce a given job;
2. Determine which suppliers are likely to give InnerWorkings the best price based on their open capacity.

In order to accomplish this, InnerWorkings keeps track of the prices that it receives from suppliers and matches that data to product specifications. As we planned our launch, the world told us that there was no way to capture open capacity information because there are over 40,000 printers in America and not only would they not tell us, but they were too antiquated in their processes to truly measure their capacity from day to day. Our hypothesis was that technology could find a way around that problem. Our theory was that if we could ping the market for pricing on a constant basis, we could establish a real-time proxy for open capacity, much like the New York Stock Exchange provides a forum to establish the real-time price of a stock.

The proof of that arbitrage: Arbitrage in this business was surprisingly clear and tangible once our model took hold. Companies found our value proposition compelling not strictly for the savings, but also for the way they could watch their jobs progress through each stage from order to assignment to fulfillment with greater control. Further, they could see their savings *at every step of the process.*

The traditional print process was reliant on individuals who worked for the printer and acted as a human funnel for all production issues—a deck already stacked against the print customer. Our technology gathered the best of what thousands of printers had to offer at any one time and added an expert production staff monitoring both the job and the supplier to reduce the chance for errors significantly. Normally, with this type of service, you would have to pay a premium. But because of our technology, leverage and scale we were actually offering premium service at a discount to the leading competitors.

As a result, InnerWorkings' revenues grew from $5 million in 2002 to an estimated $280 million in 2007, along with commensurate growth in its profits.

The foundation of Echo's arbitrage: Echo uses data captured in the open market to find the right truck moving in the right direction at the right time. This is the essence of our model. To find that right truck, we have to collect vast farms of data using automated technology and a global carrier call center. Echo analyzes the data to find the optimal carrier that has the right amount of capacity to a specific destination and is therefore able to move our customer's freight at lower costs than an average carrier. In addition, Echo's technology manages the procurement of all modes of transportation (truckload, less-than-truckload, small parcel, international, expedited and intermodal). By optimizing the supply of shipping choices within our system, Echo can truly offer its clients the ability to outsource 100 percent of their transportation needs and still receive a best-in-class solution across the entire transportation industry.

The proof of that arbitrage: Echo was founded in February 2005. In the past two years, its client base has grown from one to over 2,000. Its employees have grown to over 300. Its suppliers have grown to over 6,000. Today, Echo is one of the fastest-growing transportation firms in the United States. In addition, Echo is highly profitable with margins that are currently in line with the industry leader, C.H. Robinson, which has been in business for over a century.

The foundation of MediaBank's arbitrage: MediaBank uses technology and data to do the following:

1. Distill the broadest universe of targeted media opportunities down to the most effective subset of possibilities based on a client's customer profile, budget and advertising objectives;

2. Deliver state-of-the-art software to the largest media buyers in the world to integrate analog and digital media on a single platform while delivering full order management, accounting and analytics. We are building a media-buying superhighway upon which we hope one day the majority of the world's media will be bought and sold. To accomplish this, we constantly capture market data into a software model built to optimize media buying in a world that's going digital.

The proof of that arbitrage: MediaBank was formed in April 2006. At this writing, MediaBank has agreements with three of the five largest media buyers in the United States to manage the procurement of a substantial amount of the media they buy. In 2007, these companies were planning to migrate even more media to our new digital platform. In addition, one of our enterprise agreements is particularly unique as it's the first time a client and a software firm jointly collaborated to re-engineer the company's entire digital procurement process from the ground up.

Arbitrage is an innovation tool

At this writing, we're in the final stages of launching ThePoint.com, which we've explained is a new online tool to promote activism and problem solving. When envisioning ThePoint, we identified the problem (the Internet is filled with words but not enough action) and the solution (create an online activism site to harness the power of the Internet and allow individuals to bind together with the strength that comes from unified action). The result, we hope, will be the birth of thousands of campaigns that never had the critical mass to create vast economic, social and political change. ThePoint will provide this forum.

Fig. 11.3: A historic page from the ThePoint.com's site

This page introduces a particular issue inviting public action on the site.

ThePoint is a very different model from anything we've tried, so the natural question is, where's the arbitrage?

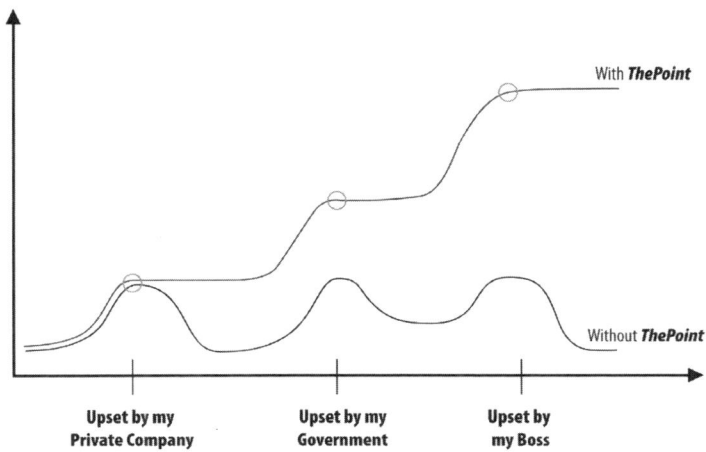

Clearly, the conventional arbitrage of buy low and sell high is missing—ThePoint doesn't plan to sell anything. Nor do its users have to spend money to join. The answer lies in understanding the true nature of arbitrage.

As we've discussed, arbitrage is not just about price—it's about value. When your model delivers new value to the market that is unique and sustainable, you have the necessary landscape to generate profits around that value.

How will we create that value in ThePoint? If the site truly works and our users are satisfied, they will frequent our site.

Let's look for a moment at the model of YouTube, according to Wikipedia in September 2007.[40]

> YouTube was founded by Chad Hurley, Steven Chen and Jawed Karim, who were among the first employees of PayPal. Like ThePoint, YouTube doesn't exist to sell anything—it has no direct revenue stream from its central idea, which is to post videos on the Internet.

The company's domain was activated February 15, 2005 and the site was developed and launched by the end of the year. Like many technology start-ups, YouTube was started as an angel-funded enterprise in a small office. Before its launch, venture capital firm Sequoia Capital invested an initial $3.5 million. By April 2006, there was significant buzz and Sequoia put an additional $8 million into the company. Its bet was correct. During summer 2006, YouTube was one of the fastest-growing websites on the Web and was ranked as the fifth most popular website on Web-tracking site Alexa, far outpacing even MySpace's growth. According to Wikipedia, by the end of 2006, 100 million clips were being viewed daily on YouTube, with an additional 65,000 new videos uploaded per 24 hours. As of mid-year 2007, Nielsen/NetRatings reported that the site had almost 20 million viewers a day. YouTube's preeminence in the online video market is staggering.

On October 9, 2006, it was announced that the company would be purchased by Google for $1.65 billion in stock. Before the Google deal, YouTube stated that its business model was advertising-based and was generating revenues of $15 million per month. Some industry commentators speculated at that time that YouTube's running costs—specifically the bandwidth required—were as high as $5 million to $6 million each month, fueling criticisms that the company, like many Internet start-ups, did not have a highly profitable business model despite the introduction of advertising (in March 2006).

That said, the company still achieved a value of $1.65 billion and by every measure is one of the most successful start-ups in history, deploying disruptive technology in a way that should be envied by all.

Arbitrage at ThePoint

ThePoint, like YouTube, will be supported by ad revenues from text-rich media ads, text-based links to an advertiser's own website, linking-based services and commerce-based initiatives. ThePoint expects to be able to offer its clients a blend of search and display, including rich media, text, video and targeted advertising.

Currently, online advertising revenue is determined by three factors: unique daily/monthly/annual visitors, the number of pages that are viewed on the site and/or the click-through rate that occurs if the site is a link to the advertiser's home page. Sites that do not attract high traffic volume often use third-party products (e.g. Google's AdSense) to generate revenue on a click-through basis at a rate that often varies between $3–$8 per thousand visitors (CPM). Accordingly, if a site had three small advertisements and 10 million monthly visitors viewing an average of five pages per visit, it would generate approximately $10 million in annual revenue. A site with 10 million visitors per month would rank among the top 200 most visited sites on the Internet.

There is not always a direct connection between current advertising revenue generated and the ultimate enterprise value of an organization. For example, as we discussed, YouTube was recently sold for $1.65 billion and yet it has generated very little advertising revenue to date. In addition, Google had a market cap well into the billions before it began to significantly monetize its search dominance through its now famous AdWords product. Like traditional media properties such as NBC, the *Washington Post* or a billboard in Times Square, the ultimate worth of the property is directly tied to the predictable and visible nature of the traffic that is associated with the property itself, more than the current advertising dollars that are being generated over any short-term period.

A property that is highly trafficked is an annuity and to determine its enterprise value, one must factor in both existing revenue being generated and revenue opportunities that are developing in the larger marketplace. With the Web's expanding social networking sites, this ladder metric is pervasive in determining enterprise value. As the Web continues to grow at dramatic rates, sites that have developed a community of traffic provide significant opportunities to monetize that traffic into future ongoing profit streams.

The pervasive Web model that exists in the market today is either largely based on total viewing audience using the traditional cost-per-thousand metric or the more action-oriented click-through approach that pays only as users take action, which is more analogous to direct response. Traffic under both of these advertising models is treated in an agnostic manner, which offline advertisers have learned, though years of measurement, is the wrong approach to attracting customers. In other words, not all eyeballs are worth the same amount to an advertiser.

ThePoint should provide the landscape to test and deploy new online advertising models that marry the right advertiser to the right body of potential clients. Such clients are uniquely motivated to switch to a new service or product based on their current frustration. Our eyeballs will have a significantly greater value to a potential advertiser as the distance between message and action will, hopefully, be significantly reduced. This paradigm could allow us to price our ads at a premium or charge a fee for every new customer that an advertiser obtains through our site.

ThePoint will allow advertisers to do more than just advertise (the very existence of their ads is part of the solution; for example there is a campaign against Blockbuster for late fees and Netflix advertises its zero late fee model). This, along with the viral nature of our traffic, creates value that should ultimately translate into significant profit.

Those that fail to find arbitrage...fail

It is essential to determine if your model creates arbitrage (value and sustainable profits) before you accelerate your plan to build the business. Earlier, we talked about some of the biggest names in Internet history that fell apart during or after the 2000 market crash. In almost all cases, a fundamental driver of their failure was the inability to generate arbitrage which led to either their failure to win clients or their failure to make money.

Webvan, the failed Internet grocer, had apparently not even *tested* its inventory model before it launched. In the grocery business, supply chain is everything. If you don't have the right food on the shelf at the right time, your customers will flock to other grocers. Within a year of its launch, the company was beginning to struggle under the weight of massive debt and its specially designed order-packing system which never got to full capacity before the company folded. In addition, in various markets where the company had a presence, it apparently didn't account for traffic patterns and other road-related or logistical issues that would slow delivery and ultimately lose customers.

Kozmo.com, as we discussed earlier, might have been helped with a similar targeted test of its services before wide deployment. The neighborhood delivery service quickly found that small items, like DVDs and cookies, were not priced high enough to justify the overall cost of human delivery.

At Starbelly, we had not finished testing our concept of distributing and designing promotional materials online and we soon found that we would have to invest far more money than we originally anticipated to build a catalog of products when the options available to our customers were nearly limitless.

In each case, the common missing element was arbitrage.

SUMMARY:

The Law of Arbitrage may be the simplest law of all—if you have arbitrage, your business will likely succeed. Arbitrage is all about value and sustainable profits. While arbitrage generally leads to price advantage in the market, it is not all about price. First and foremost, your model must deliver differentiated value that your customers need and are willing to pay for. In addition, your model must allow you to make money or all the customers in the world will not be able to keep you afloat.

NEXT CHAPTER: The Law of Velocity means that you need to constantly update the state of your technology so you're able to collect key market intelligence that keeps you in the fast lane as your business evolves. That said, you need to maintain a balance between the critical technology that drives your business forward and the necessary controls that keep you out of trouble. While disruptive companies thrive on speed, without checks and balances they can easily end up racing to the wrong finish line.

CHAPTER 12

The Law of Velocity

Only the fast survive

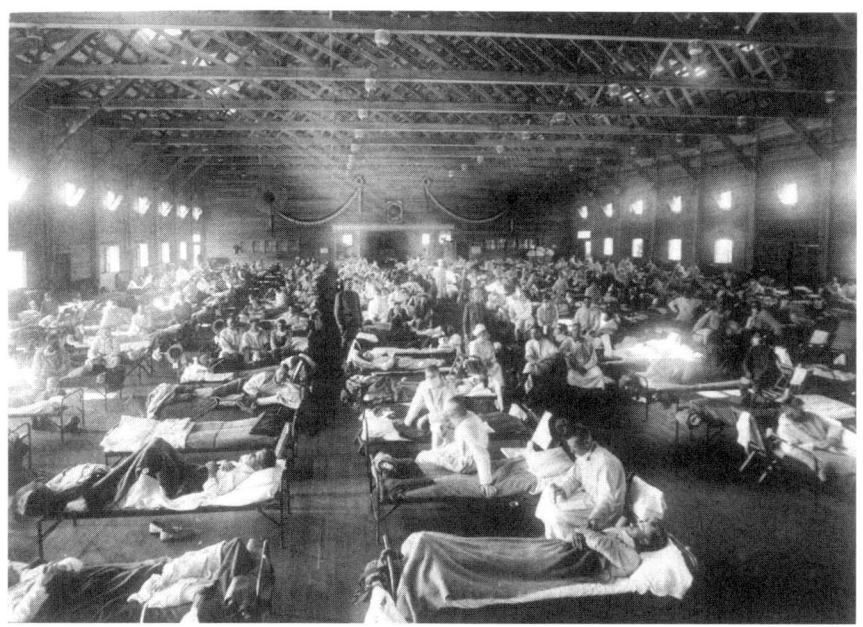

Fig. 12.1: Camp Funston, Kansas

No one ever pinpointed a cause for the 1918 influenza pandemic that killed 50 million people around the world in just 18 months. But disease specialists and historians note the horror came in three waves. Ground zero in the United States was apparently Camp Funston, Kansas where troops *reportedly picked up the virus in March of 1918 from nearby farmland and brought it overseas, infecting Poland by the summer. This wave was thought to be mild. But by August, a more virulent strain of the disease evolved. Often morphing into pneumonia, it could kill people in as little as two days. The third and final wave surfaced in the winter and finished by the spring. In that period, the flu afflicted over 25 percent of the U.S. population and cut the average life expectancy in the nation by 12 years.*

By comparison, the AIDS virus has killed 32 million people worldwide over the last 26 years, thankfully slowed by the advancement of aggressive antiviral drugs and the fact that AIDS isn't an airborne disease.

Two dreaded pandemics traveling at incredibly different speeds. Even with our advanced science nearly 100 years after the flu pandemic, experts admit there is still no way to preclude the spread of disease as viruses develop and change too rapidly.

Fast-forward to 2005. According to news reports, a Thai man named Bang-Orn Benpad stole some of his neighbor's chickens. He didn't know the chickens were carrying the Avian Flu and ate them. A couple days later he got a cough and a fever. He went to a local clinic where they took an X-ray of his lungs. Doctors suggested he go to a hospital, but he went home instead, ignoring their advice. His symptoms got worse and within a matter of days he died.

The biological superiority of many viruses is the speed at which they infect. They create a path of destruction that evolves so fast they often elude and defy treatment or containment.

The great challenge of medicine when it comes to controlling epidemics is that so often by the time the virus is detected, it has spread so significantly that it's nearly impossible to contain. "If a virus like West Nile acquires the capacity to co-opt humans as a carrier," U.S. Health and Human Services Secretary Michael Leavitt told NPR in 2005, "it will set off a pandemic struggle that will—or could—end the lives of millions. And if history holds true, it could alter the culture, the politics and the prosperity of billions more."

Speed is an unstoppable force. Welcome to the Law of Velocity.

In the opening pages of this book, we talked briefly about the speed of technology and the need to develop and deploy business models at the pace that matches the evolution of technology. It's a pace that is also accelerating exponentially.

Consider the rate at which you download updates for software on your home or office computer. If you think about it, you never really go more than a month or two without getting an update alert on something critical to your computer. When you get one, do you smack your fist on the desk and yell, "Never! I refuse to install it because they should have gotten it right the first time!" Doubtful, since it's unlikely you'd pass up the chance to make your machine run faster, add more features or see it operate more efficiently. In fact, you have probably come to expect that your software is not perfect, that there is always a version 2.0 or 3.0 or 8.0. That being said, you don't want to wait until every feature is fully developed. You want constant improvements—constant little baby steps forward.

As Sun-Tzu said in *The Art of Warfare,* "War is such that the supreme consideration is speed."

This same phenomenon holds true for developing disruptive business models. The Law of Velocity states that speed is one of the most fundamental disciplines you must master when building disruptive business models. If you can't move fast, your model will quickly become obsolete as technology forces the market to evolve around you and eventually displace you.

The days of the multi-year product cycle are dying and in many corners of the business world, dead. Longer development cycles will probably survive in companies that must assure public safety, such as pharmaceuticals. Yet even the drug industry—facing staggering costs and increasing competition from disruptive drug makers here and abroad, realizes that it has to significantly shorten its development cycle. As of 2007, industry estimates put the cost of bringing a new drug to market at $1.2 billion–$1.5 billion.

As genomics and nanotechnologies will fundamentally shift how drugs are created and deployed in the body, the large pharma companies are going to have to reinvent the manner by which they conduct their research and development and the government will have to review their regulatory procedures as well. Drug companies have long relied on federal patent protection to shield them from the open market and allow them to recover the significant cost of development. But as consumers become more demanding and governments less patient with the mounting costs of global healthcare, drug companies are going to have to increasingly rely on evolving technologies to enhance the speed at which they operate.

Note these recent comments from Steven M. Paul, the top research executive at Eli Lilly and Co.:

> Lilly has identified reducing cycle time as a very important industry initiative. Steven Paul estimates that cycle time is close to 15 years from a project inception to a molecule launch, with 10 years solely in clinical development. "We're using Six Sigma process improvement technology to reduce non-value-added work and steps that we've traditionally used in drug discovery and development that are not necessary to dramatically reduce cycle time in various phases."[41]

In a world dominated by bits of data, no one is exempt from the need to operate with efficiency and most important, speed.

If you're not moving at warp speed, you're not moving

Robert Falcon Scott, Richard Branson and Buzz Aldrin all have something in common. They all came in second at making history—Scott got to the North Pole after Roald Amundsen, Branson's hot air balloon didn't make it around the world before Steve Fossett's and Aldrin's footprints followed Neil Armstrong's on the surface of the moon.

So ask yourself this question. Each put in the proper amount of work and sacrifices to get to the pinnacle. But does anyone remember they even got there? As Vince Lombardi would say, "There is no room for second place." And that's particularly true in the world of technology. In fact, in the world of technology, we call this "first-mover advantage" and quite often it's the most significant advantage you can have in a new or evolving market.

But don't get used to it. While speed can catapult your model to the front of the pack and give you first-mover advantage, the far greater risk is missing the potential for obsolescence in your model over time if you move slowly.

The new innovation paradigm

Technology as measured through scientific breakthroughs has marked the upward surge of mankind through history. In the past, however, breakthroughs largely came from great minds that made significant individual strides, like Einstein's theory of relativity or Newton's discovery of gravity. While a disruptive idea today can be the product of one great individual's thought process, its continued dominance in the twenty-first century depends on hundreds or perhaps thousands of individuals who may never get any credit for moving it along.

This is the new paradigm of innovation—the widespread sharing of viewpoints, suggestions, criticism and even code via technologists who willingly come together through the Internet to improve something for their own advantage or the collective advantage of the entire user community.

Smart companies are listening and reacting to this paradigm shift.

The effect of this growing force on the speed of innovation is undeniable. We are in an era of accelerated evolution of disruptive theories, concepts, models and businesses. If you examine the sheer number of sites that get reviewed on TechCrunch, the pace is staggering. Each day a new model, a new site, a new business, a new feature gets reviewed in detail on that site and on other similar venues on the Web. Ideas are going from birth to death in a record pace. Just in the last year alone, millions of new websites were created. Think about that fact.

Consider the Internet a decade ago. Websites were nothing compared to the way they look and function today. Flash had just been invented but wasn't in wide use. We didn't have Ruby on Rails or other rapid application tools that are common in website production as this book was being written. There was no social networking in the way we think about it now. No text messaging. No MySpace, No Digg, No Facebook, No Craigslist and no Wikipedia. Blogs didn't exist. Google was an obscure idea that had yet to catch on. YouTube wasn't even possible five years ago—if you wanted to watch moving pictures on the Net, you settled for the strange cartoons at Icebox.com. Today, people are catching their favorite TV show on their computers and soon they'll be catching their favorite movie on their cell phone.

Progress means advancing in a collective and accelerated manner—it enriches the lives we lead and enhances the businesses which we rely on.

Balancing speed and accuracy

Think of the sheer pace of all of this innovation and the effect it inevitably has on accuracy. As we've developed the technology that's enabled the businesses we've launched, we've come to realize that there's a critical balance between speed and accuracy. You cannot release a product that's error-ridden and functionally deficient because it's impossible to fool your customers. That's true of any industry, not just ours.

But accurate does not mean perfect.

Your releases have to be rapid. Not perfect, just rapid. You'll find your customers will be reasonable (outspoken, but reasonable) if they know you're dedicated to constant improvement. That's why they'll be willing to participate in the enhancement of your product in real time if you let them. They'll deal with the imperfections so long as they can see light at the end of the tunnel and the process of improvement is rapid.

This philosophy can run counterintuitive to the culture of many companies. For example, when MediaBank acquired Datatech (the analog software provider we mentioned earlier) they had been developing software, largely written in COBOL, for nearly 30 years. Their software was highly complex, very sophisticated and exceptionally accurate and reliable.

But, their pace of development was dramatically slower than ours because their culture was all about writing error-free code with limited and centralized resources. Their products were fantastic but their lack of speed had caused them to miss the most fundamental shift in all media—the migration from analog to digital that created MediaBank in the first place. We had to get them to move at our pace without compromising their accuracy beyond an acceptable level. The last few words of that sentence mean everything—"beyond an acceptable level."

In other words, there was no way to get them to move twice as fast without any compromise to accuracy, as accuracy and speed are often countercyclical forces. But, we could get them to move twice as fast and only compromise 10 percent of their accuracy. That trade-off, especially in light of our user testing and quality control processes, would be more than acceptable. It would allow them to deploy more rapidly and ultimately meet the needs of the market.

Bill Gates puts it this way:

> You not only need to develop quickly. You need to develop in small doses. Projects of only three to four months' duration are going to have much lower failure rates. With short projects you're forced to make important trade-offs that will drive you to simplicity and focus. You'll end up with goals that can be executed. In addition, it's far easier psychologically to pull out and redirect your development team when people haven't spent a year of their lives working on a project that's now going down the tubes.[42]

You need speed, but if the foundation of your disruptive model is cracked, you'll be left behind in record time.

Take Friendster, founded in 2002 and the grandfather of the current crop of social networking sites. The Mountain View, California, company squandered its most valuable asset: first-mover advantage.

They introduced a great model for the moment—and stopped. Their technology advantage seemed to come to a screeching halt just as other social networking sites came to the market with new features like sharing of videos, photos and music. Today, they've been eclipsed by MySpace and Facebook, which combined have created billions of dollars of value off an idea that Friendster brought to market.

Friendster was too slow to react to the changing Web and it suffered accordingly. While we would love to have all the time in the world to develop software products at 100 percent accuracy and completeness, that's an impractical goal. Today's significant technology advancements rarely occur behind a secret bunker—initial developments might, but not over time. You have to test and tweak, test and tweak, not only as your product is being introduced into the market, but long after it's been in the market. The new life cycle of innovation is vastly different than in the past. In today's market you have to incorporate both what the customer needs and what technology will allow you to deliver and you have to do both in little iterations all the time.

Your product is never finished.

And because technology changes so rapidly, you need to innovate at a rapid pace. And that's where the accuracy/speed balance comes in. If you gave me the choice of being 100 percent accurate in my solution yet only at a speed of 30 miles per hour or be 80 percent accurate and move at 60 miles per hour, I'd take the latter every day of the week and twice on Sunday. Yes, there's risk to moving fast without 100 percent accuracy. However, the risk is far less than missing the chance entirely to compete in the marketplace. You can always issue updates and solicit feedback from your customers to fix bugs or advance even farther the next time. But if your technology solution doesn't get to customers in the first place, then you've obliterated your business opportunity.

My Uncle Irwin used to say, "When you're driving and you get lost, speed up, so at least you will get somewhere faster." You'll either find your way or get more lost, but you'll get to an answer quicker than by squinting at a map by the side of the road, watching the other cars pass you by.

When giants sleep

Perhaps the best way to understand how critical speed is in the modern economy is by looking at examples of leaders who lost by moving too slowly. What would have happened if Microsoft used all its powers to get a revolutionary search product out in the marketplace before Google opened its doors in 1998? Nearly a decade later, Microsoft keeps throwing money at Windows Live, which sits alongside its MSN business product. It has decided to develop its own technology in recent years for the underlying search engine and to try and gain market share in the ever-expanding universe of paid search.

As this book was going to the printer, Microsoft still didn't have a winning horse in the search race that Google continues to redefine each day. Microsoft's market cap has gone from $231 billion five years ago to $275.7 billion today, up 19 percent, while Google has taken its lead in search from a $50 billion market cap at yearend 2004 (the year of its IPO) to $153 million at the end of July 2007, up more than 200 percent. In less than three years, Google amassed more than half the market capitalization of Microsoft, one of the most successful companies of all time.

Microsoft, for frame of reference, was founded in 1975.

Think about Motorola. Thanks to its RAZR phone, Motorola gained traction in the cell phone business it helped create. It was riding high in 2004 and 2005 and by the second quarter of 2006, Motorola had about 22 percent of the global cell phone market, a significant improvement from where it was in 2004, when Samsung was taking market share from Motorola every day. Praise was rolling in and article after article saluted the company's comeback and forecast even larger gains in the future. But by the first quarter of 2007, Motorola's market share started to slide, falling to just over 17 percent.

Motorola had failed to build and maintain a rapid product development cycle. It never produced a high-end successor to the RAZR, which was eventually battered in price wars with lower-end alternatives. In addition, its competitors quickly shifted their focus to PDAs, which integrated entertainment, phone, Internet and e-mail into one device. And to make matters worse, Apple announced the release of its iPhone, which further raised the bar for mobile innovation. Motorola, like so many others, was caught trying to understand and react to a market that had fundamentally been shifted by technology.

In the simplest of terms—if you are not disrupting, you are being disrupted.

Lightning cycle time

Rumor has it that eBay operates on a *two-week* development cycle. And if you know anyone, particularly a teenager or twenty-something, who spends time on MySpace, he or she will tell you that one of the reasons the environment is so addictive is because it's constantly updating, changing and addressing users' needs. While these are consumer sites and B2B often requires more depth and development time, there's no denying the pressure for speed. The pace of development on the Internet is setting the standard by which we should measure the pace of development in the off-line business world as well.

The most necessary and time-consuming development practices need to get faster and even Washington is catching on. For the pharmaceutical industry, the U.S. Food and Drug Administration developed its 2006 Critical Path initiative to reform the process of getting drugs to market. It explains the reasons this way:

> Despite important investments in basic biomedical research, the number of applications to the FDA for new drugs and biologics has declined over the past decade. Of more concern, product development is not becoming more efficient over time—a drug entering Phase 1 trials in 2000 was not more likely to reach the market than one entering Phase 1 trials in 1985. And we are seeing more product candidate failures in the later stages of product development—the most expensive way to fail. Recent biomedical research breakthroughs have not improved the ability to identify successful candidates and

bring the most promising products to patients in a timely and affordable manner.[43]

Cynics might say this process is intended to drive drug companies to earlier profits. But if the overall cost of development can be streamlined with no loss of accuracy, as the markets correct themselves the savings should eventually be pushed down to the patient. The end product of real innovation is typically lower cost or greater value.

In addition, this vortex of wasted time and resources during the journey for perfection is another example of both what is wrong with the process of bringing drugs to market and what is wrong with many companies who fall victim to the same paradigm. Now in the case of drugs, the end result of 98 percent accuracy might be hundreds of lives that are lost, which is a cost that is too high for society to bear. But in the case of companies bringing consumer products or business applications to market, the cost of near perfection is relatively small and is far outweighed by the danger of moving too slowly and missing market opportunities.

The development cycle of MediaBank is a perfect example of how necessary speed is when bringing a disruptive technology solution to market.

Based on fortuitous timing, we had to build a state-of-the-art digital and analog system with full analytical capabilities within one year. This grew the scope of our initial project by 400 percent. We were knee-deep in building a digital order management tool when suddenly our plans changed overnight and we had to expand our scope exponentially. The reason for this acceleration of pace was because one of our first clients told us they wanted to roll our solution out to a much broader audience in the same time frame, so we responded by acquiring an analog software provider (Datatech) and an analytics solution (Blackfoot) to help us address their needs.

By July 1, 2007, we were on a journey to modify and update our analog software while conducting and completing wide sweeping gap analysis for our new client. The project involved over 100 people within their organization. In addition, we had to finalize, test and deploy our digital platform and we had to integrate in the analytic offering of Blackfoot, which in and of itself would have been a monumental undertaking. All the while, we had to service the day-to-day needs of every other agency that was relying on our suite of software.

There was no time to waste. Not a minute. We set in motion a hiring plan that involved adding nearly 50 people over four months. We hired an internal recruiter, reached out to everyone we knew and began marshalling the talent we needed. We built an automated development-tracking tool to allow us to maintain control of the project at a micro yet decentralized level. We needed to achieve organized chaos, which by definition allows an enormous number of variables to run free without structure within a larger confined space. It might sound a bit frantic, but if you maintain discipline around the key drivers (timeline, budget, delivery date, dependencies, testing, etc.), you can actually encourage a great deal of freedom and speed among the team that has to do a year's worth of work in half the time.

Look at a Google. At $10 billion in 2006 revenues it aggressively hires bright people and *makes* them spend one day of the workweek working on projects that interest them. Indeed, "20 percent time" has resulted in many new wrinkles in search at Google and a plethora of innovations the company needs to stay fresh in the marketplace. Such organized chaos has helped keep Google's growth rate at 40 percent a year.

If an organization becomes too big to accomplish short cycle times and encourage this type of freedom, maybe it's time to jettison the pieces that are slowing it down. Those pieces tend to have names like micromanagement, reports, meetings, hierarchy and politics. Organizations should always think in terms of whatever will give them optimal speed to keep innovating and therefore disrupting businesses—especially their own.

Speed leadership

We'll get to the Law of Promotion in the next chapter, but CEOs need more than an ability to sell a business concept. They need to drive development velocity from the top. Former GE chief Jack Welch practiced tough love on his business models—if a division was not performing at a consistent first or second place in its industry, it was on the sale block or primed for a shutdown. In order to achieve that status, you need constant dedication to product development and velocity. In his words:

> An organization's ability to learn and translate that learning into action rapidly is the ultimate competitive advantage.

And Steve Jobs, leading the charge at Apple with a mix of groundbreaking consumer software and hardware, understands the need for speed as well as the need for flexibility:

> Sometimes when you innovate, you make mistakes. It is best to admit them quickly and get on with improving your other innovations.

Since 2005, we have been hiring a new employee nearly every workday of the year at Echo. In September 2007, our total employee count (including our employees in India) was approaching 300. The sheer force that is necessary to add a new body every workday is almost beyond comprehension. Your organization is growing by the day, the week, the month, over and over again. There are always new faces, always new roles and responsibilities. Just when you unpack your desk, you have to pack again, because you are constantly moving to accommodate new hires. In that type of culture, moving fast isn't an alternative, it's simply a state of existence. Like driving on the highway: the only way to travel long distances in short amounts of time is by going fast.

Technology unites our businesses and defines their potential. Speed allows us to garner advantage in the marketplace as we have come to master the concept of moving quickly, learning, reacting and then moving quickly again.

SUMMARY:

Businesses no longer have the option of long development times. Exponential gains in technology—and the willingness of customers to be a part of that advancement—make it necessary for companies to do basic product introductions with the promise of constant and regular upgrades and updates. Organizations have to learn to react to the new technology-enriched climate and force innovation to move at the speed of technology.

NEXT CHAPTER: The Law of Promotion is all about leadership, not salesmanship. As business speeds up, managers and entrepreneurs need to master the art of product evangelism at all costs: Believing when no one else does, keeping people on a fast-paced development track and most important, keeping on point when there's extreme criticism in the marketplace.

CHAPTER 13

The Law of Promotion

Be a tireless evangelist for your idea

In the late 1970s, U.S. Congressman Al Gore began holding hearings on the then-arcane subject of global warming, the gradual increase in the average temperature of the earth's air and water supply due to rising emissions of carbon gases. Gore became obsessed with the topic in college. For the next three decades and right through his two terms as vice president, Gore would keep speaking about global warming despite reactions ranging from silence to ridicule wherever he went.

*Today, Gore has a hit movie (*An Inconvenient Truth*) and an Oscar to show for his adherence to a single message over the past 30 years—that without change in individual, business and government behavior, global warming will endanger life on the planet. Gore has been a driving force in turning around national opinion on the topic. People are beginning to understand the risks—an April 2007 ABC News/Washington Post/Stanford University poll showed that 33 percent of the American public placed climate change ahead of any other environmental problem; that's up from 16 percent during the same time in 2006.*

Despite these numbers, there are still many doubters about global warming. A simple Google search of "Al Gore" and "global warming" turns up an almost even split of websites with positive and negative viewpoints on the hot environmental subject. Even still, Al Gore keeps spreading the message despite the obstacles. He marches on without being deterred and remains steadfast in his beliefs despite continued claims that his data is inaccurate and that science doesn't support his assertions.

Welcome to the Law of Promotion: the need to stay on message no matter who tells you you're wrong and no matter how often you hear it.

There are two critical moments when you need to be an evangelist at all costs. The first is when you launch a business. The second is when something goes wrong in that business, as it inevitably will.

When the unexpected dominates

The first example is one we'll get to in a minute, which is something that all disruptive businesses have to overcome.

But we'll start with our second example first—when something goes wrong. The story involves the management of InnerWorkings and how their 2007 began. On January 12, a Friday, the company got a call from *Barron's*, the financial weekly, asking for comment on an article about InnerWorkings that was about to go to press. Given that InnerWorkings' management was in the midst of a quiet period in advance of the company's secondary public stock offering, they had to decline. On Saturday, just a few hours after they received the call, the piece was published and they—and I—were in for quite a shock. Among other things, the article said:

> You see, InnerWorkings goes to great lengths to obscure its ownership and control by a chap named Eric P. Lefkofsky who has a history of busting investors after promising to radically transform bricks-and-mortar industries. He seems to identify with Dr. Seuss's huckster: he called his last business Starbelly.com, a venture that rapidly went into bankruptcy…The current InnerWorkings road show and stock-offering is, in part, aimed at cashing out much of Lefkofsky's stock while InnerWorkings' shares teeter at stilted levels.[44]

Chapter 13: The Law of Promotion

It was not the kind of thing any of us wanted to read over breakfast on a Saturday morning.

In the first place, the article was loaded with inaccuracies, half-truths and incorrect statements too numerous to go through in detail here. The underwriters went to great lengths to insure that all of InnerWorkings' public filings were detailed and accurate, including the sections regarding me and the fact that my wife invested money in InnerWorkings when it was formed and therefore was a large shareholder through an entity that she owned, Orange Media.

The *Barron's* reporter's thesis that InnerWorkings went out of its way to obscure my involvement assumes that investors don't read the public filings of the businesses they invest in. It also assumes that somehow my involvement or lack of involvement was material to the company's performance. Since InnerWorkings went public, the company has met or exceeded its financial guidance, often by significant double-digit percentages and achieved levels of growth and profitability that were well above my expectations when I was still involved. Unfortunately for my ego, InnerWorkings' management did this during a period when I was no longer responsible for the day-to-day operations of the company, so the credit belongs to them.

Despite how troubling the article was as a purely personal attack from someone I had never met or spoken with, there was a much more worrisome situation as the story ran. InnerWorkings' top management—led by CEO Steven Zuccarini and CFO Nick Galassi—were in the middle of their road show in advance of the company's secondary offering. They were meeting with nearly 10 investors a day.

Lousy press—however inaccurate—is not how you want to start the day with a room full of investors when you are in the middle of marketing a deal.

On that Saturday, the company's Board of Directors and Officers debated whether or not they should proceed with the transaction. They had been caught off guard to say the least and given the quiet period restrictions, the company was not allowed to fully combat the accusations in the article. But in a pivotal moment, they decided to go ahead. You can't let inaccurate press stop you from going about your affairs and doing what is right for the business. The company had committed to raising proceeds—it was the right thing to do for the business—and so it marched on.

Advancing without a script

Even though Steve had spent 25 years in the printing industry at RR Donnelley & Sons before joining us, overseeing its catalog, retail and global services business, he could not have been fully prepared for an event such as this. The public markets have a momentum all their own and that morning, our stock reacted as if we were in the midst of a hurricane. The company's stock dropped by 25 percent within hours.

Steve and Nick met with nearly 50 investors that week. In each meeting, if they weren't attacked when they walked in the door, Steve at some point would say, "OK folks, I know everyone is thinking about that article so let's just get it out of the way and talk about it." With courage and conviction, Steve would respond to every inaccurate element of the article and try and get the investors focused on the fundamentals of the company, which were and are extraordinary.

The stock rose to about $13.80 toward the end of that tough week, gaining back much of the value it had lost, and the company was able to complete its secondary offering, selling an additional 8 million shares, and the stock was trading at $18.50 as of October 2007.

When things go badly and they always do at some point, you have to bring to bear every ounce of promotional talent you have, because everyone will look to you as the business leader for stability. If the fundamentals are still good, you have to be as passionate about your message when things are bad as when they are good. You have to convince yourself that the troubling news is temporary or irrelevant and you have to shout your message at the top of your lungs from the highest mountaintop. If you crawl into a hole, you risk everything you've worked for because you've lost perspective.

I have been in business for nearly 20 years. I have had a thousand things go right and a thousand things go wrong. I believe that building a business is every bit as messy as raising a child. Kids are fragile when they are first born, they have to learn to crawl before they walk or run, they go through growth spurts and growing pains, they evolve and eventually they outgrow you. Above everything, you have to try and maintain perspective.

Jack Greenberg, the former CEO of McDonald's and a Director of InnerWorkings, once told me, "I used to tell my kids when they would read something glowing about their dad—I'm not that smart. And when the day comes when you read something mean about me I'll tell you now—I'm not that stupid either."

It's easy to let the waves rock your confidence, but you have to keep promoting your ideas, your vision and your model through even the roughest waters.

Your beliefs are your message

Charles Schwab said, "I consider my ability to arouse enthusiasm among men the greatest asset I possess. The way to develop the best that is in a man is by appreciation and encouragement."

I don't believe leadership or salesmanship comes naturally to a lot of people. I've met CEOs who weren't necessarily the best speakers or the most magnanimous men and women in the room. What sets them apart, at least for me, is their central belief in what they're doing and their passion for communicating that belief. In other words, what's valuable is their ability to galvanize people around the mission of their company and the potential of their products and services.

While we're not excessive about the use of public relations—we believe growing sales and earnings provides the best PR results so we tend to focus on that—we do believe that you have to find a way to get your message out to the broadest audience possible. For us, it begins with being passionate about open communication.

Once you have come up with a disruptive idea, you have to share it with everyone who will listen and you have to share all the facts and not only with people who support your particular point of view. I often get criticized for discussing issues like ownership or salaries with people who might not normally be privileged to that level of information. My attitude is simple: If I have to filter what I am saying, something is wrong. I'm not smart enough to remember who I should or shouldn't say something to so I choose the alternative—I say everything to everyone and I get feedback, hopefully honest feedback, from anyone and everyone who will provide it.

Besides open communication internally, you have to preach your message to the outside world every chance you get. You have to take every meeting you can and jump at every opportunity to tell people about your business model and solicit their feedback.

When you have a high-growth model, you need to create momentum. If you're a start-up, you have to create that momentum from a standstill. That takes an enormous amount of energy and to create that energy you need a network of people to help you. It goes beyond those you hire. You have to think in terms of contacts who can introduce you to a world of suppliers, customers, employees or investors. You need to create buzz. You need to create enthusiasm and excitement. That takes promotion—constant promotion.

My longtime partner, Brad Keywell, is as good at creating momentum in a start-up business as anyone I have ever met or seen in business. He is raw energy and in an exceptionally compressed period of time, he can take an idea and give it life. The mastery of accomplishing this is to spread the word like gospel. You have to tell your story to a thousand people, some of them ideally situated to help you and some of them way off base. Brad turns over every stone and takes every opportunity to try to build a connection and a bridge between what he needs and what the person he is talking to can offer. It takes real passion and near boundless dedication to jump-start a disruptive idea from conception. Some people have the gift; others need to learn from those who do.

Every promoter needs a message. In the case of disruptive business models, your message has to be very tight because the concepts tend to be very broad, often unconventional and the recipient is either unfamiliar with the industry, predisposed to think your model won't work or otherwise distracted. So, since you have a lot going against you, your message has to be clear and your conviction has to be steadfast.

Here are the core messages for each of the three businesses we've helped build:

InnerWorkings: Delivering More

> InnerWorkings is a leading provider of outsourced print procurement solutions to corporate clients in the United States. We leverage our substantial buying power to work with companies like yours to save time and money on all your printing needs and we do this through our proprietary technology and database as well as our extensive industry expertise. We've created a transparent competitive bid process to procure, purchase and deliver print in individual transactions as well as for your entire enterprise.

Echo: Evolved Transportation Management

> Echo Global Logistics is a transportation management firm that provides superior cost-saving technology and services for companies ranging from small enterprises to the Fortune 500. Our proprietary technology and integrated systems manage our vast carrier base, matching every tendered load to the carriers that are most appropriate and efficient. We save our customers an average of 10 percent or more off their existing transportation cost with real-time access to all of our technological advantages which include freight optimization, order tracking, automated order entry and management, back office integration and full audit and reporting capabilities.

MediaBank: Technology-Enabled Media Performance

> MediaBank helps media buyers, advertising agencies, associations and corporate clients identify, negotiate, buy and track advertising media more effectively and efficiently. We do this through our MediaBank Order Management and Analytics Suite, a scalable procurement platform that provides agencies and advertisers a holistic view of digital and analog media spend through an integrated order management and accounting tool. In addition, we collect and offer data on all media—including emerging technologies—and we offer advertiser-focused tools that streamline the management of complex multimedia campaigns for global advertisers. With our product portfolio, MediaBank addresses both ends of the buying and planning spectrum across all media types.

A good, tight message is critical, but it's only half the battle. It is one thing to memorize short sound bites of the advantages of your business or model, but the real challenge for any corporate leader is to make that message so organic that it's part of you. Without the natural ability to promote your business—no matter what else you do right—you will find yourself behind the eight ball. So how do you get good at promoting your business, especially if you are not comfortable with the act of promotion in general? The answer lies in one word—information.

Overcoming the Law of Convention, Part II

I took a negotiation class when I was at University of Michigan's Law School. The class was taught by one of the finest professors and legal minds alive today, James J. White. The idea behind the class was to create live simulations whereby law students would have to negotiate in small forums against each other and those who achieved the most optimal result would win the negotiation and get the best grade in the class. Professor White's thesis, or at least one of them, was that all things being equal the most prepared students would win the negotiations because they would "know" the outcomes they were trying to achieve. My theory, as it related to that class, was that a good negotiator could out-negotiate even a more knowledgeable opponent by simply reading and reacting to his or her posture and position. My theory was proven right—I received an A in the class without researching topics before the negotiations at all. But that was life in the classroom and I came to realize that my theory was actually dead wrong.

In the real world, knowledge and information create advantage because they prepare you for the unknown. As students, we actually knew much more about each other than we acknowledged. Outside, beyond name and affiliation, most of the people you will negotiate against will largely be strangers and information is your armor. The more you truly understand a topic, the more ingrained it is in your thought process, the better off you are, not just in negotiation but promotion as well.

When you come up with a new and disruptive idea, you have to do two things to promote it: First, believe it and second, live it. Let's focus on the second, because I think we would all agree it's nearly impossible to promote something you truly don't have faith in. So what does it mean to live it? We tell our sales staff that in order to sell a solution you have to become immersed in it. You have to know everything about it. You have to read about it, ask questions about it and explore every aspect of it. You should become so knowledgeable about the topic that people say to you, "How do you know so much about this? You must have been doing this for years."

Building passion into a disruptive idea

If you have a disruptive idea that goes against the grain, you have to find a way to passionately communicate that message in all weather—just like Steve and Nick had to do when they faced bad press at InnerWorkings. No one can make you articulate or dynamic, but you can certainly be knowledgeable as a starting point and grow your communications skills from there.

Style is irrelevant. We have two completely different styles represented by the two CEOs that run InnerWorkings and Echo. Steve Zuccarini, InnerWorkings' CEO, is larger than life, a natural salesman, very polished and very commanding. Doug Waggoner, Echo's CEO, is much more reserved and understated, a natural operator and brilliant technician. What is fascinating to me is that both are highly effective at promoting their companies. Both do a fantastic job, in my opinion, of communicating the central value and proposition of each model, but they do it in ways that are polar opposites of each other. How? Because both are extremely knowledgeable about the businesses they run. They live their business models and so promoting them is second nature, like parents promoting the achievements of their sons or daughters.

Convince others by convincing yourself

Both have immersed themselves in their individual messages that give their audience the confidence that they understand their businesses and the impact they have in the broader market. They are literally the most knowledgeable guys in the room when they talk about their companies. That's exactly what you want.

So how do you get informed? Not to sound repetitive, but you ask stupid questions and lots of them. That's really the first step in learning to promote your business—you have to learn about your business. To get good at answering tough questions you have to first get good at knowing how to ask them. Our management teams get praise for their deep knowledge of the industries they're in partly due to the practice we discussed earlier in the book—asking hundreds of questions (some tough, some easy) as they research their industry and their model.

The second step in mastering promotion is reaction. When you are out there standing on your soapbox shouting about how great your new model is, you have to be able to react to your audience. This might sound like a cliché, but there is no substitute in selling for listening. If you aren't listening to your audience, really listening, you are at a huge disadvantage. Selling is a two-person sport and if you can't adjust to the nuances of your audience, your message will get lost far too often. If on the other hand your audience is getting your message, there are typically telltale signs. If they're nodding, contributing, asking questions, you

you know they are engaged. If they seem disinterested or combative, you have to change and tweak your pitch to try to win them back over. The process is not static, at least not if it's being done right.

Third, when you convey your message to people, convey it with confidence. You have to be willing to stand up and tell everyone they're wrong and you're right. There is often no way around this and the more disruptive your idea is the more people will think you're crazy. If you are well informed, you should be convinced that your new model has merits and that conviction should give you confidence.

As we prepared to launch Echo back in February of 2005, we had to explain to people how companies would be willing to communicate with customer service representatives located overseas to at times negotiate transportation in the United States. There was skepticism, to say the least. We were able to respond with the results of all of the exhaustive research and testing we did, including running business through our call center in India and our statistically valid proof that our Indian operators were able to efficiently find trucks and negotiate with U.S. carriers. The more information we provided to our skeptical audience, the more we saw them begin to backpedal. They had opinions. We had facts. Lawyers have to develop this same skill. My brother Steve, one of the best litigators I have ever seen in action, is a master of building a case that fosters spirited advocacy.

Again, it's all about how passionate, how informed and how confident you are in the presentation. But there's another half to what makes promotion effective—performance. Your business needs to continue to be disruptive over time, which means you need to execute in the market. Ultimately, no matter how passionate you are at promoting your idea, there is no substitute for performance. In the end, execution will win over all of those who doubted you.

Summary:

The Law of Promotion is about balancing superior technology, infrastructure and performance with a passionate message about your business and its potential. Creating that message requires not only information and practice, but also a continuous effort to pick apart your business so you can address any resistance in the marketplace to your disruptive idea and insure solid execution of your strategy.

Next Chapter: The Law of Experience states that a business should operate in two hemispheres—the hemisphere of optimism that's outward facing and the hemisphere of pessimism and paranoia that faces inward. For technology-driven companies, seeking out the potential for errors, mistakes and failure is one of the most critical skills you need to develop. You have to create a pathway for bad information to surface so you can examine it and react to it.

CHAPTER 14

The Law of Experience

Optimism, pessimism and paranoia

From 1998 to 2000, legendary investor Warren Buffett's stock, Berkshire Hathaway, had dropped nearly 40 percent as technology stocks were at their zenith. And still, Buffett wasn't investing in tech stocks even though the rest of the world was caught in a state of Internet euphoria. When asked whether there were any technology targets on his radar screen, the Oracle of Omaha kept repeating the same frustrating response: "If we can't find things within our circle of competence, we don't expand the circle. We wait."

How could Buffett, one of the most brilliant minds in the history of Wall Street, sit out during one of the greatest investment booms in American history, literally the ground floor of the Internet economy? He gave his shareholders at the 2000 Berkshire Hathaway annual meeting—held a few days after the NASDAQ crash—this explanation: "We understand technology, how businesses can apply it, its benefits, impact on society, etc. It's the predictability of the economics of the situation 10 years out that we don't understand. We would be skeptical that anyone can. I've spent a lot of time with Bill Gates and Andy Grove and they would say the same thing."

In truth, this wasn't the first time Buffett looked like he was losing his touch. In the late 1960s, he wrote his investment partners telling them he wasn't buying because nothing was priced attractively. He waited until the stock market slid in 1973 and finally got out his checkbook. In 2001,

Buffett would get out his checkbook again, but only after the markets went through one of the most significant corrections in history.

Buffet has demonstrated patience over and over again. At publication, he was sitting on a whopping $46 billion in cash—at any other company, investors would be irate if management failed to put that money to work. Indeed, patience hasn't always served Buffet well; there's no denying the value creation that could have occurred had Buffet invested in companies like Microsoft, Apple, Oracle, Cisco Systems, Google, Yahoo or eBay.

Yet Buffett is the rare billionaire who admits his mistakes and has said publicly that while he hates a high cash position, he refuses to overreact when he just can't find companies he feels are worth buying. As for Berkshire Hathaway's stock price, that slumping $47,000 per share price in early 2000 had recovered to $110,000 by August 2007.

Welcome to the Law of Experience—the realization that there is value to gray hair and with time, mistakes and second chances, you do gain wisdom.

I believe in this philosophy: You have to be optimistic when you sell, pessimistic when you buy and paranoid in between. This basically means that you have to have a positive outlook when dealing with your customers, but a negative outlook when dealing with suppliers or internal operations. In other words, you have to be waiting for the next disaster to occur at all times and you have to constantly be taking any and all actions that will help you avoid its occurrence.

This is especially true for technology-based businesses since no customer remembers the 364 days of flawless service you provided when your system was up and running and stable, but they will never forget the single day your system was down. To have your technology performing is acceptable; to have it fail is unacceptable. This is the standard by which all technology companies are forced to live. There's another Warren Buffett quote that explains this paradigm perfectly:

> It takes 20 years to build a reputation and five minutes to ruin it. If you think about that, you'll do things differently.

The Law of Experience requires you to be compulsive about customer satisfaction while keeping an equally compulsive eye on everything that can, and inevitably will, go wrong.

Andy Grove was right

The former Intel chief hit the nail on the head with his book *Only the Paranoid Survive*, because it's an idea we live every day. Your responsibility is to create a company with two faces. Your outward face needs to be optimistic in nature or you will end up terrifying your customers and investors and partners for no reason. Chicken Little is not the side you show to the market. On the other hand, it's perfectly acceptable inside your company. Your inward face should be pessimistic and paranoid in nature. By assuming that disaster is always around the corner, you will end up taking actions that are proactive in nature instead of reactive after the problem has occurred. Although it might sound a bit pathetic, we simply assume at all times that things are going to go wrong.

As an aside, I don't think that makes for a negative culture. The way we use pessimism makes for a workplace focused on finding problems, solutions and profitable new ideas. Granted, we're serious at times, but that's because we're dedicated to avoiding failure and not getting blindsided by issues. Our culture, work environment and internal controls are designed around anticipating problems in everything we do, every day, so we get the chance to fix them before they escalate.

In the summer of 2007, our executives at MediaBank were working on a major software project for a media buyer within one of the largest advertising holding companies in the world. It was a status meeting with their senior management after a month of intense work. There were roughly 30 of our people and theirs in attendance and I started the meeting by discussing the fundamental difference between a creative culture and a technology culture. I raised the point that we brought up earlier in this book, that ad agencies are by nature focused on relationships—everything is very people-centric, creative, visceral, optimistic and centered around servicing the unique requirements of the client. Tech companies by contrast are focused on the deliverable—everything is very data-driven, logical, sequential, empirical, pessimistic and centered around meeting commitments and deadlines.

In order to keep our cultures from clashing we had to adjust our style and provide a cloak of optimism to clients, meeting every unique need with an educated but accommodating approach to their business. We tried not to inundate them with the real "us"—the constant fretting over every detail, the concern over what potentially could go wrong, the constant search for stress points in the project. Looking inside the belly of the technology beast can be a terrifying experience, particularly if you're looking in from the outside.

You learn to master the art of turning optimism on and off, just like you learn how to promote your business. For example, Brian McCormack and Barry Friedland, two of InnerWorkings' founders, orchestrated InnerWorkings' first order, a sports book. They knew a lot about print in general but very little about printing books and they still took the order believing that hard work and our model would deliver a positive result to the client. Over the past five years, InnerWorkings has probably bought and sold over 10 million books in the market and they are still to this day one of the largest buyers of book printing in the country.

Despite our outward optimism, our dominant thought process has always been to focus on our weaknesses and try and *stomp them out*. That's why the leadership in a technology-driven business needs to have something of a split personality—the ability to cheerlead for a disruptive business concept while anticipating the 101 different ways the model could blow up.

Protecting a disruptive idea

When you incubate a new idea, especially one that could disrupt an entire industry, you have to assume that others will try and derail your model at some point, especially early in your development. We've obviously spent considerable time in previous chapters pointing out examples of product innovators who couldn't maintain their momentum. The question is: What can you do to protect yourself during the stage in which you are new and vulnerable?

Here are some basic steps:

- ✔ You have to protect your intellectual property at all times. Talented legal and strategic advisors are critical. You should only be sharing sensitive information with those that have signed non-disclosure agreements. Every employer or contractor you hire should sign an Employee Innovations and Proprietary Rights Agreement that guarantees that everything you pay them to develop belongs to you.

- ✔ You need to hire talented employees, especially early on and you have to try and keep your first-generation employees happy and engaged so they don't leave. Departures only slow you down and force you to spend more time educating and training at a juncture in your lifecycle when time is the most precious.

- ✔ You need more than a few key suppliers in case of problems—and there will always be problems. If you are reliant on a small number of suppliers you are vulnerable. Find redundancy in your supply chain.

- ✔ Make sure you have plenty of cash on hand and do whatever it takes to avoid crippling debt at the outset of starting your business. There is no substitute for financial security. If you're developing on a shoestring budget and one thing goes wrong, you could find yourself out of business or severely handicapped in your execution.

- ✔ You need to keep your ideas relatively quiet until you have amassed enough strength and scale that you can thwart off competitive threats. It's a very small example, but I try to avoid sending our business plans or financial models via e-mail. Some people might think this is crazy given how much we love technology, but I always send them via overnight mail. Sensitive data online is vulnerable the minute it leaves your firewall. I'd rather ship a hard copy with a responsible carrier. While it might sound a bit paranoid, it's added protection against the widespread dissemination of sensitive information when a business is young and therefore fragile.

This is what we call constructive pessimism—building a company while steering around potentially lethal business obstacles. Technology-driven companies have to be especially secretive early on and protective of their value proposition. Disruption is painful. Innovation is painful. As a result, you will end up with far more enemies than friends.

Debt: The not-so-silent killer

In 1994 my partner and I bought an apparel manufacturer in Wisconsin and discovered how dangerous debt can be to your ability to think quickly and adjust strategy. Businesses are typically financed with either debt or equity, which basically means that you have to make a choice as to whether or not you want to sell stock to raise money or take on debt that must be repaid at some point in the future. Many entrepreneurs are scared of selling equity as they fear giving up control of their idea or taking on partners who might end up dictating how their vision comes to life.

We prefer raising money through equity financing as we have come to believe that debt is a layer of instability that is nearly impossible to predict or control. It's a distraction while you're building your product, assembling your team and dealing with significant growing pains to have to also manage a balance sheet that is weighted down in debt. Banks, unlike shareholders, are not aligned with the founders of the business. Banks don't care how the shareholders or unsecured creditors make out as long as they collect their principal and interest. Shareholders, on the other hand—even shareholders with certain vested interests—tend to be aligned with the other common shareholders in that all parties rise or fall in a more uniform manner. While this is not always true (i.e. a shareholder who has preferences whereby he makes out like a bandit even if you don't), the vast majority of the time there is a wall with equity on one side and debt on the other.

To some, our attitude about debt is very strange. We believe that if you need to take on debt, you'd better be certain you can extinguish it quickly. In other words, if you have borrowed more than you can repay, you have overextended your balance sheet and you are now at the mercy of your lender or the lending community in general. As unconventional as it might sound, I always advise people to do whatever it takes to make sure their businesses don't become subservient to debt. As this book was being written, the nation was in the throes of a liquidity crisis brought on by poor lending practices during the real estate boom—another example of the unpredictable nature of debt.

In virtually every scenario, we prefer equity as a primary funding vehicle.

As an example of our constructive pessimism in finance, when we did a Series E financing round for InnerWorkings in January 2006, people asked us why we raised money when the company was so clearly on a path to go public a few months later. We raised money at $4.92 per share in January and we went public at $9 a share in August. At the time we sold the stock, we knew it was at a 40-50 percent discount off an IPO price and we could have waited a few months and just gone public. We knew we would probably take a hit, but we were more worried about the unknown variables that could have occurred before we went public. One was a bird in the hand and other was two birds in the bush.

Again, this may be paranoid but it is part of our overall culture and it is ingrained in our behavior. The bottom line: Remove anything that is unpredictable and hostile to your business formation and ongoing execution. That's constructive paranoia. You need to look over the entire landscape of your business and determine what can cause you harm. Paranoia is a skill that most businesspeople have not mastered and those that have tend to find their failure rate is dramatically reduced.

What is business wisdom?

The Scottish author Samuel Smiles once said, "We learn wisdom from failure much more than from success. We often discover what we will do, by finding out what we will not do; and probably he who never made a mistake, never made a discovery."

That's the experience of most successful entrepreneurs and business leaders in a nutshell. What is business wisdom and at what point do you attain it? Business wisdom is the hard-won proof of success—the learning of techniques and discovery of new practices that makes a business viable, unique and successful. You embrace elements of business decision-making that produce positive results and jettison those that produced negative ones.

The technology bubble actually produced dozens of truly great ideas and models within a sea of failed businesses. Back in 2001, when we launched InnerWorkings, we were in the first baby steps of the now-ubiquitous wireless age. Mobile computing simply couldn't match the promise of terrestrial broadband networks at that point, so when the Ricochet network appeared that year, there was excitement. The company launched 128K wireless service for notebooks and some PDAs in about a dozen cities. But at $80 a month without a compatible modem, it never made the leap to ubiquity. A story in *PC Magazine* in 2002 noted, "…now Ricochet is gone and high-speed wireless connectivity is nothing more than an urban legend."[45]

In any failed enterprise, it's critical to figure out the elements within the failure that were nonetheless beneficial to your experience. You have to learn to dissect the outcomes of the business and review each one in an objective and independent manner.

However, good ideas don't die a permanent death. Cellular providers led the charge to turn urban legend into reality and now, wireless Internet is free in an increasing number of regions.

"Fundamentally, everything we do is an experiment," Douglas Merrill, a Google vice president for engineering, told *Business 2.0* magazine, "The thing with experimentation is that you have to get data and then be brutally honest when you're assessing it." When introducing new features, Google has remained true to a "fail fast" strategy: Launch, listen, improve, launch again.[46]

Constructive pessimism attracts capital

In our role as venture capitalists, we look for companies that have complete belief in their idea but also have the ability to be realistic about its potential for disruption and the resources that will be required to achieve the desired end state. We are exposed to nearly 50 companies a year and one of the amazing things we see over and over again is a complete ignorance of cash needs.

When the majority of people come in to talk with us, we see tons of energy but very little realism about capital and the resources that are going to be necessary to turn their ideas into a viable business. Entrepreneurs will walk in and say, "I need $500,000," and we'll say, "That doesn't seem like enough," and they'll blink and look at us like we're nuts. Telling them that they need more money is not an indication that we want to throw money at them; it's simply a reflection of our experience and our belief that they have not yet learned to be pessimistic when it comes to their internal operations and requirements. The single truth among most young companies is that they will all run out of money at some point and because they haven't lived through that experience, they have no true appreciation for cash flow and how critical it is to conserve financial resources.

The entrepreneurs shake off our "you-didn't-ask-for-enough-money" comments and then go on with their tale of how great the product is and how many units will sell within a specified period of time with a relatively problem-free outlook. We ask about anticipated quality defects and potential for packaging and transportation errors. We ask how much of their current business is signed up with one customer. We ask about production problems or their lack of experience. We ask about their intellectual property concerns. We ask about their ability to staff the business properly. We ask about competitive threats and scalability. We ask about dozens of other operational, technological and financial issues.

But in the end, they're still hopelessly *hopeful*. They believe the idea is so great that it will circumvent all of our concerns.

Sometimes it actually will. But we know from our own failures that most of the time a great idea cannot survive poor analysis and execution. A failure to counteract all the negative things that could happen in a business is the result of a lack of experience.

And this is especially critical in an environment that is experiencing accelerated technological advancement because technology creates two layers of instability—speed and change. It is hard enough to compensate for a lack of experience, but to do so in a market that is experiencing accelerated disruption is especially difficult and requires an even greater appreciation for what can go wrong.

Take for example financial projections. We see plenty of hockey sticks when we look at financial projections of high-growth technology companies. This means that an individual comes to us with a financial projection that literally looks like a hockey stick—the company is currently generating very little revenue and no profit but at some point in the near future its revenues and profits skyrocket up. Unlike a less-severe escalating line which gives you the comfort that gains are expected to be gradual and predicable, a hockey stick implies that a new company's finances will accelerate in a sudden and speculative manner.

We hate hockey sticks. They're generally unrealistic. We want to see financial projections with more reality in them. We need to see evidence of significant growth in revenues and profits on a gradual scale. Seeing no rise in revenues for eight quarters means that there is very little likelihood that you will see significant rises in quarter nine, unless something explains the sudden escalation like a product launch that's years in the making.

So where do new entrepreneurs get experience when they simply don't have it? The answer, unfortunately, is that there is no substitute for experience or Cliffs Notes for wisdom. Yet there are things you can do to hedge your lack of experience.

Find mentors: Find people who have experienced what you haven't and let them rake your ideas over the coals. Still to this day, we seek out people who know failure—those who have navigated a tough spot and come out of it—to review our ideas and think of nuances in new opportunities we might have overlooked.

Find your No. 1 pessimist: Designate a world-class pessimist within your business who can be counted on to shoot bullet holes through virtually every aspect of your plan. You want to know every potential misstep, production problem, financial, legal and competitive risk out there. If you've never stepped in such a minefield personally, you need to find someone who has or someone who has the natural tendency to be pessimistic and cautious.

We find that new entrepreneurs are often great salesmen. Yet we've found over time that salespeople are the easiest people to sell to in an organization. They're quick to rationalize every failure, every setback, every event that should cause them to re-evaluate the model and the business. New entrepreneurs are most likely to burn cash because they are the most likely to sell themselves on the notion that their idea is so fantastic everything will work out OK in the end. In today's fast-paced climate, by the time you realize you have spent too much or wasted too much, it could be too late to recover. Believe in your solution, not the hype.

However, we have to acknowledge that there will be some folks who hit the cover off the ball the first time they get up to bat. Sergey Brin and Larry Page of Google are two great examples of enormous success without historic failure. But I like getting to know people who have dropped the ball and learned to pick it up. To me, the real magic occurs when we meet someone with a great business model who's a paranoid leader looking for smoke from a fire that hasn't yet started.

Summary:

The Law of Experience could also be called the Law of Failure—And What it Teaches Us. As you're developing a business, you're making a mistake if you don't ask tough questions and focus on what could and inevitably will go wrong. Experience is all about predicting and managing against failure while all the time maintaining a positive and optimistic outlook as you improve your model and capture more share in the market.

Next Chapter: The Law of Accretion describes how technology-driven businesses should be built—quickly, accurately and in stages that can be released to customers the second they're ready for use. Gone are the days when a company's product can undergo years of experimenting and testing behind closed doors and secrecy. You need customers to be directly involved in your product development because they're truly the best experts you have at what will and what will not work for your business.

Chapter 15

The Law of Accretion

Lots of little adds up to a lot

A construction site evolves over time in small increments. From the day the ground is cleared, people pass by looking for signs of activity. A foundation is poured, pillars and supports go up, then floor by floor, the structure heads toward the sky toward completion. There's always change, something to see, but it's a while before the structure takes shape.

This process hasn't changed in thousands of years from the time they built the pyramids at Giza to the days of erecting the Sears Tower in Chicago. Thousands of tools and parts and thousands of individuals make a contribution. Creating a building from the ground up is much like writing a piece of software, with one critical difference. It's typically not safe to go into a building until it's done. With a piece of software, however, customers don't want to wait until every last painting is hung on the walls—they're looking for a product they can use right now, even if some walls are empty.

Whether it's an iPhone or an ERP system, today's customers are content to accept innovation in small bites adding up to an increasingly bigger, more important whole. The essence of disruption is constant, significant progress toward the end state.

Welcome to the Law of Accretion—the expectation of your customers that change will happen in small, constant and significant increments.

Our customers are the most important change agents in each of the companies we've founded or funded. There's no question that our management and employees have worked hard to develop disruptive, successful business ideas, but to say we've done it alone, in secret, with no customer direction would be inaccurate.

When you shut out the customer, you have literally exiled the most productive avenue of feedback and direction in your business. Successful businesses create opportunities for customer participation and development in their model for one simple reason—the model exists to attract customers in the first place.

In my opinion, the day of the focus group is waning. Granted, the focus group is largely a business-to-consumer function, but whether it's B2B or B2C, the Internet has made it possible not only to solicit direct customer feedback, but to keep the door open for customers to test your product and share spontaneous ideas and input about what you're doing right and what you're doing wrong. There's no reason to gather customers into any artificial setting anymore to get their opinions and reactions. Traditional surveys are losing their utility as technology allows your company to put your product in front of customers and let them go to work in their everyday setting.

But it's critical to not only listen but to react to that feedback in real time. The Law of Accretion states that you not only build at the speed of technology, but that you build at the speed of customer demand. You'll need to update your model quickly to keep up with both.

Simple solutions require complex thinking

One of the fascinating features of Google is its simplicity starting with that sparse interface. Granted, you can dress it up with weather reports and celebrity news if you want, but Google is probably the world's most disruptive solution dressed in a simple white wrapper. However, beneath the elementary graphic interface of Google's home page is one of the most complex algorithms in the world. That algorithm navigates a server farm of 450,000 throughout their worldwide supercomputer cluster holding an estimated four petabytes of memory.

The greatest business ideas are very simple. But look behind the curtain—or the landing page, as it were—and you'll see the technology that delivers those ideas is often very, very complex.

This is the work we do and what any disruptive technology-driven solution requires. The idea of creating a Web-based marketplace for efficiently priced real-time media data is simple. But the execution is monumentally complex.

MediaBank and its subsidiary DataTech were already revolutionizing the procurement software at some of the world's largest media-buying agencies. But to take our solution to the next level, we had to construct a portal to gather critical market data every second so that those agencies could use that information to effectively buy media on behalf of their clients. The gathering process requires constant testing and monitoring of the quality and usefulness of that data. It's an extraordinary amount of work, but in the end we will have constructed a quasi-exchange upon which media can be bought and sold more effectively for our clients than through any other solution available to them at present.

The design process for our solutions

We build technology systems like a kid builds Legos—one block at a time—until our vision starts to take shape. As we discussed previously, we have utilized rapid application software in most of our business technology prototypes that we've allowed our customers to test at each stage of development.

We've used rapid application tools like FileMaker to build our prototype systems. In each case, the process is similar:

- ✔ We determine the business requirements that are necessary to bring our idea to life. In other words, we gather tons of information and data and we try and design at 30,000 feet what we want the system to do.

- ✔ We draft a functional spec that details what each screen is supposed to do, how it is supposed to look and how the system is supposed to perform.

- ✔ We model a database and test it to determine if we can extract the necessary information that we are going to need in order to gather data that should provide us an informational advantage.

- ✔ Then—and this is the part that is atypical—we build an entire functioning system using a rapid application toolset that by design will only be used for a very short period of time, at most three–nine months.

- ✔ We build a working prototype system that is fully functional without security or scale and start conducting business through the application—taking orders, managing procurement and tracking inventory so we can test its workings and incorporate what we learn.

- ✔ We let our customers become our power users and through their real use of our system we essentially let them design the final product that we'll use to code the secure and scalable system for mass deployment.

These initial prototypes are not scalable enough or secure enough to run Wal-Mart, but who starts off at the size of Wal-Mart? We build complex solutions by starting with simple technology applications that rely on the richness of their data and the architecture of the business solution to add value. Then we enhance the interface with lots of bells and whistles, which are often much easier to develop but viewed by our customers as much more valuable, given that they enhance their experience more than the guts of the system which they can't see or touch.

As our customers find flaws or issues, we modify the system at speeds that are simply unattainable unless you are using rapid application tools like FileMaker. Through this process, we take a working prototype and mold the application in real time to the desired final product within months, instead of years.

Joe Keller, Sun Microsystems VP of Java Technology, Web Services and Tools Marketing, sees this as a trend:

The trend in IT continues to be to look for ways to stretch investment dollars by purchasing off-the-shelf software where possible, but at the same time ensuring that this off-the-shelf software works in such a way that is a competitive advantage for the company. If you have exactly the same systems as your competitors, then there isn't an advantage. So many companies will take off-the-shelf software and customize it to gain an advantage. Looking at next year, eight in ten developers expect that their IT projects will involve at least some custom development, either start-from-scratch custom applications (48 percent) or as integration into existing systems (34 percent). Only 11 percent expect that IT projects will focus on packaged application installation or upgrades. [47]

As you can see, companies are using a hybrid approach, purchasing applications off the shelf and then integrating them in a way that brings competitive advantage while simultaneously building a custom application that drives uniqueness in the business.

If you look at the most competitive companies in a particular industry, you'll see that they are highly automated, they grow unique capability with their systems and they use this as a competitive advantage. It doesn't matter if you're in telecommunications, financial services, hospitality or travel—it's how you invest in and use the system for competitive advantage.

Real-time software development

We've engineered an on-the-fly approach to developing software that encompasses the use of rapid application tools and constant feedback before the final secure and scalable product is constructed. We didn't just stumble onto this approach. We tried the conventional approach and failed.

In 1999, when we began constructing our e-commerce site for Starbelly, we hired our way into a dedicated 100-plus member software development staff that consumed millions of dollars building a functional prototype. We had Rational-Rose use-case models, we had a huge quality assurance staff, we were working with Oracle 11i, we had a team of enterprise architects and nearly a dozen different vice presidents of various departments within technology—we had all the elements in place for a large scale, conventional late-1990s business launch. At our peak, we were investing more than $5 million a month on technology, hiring the best of the best at a clip of nearly one software engineer for every business day of the week.

And yet, for all of the time and money we spent, the results were underwhelming. We literally had over-engineered our systems, over-staffed our projects and over-thought our solutions.

Today, we build mini working systems in small iterations where the development cycle is never more than a few months. We use every system we build day in and day out. We punish them, we let our customers punish them and within a short time after launching our prototypes, we start writing code to a parallel and more stable database (SQL Server, Oracle) using more customizable, secure and robust programming languages (.Net, Java).

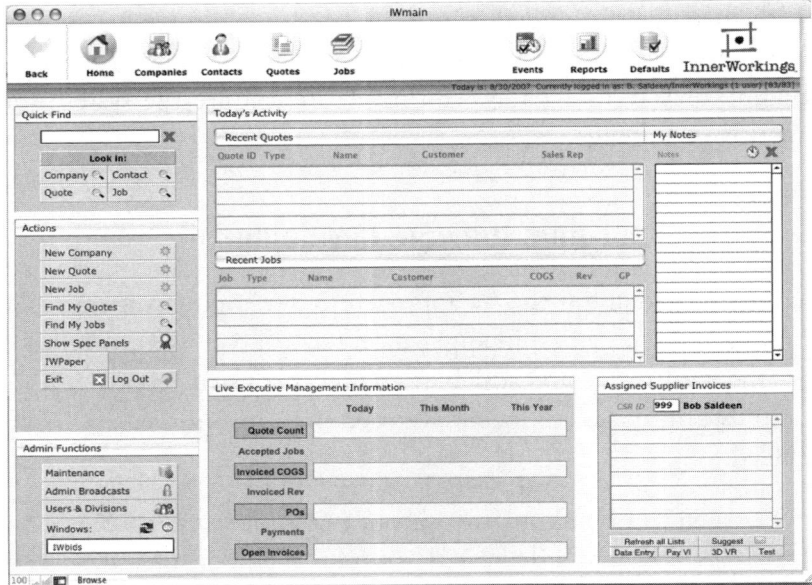

Fig. 15.1: A historic version of our FileMaker application for InnerWorkings

Chapter 15: The Law of Accretion

InnerWorkings, Echo and MediaBank were all launched initially using FileMaker, a cross-platform database and toolset that's now a subsidiary of Apple. It was an off-the-shelf product designed to allow limited but rapid application scripting that had its roots in the early 1980s.

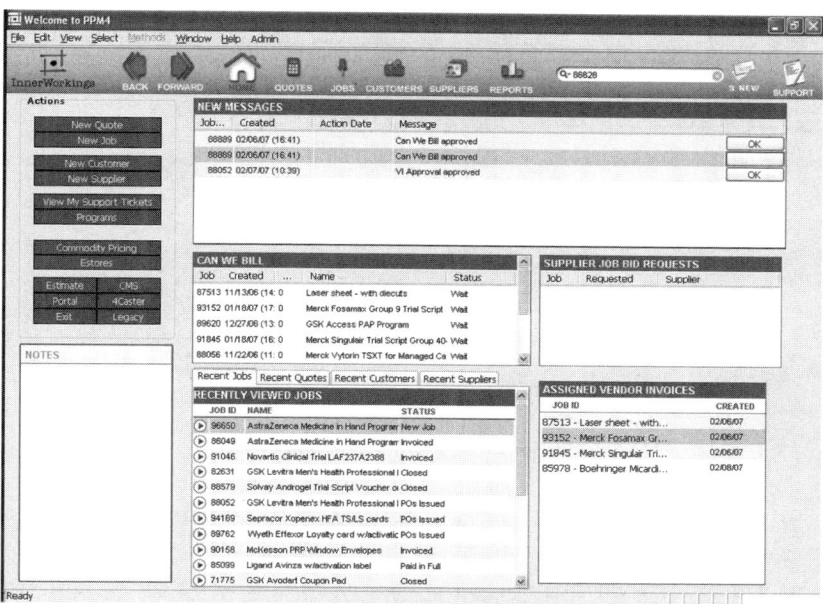

Fig. 15.2: A historic version of our Servoy application for InnerWorkings

At InnerWorkings, we had the FileMaker prototype up and running for customer use within two months. We actually built multiple prototypes in FileMaker until we got the application to the state we needed, ultimately migrating to Servoy (another rapid application Java toolset) and a secure and robust SQL server database. In addition, InnerWorkings had applications that were written in .Net and Java. For example, InnerWorkings' Supplier Portal was a Web application written in .Net communicating with their SQL server database.

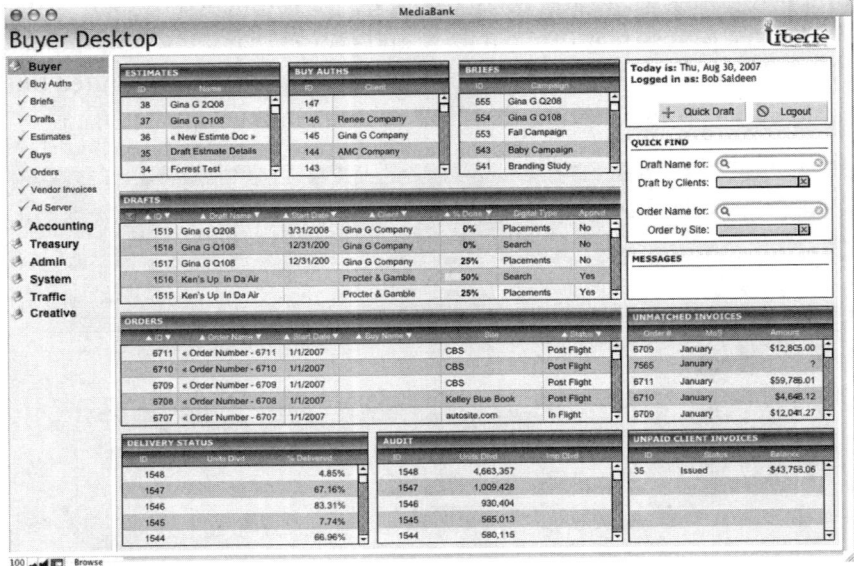

Fig. 15.3: A historic version of MediaBank's digital prototype

In addition to the day-to-day order management and analytics system, InnerWorkings also needed to maintain server capacity via its FTP site to interface with various software applications that enable clients to effectively store, retrieve, present and manage large volumes of digital content and imagery, such as their creative print files or the advertisements that get placed in a printed magazine or their mail file (the file that stores their mailing lists). Print production and digital imagery are interlinked. Companies are increasingly concerned about the storage and maintenance of their digital repository. InnerWorkings' systems allow their clients to manage, retrieve and distribute multimedia and static files, via the Internet, to upload or share logos, artwork, brochures, presentations, photos, video and text documents.

Scale is everything

The key to managing scale is to eat the elephant one bite at a time. There is no point building a system to handle a billion transactions a day when you only have ten a day at the start. There is no point building a system to accommodate a thousand users when you only have five. Everything starts small and grows over time. The key is to build systems that are appropriate for each cycle of your growth. You need to build a small house before you build a big one.

At MediaBank, we set out to construct a digital media-buying tool with no industry forerunner that we could lean on or learn from. We were in uncharted territory trying to build a piece of technology to define buying standards and optimization in a field that was only a handful of years old in the first place. There was no true working prototype or comparable for what we wanted to build. We interviewed hundreds of people to come up with the architecture for the system.

Again, we built the application in FileMaker, deployed it, tested it, refined it, tweaked it and retested it until we felt that the prototype was complete. At that moment, we deployed a team of developers who began construction of a copycat version of our FileMaker digital system written in Java connecting to an Oracle database. Given that our main system had to support thousands of concurrent users and house nearly 80 terabytes of data at a time, we needed robust, scalable and secure tools for the live operating system.

With Echo, we launched in February 2005 in FileMaker and by January 2006, we began rebuilding the entire system in .Net connecting to a SQL Server database. In the case of Echo, we had literally grown so fast that we actually stressed the physical limitations of FileMaker both in terms of number of concurrent users (we had approximately 200 on the system) and the amount of data that can be stored and retrieved. Because of these limitations, the initial FileMaker system was crashing several times a day and all users would have to log back into the system to continue working. We were dealing with speed and overcapacity at the same time and we just couldn't develop our scalable secure platform (known as Optimizer) fast enough.

Echo's systems house vast amounts of data. In addition to housing, TL (Truck Load), LTL (Less Than Truckload), small pack, international, intermodal and expedited pricing data as well as a mountain of internal accounting and administrative data (bills of lading, packing slips, invoices, supplier insurance forms and more) they collect information on available empty truck capacity by applying their offshore labor pool to the time-consuming task of calling, discussing and negotiating truckload availability from thousands of carriers across the United States. No Internet truck posting board, no global positioning system technology and no public marketplace solution has solved the problem of capturing this disparate, fragmented and carrier-specific, equipment-specific and trucker-specific information. The only way to capture this valuable data about truckload opportunities is through one-to-one calls with carriers, which creates large pools of data that must be stored, retrieved, analyzed and optimized.

People have asked us why we would go to the effort of duplicate development—some have even told us we were crazy to do so. But in our opinion, there is no other way to insure success when you are dealing with disruptive technology solutions that are revolutionizing a process without an effective roadmap to the software needed to accomplish that objective.

As we were writing this book, the technology for ThePoint.com was being constructed in a rapid application Web-development language called Ruby on Rails. What is most fascinating about Ruby on Rails is that it's a rapid application toolset for the underlying language Ruby, but unlike the scale limitations of FileMaker, Ruby on Rails is both fast and scalable. Sites of enormous magnitude can be fully developed and maintained in Ruby on Rails. That's why we're so excited about what could represent a new paradigm for us. The way the software industry is moving, one day we might find rapid application tools so robust in nature that they can be used for both the prototype and our final system.

Lots of little adds up to a lot

I first heard the term from David Kalt, the founder and former CEO of optionsXpress, when he was guest lecturing in one of my classes. It caught my attention as I thought it described the process of rapid application development in a succinct manner.

Instead of waiting for a massive release, every time you have a feature ready to go, you should deploy it. Enhancements don't have to be major or significant. The user experience is enhanced by tons of little features that make their lives better or make navigation a bit more fluid. If you look at great websites like Yahoo, eBay or MySpace, you will notice over time a constant pattern of releases to the overall functionality and user experience, most of them very subtle. No one release is so significant that you feel like you are at a new site, but your experience is constantly enhanced.

Too often, too many companies get stuck thinking that to change their product they have to take a quantum leap forward. To hide this work from the public, they maintain the status quo until they are ready to release an entirely new product or system. This is risky and at odds with the pace of accelerated disruption.

A far better approach is getting a working system up and running and getting your customers to interact and supply their ideas and feedback. That's exactly why features and enhancements need to come quickly, no matter how small they are. Good things come in small packages.

When it comes to enhancing service-oriented technologies, this philosophy is even more crucial. Whatever we do in the development cycle of these businesses, we plan to maintain a quick turnaround system in place for improvements and new versions of our software. Our technology will accurately mirror business conditions in their respective industries because our software development efforts will constantly keep current with the feedback we get from our customers.

Even if that feedback is minor, a simple enhancement can go a long way to improving the overall effectiveness of our products. That's the benefit of incremental, ongoing improvement—you're less likely to miss major shifts in the demand of your customers or major threats from your competitors because your products stay on the cutting edge. By waiting until you have something big, you lose your ability to react to changes in the market and you lose the advantage of speed. Things that move slowly eventually die—just look at the dinosaurs.

Summary:

The Law of Accretion demands a whole new approach in programming the technology of technology-driven businesses. Updates cannot wait for months or years. Constant updates and development are necessary to keep up with not just customer demand, but with the ever-quickening pace of technology available to every competitor in your market.

Next Chapter: As technology advances, there are more opportunities to automate nearly every aspect of your business. The Law of Automation states that technology-driven businesses have the best opportunity to support their people with solutions that allow staff more opportunities to serve customers and seek out new market opportunities.

CHAPTER 16

The Law of Automation

Automate everything you can

On Election Day, the nation screeches to a halt as registered voters trudge to their local polls to stand in line, sign their names and wait to step up to a little plastic carrel so they can squint at a lever or a punch card to select a president, a senator or an alderman.

The process is so antiquated it is almost comical. You drive to a local school or community building. You stand in line and eventually go up to the table according to the spelling of your last name to present your voter registration card. You sign your name and receive a paper ballot. After spending time in a different line, you eventually make your way into the voting booth where you face an attached binder with dozens of races listed, Republicans in one box, Democrats in another. You attempt to line up your ballot with the little holes that coincide with the candidate you want to vote for and race by race, you punch out the holes in your ballot. Since your ballot has no names, only holes, you're never quite sure you hit the right spot.

This historic tradition remains in a country where a quick cell phone text message can register your vote for American Idol—*which in 2006 registered more votes than were recorded when Ronald Reagan was elected president in 1984, the biggest presidential landslide ever.*

Maybe Americans really liked Taylor Hicks more than any choice on the presidential ballot.

Or maybe it was just easier to vote.

Automation can revolutionize any process. It is the reason we have cars, washing machines, telephones and thousands of other mechanical and electrical devices that make our lives easier. But the voting booth is one glaring piece of evidence that the landscape for automation is still wide open. Will Americans ever trust a central technological solution to collect their votes for the most important office in the land? If they do, it's possible that more than half the people in this country eligible to vote might finally elect to do so. And that might produce far more change than just no more long waits on Election Day.

Welcome to the Law of Automation—the willingness to sniff out the potential for automation in the most obvious and hidden processes we have.

It was 1946 and D.S. Harder, an engineering manager at Ford Motor Co., coined a term that would forever describe the benefit technology would have on the world—automation. Automation happens when machinery is programmed not only to complete a task, but also to perform the task consistently over and over.

The twentieth century was staggering for the sheer number of tasks automated within our society. In the opening chapters of this book, we discussed Ray Kurzweil's theory of the Singularity—the approaching day when computers will finally match human intelligence. Based on that expectation, humans have not yet begun to experience the impact automation will eventually have on their lives.

As we discussed in Chapter 3, pain is the motivator for modernization and automation. This chapter deals with finding the specific pain points and the specific opportunity for automation within your internal operations.

Identifying pain

When you're starting a business, there's a world of pain out there that you can't fully envision. But it does become clear in a relatively short time as you develop processes and systems to run your business. We spoke in Chapter 3 about sensing pain in processes within an industry. In this chapter, we're moving that issue indoors to the processes you will develop and use to operate your business and reach out to suppliers and customers.

Pain, in this context, is the discomfort that comes from processes and practices that take time, energy and financial resources from your business. Painful processes not only distance you from your customers and the best suppliers in the marketplace, but they prevent you from using your staff resources in the most efficient way possible.

You have to identify key sources of pain within your business and wipe them out through automated solutions. Such solutions can give your company the agility it needs to launch a disruptive solution within a chosen industry. Automation doesn't just block distractions—it fuels your entire business.

The key here is to move from the general to the specific. Focus on every aspect of every operational procedure from order inception to completion and determine which components can be improved upon and which are already optimally efficient. Start with your employees. Ask what slows them down. You'll hear loud and clear about manual processes that are inefficient—they tend to stick out like a sore thumb. Don't waste time digging—just walk up to your people and ask them. They're at ground level. They deal with your systems on a minute-by-minute basis; they know where your problems are.

Humans should be thinking

It sounds a bit sci-fi, but what jobs within your business are absolutely necessary for humans to do? To get a correct answer to this question, you have to look at every single process within your organization from cradle to grave, order to close-out.

Every point in your organization where a human touches something is an opportunity for automation. For example, in several of the companies we've launched, human hands don't touch invoices unless somebody needs a printout. Our systems are so automated that a customer's keystroke sets in motion a domino effect of actions that instigate ordering, billing, payment and most important, data gathering at every stage of the transaction. Our system gets smarter with every call and response, all during an order management phase that is largely devoid of human interaction.

What do our employees do then? They figure out how to make these processes work even better and faster and they spend their time making sure our customers are satisfied—that's their highest and best use.

Here's is the main trigger point for us to study automating a particular task: If a person is doing something more than two to three times a day, we either find a way to automate it or make sure we are collecting data from it.

Consider the following tasks that happen in every business, every day:

- ✔ Data entry of the specs of an order
- ✔ Sending out a quote to various suppliers to bid
- ✔ Entering price data into the system to compare prices
- ✔ Communicating with vendors to determine where your order is
- ✔ Issuing customer invoices
- ✔ Reconciling your invoice against the vendor invoices you receive
- ✔ Applying cash to your open accounts receivable
- ✔ Paying your vendors
- ✔ Passing information from your operating system to your accounting software
- ✔ Generating customer reports

These are all examples of time-consuming processes that can and should be automated. And this list is only a fraction of what we'll attack in our own businesses over time as our technology continually improves.

MediaBank's journey has been fascinating simply because we discovered how poorly automated the media business had historically been. We conducted an audit of where data was stored at the largest media buyers in the world and we found that the vast majority of valuable data was held within an endless variety of custom Access and Excel programs. Even worse, they told us they couldn't fully manipulate the data, sort or clean it because it all contained different coding based on which managers were pulling the data sets at the particular moment in time when the data was collected.

Until MediaBank, the advertising industry was walking into the digital age with endless silos of proprietary data on databases that didn't talk to each other, had size and scale limitations and required significant user involvement and time to even query in the first place. Our challenge was to break apart every aspect of the order management process from inventory allocation through cash application and accounting and re-engineer the process to be less reliant on people.

To do this, we met with hundreds of power users within the media-buying agency setting and began to explore what they did efficiently and what they did that was inefficient—minute by minute, process by process. We had to reconstruct how an order would flow through a system that was automated and build our system to emulate that.

For example, just look at the process of generating an invoice. In most companies, invoices have to be generated by users in a one-off manner. Data has to be keyed in, items have to be reconciled, things have be checked and double-checked and then, once all of the information is correct, an invoice is sent out to the customer either electronically or by some other means.

At most of our companies, we have no billing departments. Bills generate themselves. At Echo, for example, we should process well over a million transactions in the next year—a number which is currently growing by over 100 percent annually. We do this with a billing staff of three people at present who do not generate bills, but manage variances that come in from our suppliers. Each transaction invoices itself if possible as our rule-based application auto-matches vendor invoices that come in, checks them against purchase orders we have issued and automatically generates invoices to our customers.

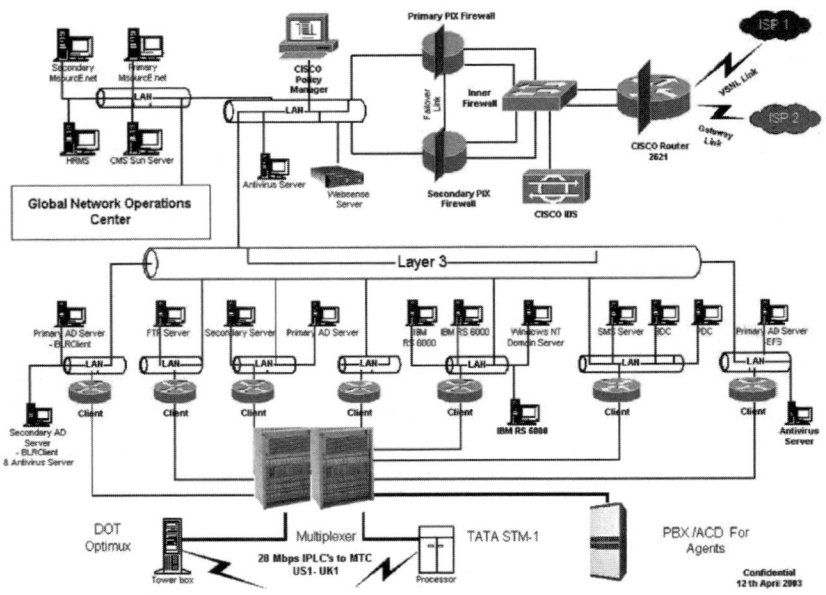

Fig. 16.1: Historic Echo Infrastructure Diagram

This is just one example of how we are able to build businesses that are more profitable than their longtime industry counterparts. We identify repetitive or extremely time-consuming human tasks, abnormally large stacks of paper or anything that slows down the user experience and we match it to an automated solution that provides significant scale and leverage to our back office operations. Everyday, we identify weaknesses where we need to improve.

When the expertise resides in the code, it's much easier to push change through an organization. People have to be trained and old habits have to be broken whereas code can simply be upgraded.

Most of the recent companies we've started are business-outsourcing solutions. We make it easy for companies to outsource their print, transportation and media-buying services. Not only do we sell outsourced solutions, but we also buy them from others from time to time. We consider outsourced solutions to run non-core components of our own business as well. Why? Because the ultimate in efficiency is to completely remove the task altogether. In other words, there is nothing more efficient for an organization than to not have to do something in the first place.

The challenge is that it's often impossible to maintain control and price advantage in outsourcing the core components of your business. For example, the *Chicago Tribune* can and should outsource many elements of its business but it probably makes no sense to outsource the printing of the newspaper itself. If you have lost efficiency in various lines of your core operation, you should invest money to improve efficiency and gain competitive advantage or dump the business line altogether. If there are business elements that are not core, you need to automate or outsource those functions.

Putting process under a magnifying glass

Disruptive technologies need to serve as bridges that span all aspects of your operation to your suppliers, internal operations and most important, your customers. Automation is the connective tissue that pushes down cost and builds efficiency. If you fail to find these opportunities for mass automation throughout your operation, you'll risk disruption from a competitor with a more fully integrated solution, because the more fully integrated and automated you are, the lower your internal cost of operations and the more efficiently you can price your products to gain market share.

Automation needs to extend not just inward but outward to your customers as well. Conventional systems that address customer automation or connectivity have typically taken one of two major approaches: They've connected one system to another through integration or they've added Customer Relationship Management (CRM) as a way to track and analyze their customer base. We do both because it is exponentially more beneficial to not only track your customers' behavior but also integrate with their operations every chance you get.

If your model is truly disruptive, you'll likely gain market share in the early stages of your model as customers test your solution. Yet from day one, it is essential to connect your business to theirs with an easy technology solution that assures maximum stickiness. If a competitor is coming after your customers with its own disruptive solution, it's your best defense to be as technologically ingrained as possible inside your customers' organization. If customers are thinking about leaving you, the process should be both cumbersome and risky for them because your systems are doing so much behind the scenes that your customers rely on, that they are hesitant to just up and leave you without serious consideration.

To make CRM and customer automation really effective, you can't stand outside your customers' building waiting for them to tell you something. That's why you need your automated solution to invade your customers' work environment. You need your system to solve deficiencies within *their* system. This is how you make yourself irreplaceable.

For example, Scott Frisoni, InnerWorkings' EVP of Sales, who was both instrumental and invaluable to the formation and development of the company, helped InnerWorkings land a contract with Circuit City to manage their store signage in early 2005. Circuit City was using a large ERP system to manage their back office operations. We developed a capability within our system to break down their invoice totals at the store level so that we could invoice them in denominations of 650 (both at a dollar level and a job level) every time we sent them an invoice. This allowed our invoices to be automatically integrated into the cost-accounting side of their system which was designed to allocate costs at the store level. When we began building this capability, it took our customer service representatives nearly a day to generate one invoice to Circuit City.

By the time we were done automating the process, we had it down to five minutes.

Revolutionizing your customer's supply chain

Wal-Mart is an organization that's arguably made the greatest strides in this area, using customer data as the carrot and pricing as the stick to get manufacturers to provide just-in-time inventory and keep its aisles stocked with the right merchandise at the right time. We've brought this approach to printing, transportation and media buying by creating a completely transparent solution between customer and supplier.

At InnerWorkings, we built a portal that allows suppliers to upload their equipment profiles, pricing, capabilities and capacity and it allows them to review their open invoices, bid on open jobs that have yet to be awarded and communicate in a host of other material ways with the company. Why? Because vendor/supplier automation is critical to removing barriers to how your disruptive solution gets to market throughout its entire lifecycle, from the earliest inception of supply to final delivery.

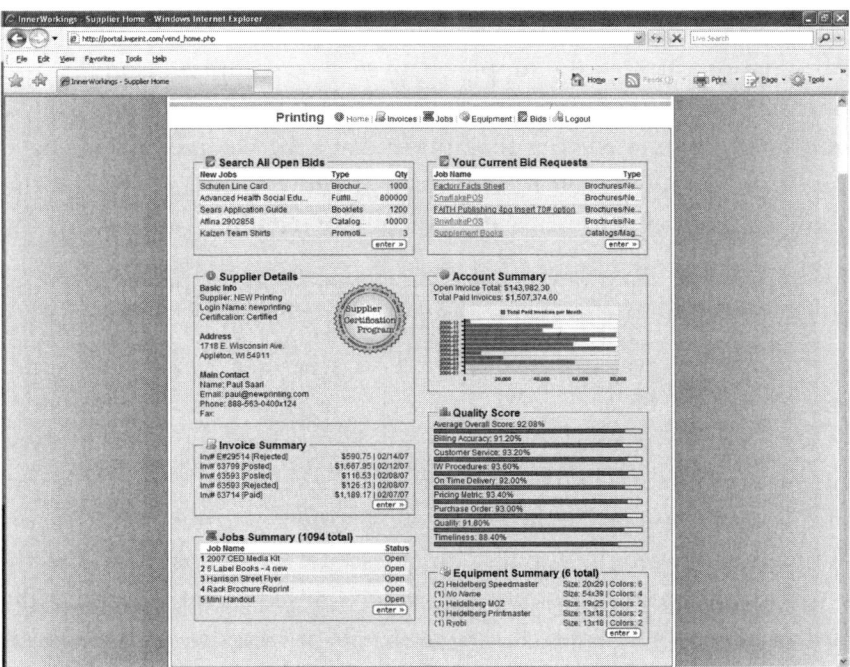

Fig. 16.1: A historic version of InnerWorkings' supplier portal

By automating the manner in which suppliers communicate with InnerWorkings, friction is removed, time is saved, costs are reduced and the overall process is more streamlined and efficient.

In older, more-established industries like printing, the supply chain is typically not automated—at least not to current standards. Communication is typically via phone or e-mail and you rely on trained personnel for the process to be successful. What's more is that because the process is manual, it lacks transparency. In other words, like with many other industries, the only way you know your order is on time is to consistently check in with someone who has more information about the status of your order than you do. You call or e-mail and have to repeat the process over and over again. Between each moment when you check in, you are again in the dark. Not only is the process inefficient in that it takes too much time, it is also frustrating for you and your customer. By building information pathways for information to flow throughout your entire supply chain, you reduce this friction and enhance the overall process.

Automation through the supply chain may be complex (as in the case of InnerWorkings' supplier portal) or it may be quite simple as in a one-sided automated tool to capture data. At MediaBank, we have developed a tool we call MediaInfo that allows media properties the ability to upload their price and availability data into our system.

At first, we went about collecting this information manually—calling thousands of properties asking them to send us their rate card and their catalog of available properties. This process, as you can imagine, was quite labor intensive. We knew that it needed to be automated, so we constructed an e-mail that would be randomly sent out to all of the media outlets we knew of with a letter asking them to take a few minutes and update the inventory we had in our database for them. When they opened the e-mail, a unique secure URL took them directly into a separate area of our database which housed their price and availability records. They were able to change their records which we could then review for quality purposes and then automatically upload into our main database. This process was not completely automated, but required a fraction of the time the old process did.

Creating an automated business from start-up

The order management and administrative costs of a new business can be more expensive than any other category of your overhead. If you're starting up a new company, it's best to set up an automation strategy from day one. Create a customer and supplier solution that reaches from your organization into theirs, makes their lives easier and collects specific data that will be valuable to your organization every step of the way.

Automation is not just for large companies. You have to start automated from day one, even when you are small. According to information on PayStream Advisor's website, by the end of 2006, only 10 percent of small and 25 percent of medium-sized businesses had implemented an automated expense control solution compared to 40 percent of companies with $2 billion or more in revenue. The irony is that smaller organizations really need automation to grow quickly.

As for physically creating the system, the process works no differently than creating any other form of custom software in your organization. If an out-of-the-box solution won't do for the long term, create a functional spec first, build a prototype, bring certain customers and suppliers into the system to test its flaws and capabilities and if necessary reconstruct the system once it is fully functional on a more robust, scalable and secure platform.

Focus on these key automation opportunities:
- ✔ Internal accounting functions
- ✔ Order management and processing
- ✔ Lead and proposal generation
- ✔ Customer and supplier records
- ✔ Customer feedback and marketing information
- ✔ Administration
- ✔ Order tracking
- ✔ Digital asset management and repository
- ✔ Salesforce data
- ✔ Legal and compliance

We don't believe, as some purists do, that you can automate humans out of the equation. But think about how much more productive you can make a business out of the box by focusing on optimal tasking for staff as opposed to nuts-and-bolts manual operations. When you automate your processes you optimize the human capital that you have working at your company. This too creates a significant gain in productivity in that you are able to utilize your personnel more effectively.

You will always be paying people to work in your business, but why would you want to hire gofers when you can focus your recruitment on strategic thinkers, good managers and creative people who can keep the automation ball rolling? Allowing people to keep the more interesting and challenging parts of their jobs while dumping the menial tasks might actually help you retain talented employees and attract new ones.

Think about the intangible functions your business relies on to be successful. That's where you need to put the best people you can find. A computer can't say, "Don't worry, you'll be OK, I'll make sure I personally get involved to make this problem go away." When you think about it, that's the key message you need to deliver at every human touch-point in your company—you're always encouraging customers, supporting them or diffusing their anger or worry.

The best companies you deal with are those that are able to deliver the human element in the smartest ways and at the most convenient and critical times for you. They do this because they allocate people to problem-solving rather than manual processes that would otherwise take all of their time. Some people think the benefit of automation is staff reduction and that's shortsighted. The real benefit is staff redeployment and optimization. It's about making your labor force more efficient and effective, not smaller.

In January 2007, IntelligentEnterprise.com came up with a series of IT trends that both old and new companies might consider when thinking about ways to make their businesses smarter and more agile. Here are two additional concepts that you should consider when you think about automation: [48]

Capture knowledge before employees leave. The average retirement age is 62, but losing experienced employees at any age can be costly in terms of knowledge they take out the door. Come up with a portal-like workspace where all your employees can store their knowledge, documents and correspondence so you don't lose key data on customers, products or operations when they leave their desks for good.

Make process analysis constant. Companies are looking to business analysts to constantly streamline their processes. The analyst role is evolving into something more akin to a product designer. Your business analysts—whether they're internal or consultants—are at the vanguard of pinpointing problems and redesigning systems and functions to speed your development cycle and deliver design refreshes quickly. Don't assume the automation solution you implement today will be cutting edge six months from now. The best automation gets constant reviews and upgrades just like the solutions you sell your customers.

The most critical aspect to automation, regardless of which strategy you focus on or which piece of advice you follow, is to make sure that you are passionate about automating everything you can. In this case, half the battle is simply refusing to accept manual slow processes that are inherent to your operations. Study them, pick them apart and find ways to infuse technology into them. In the world of accelerated disruption, businesses that do not embrace automation will be at a severe disadvantage as markets and market conditions evolve more rapidly than ever before.

SUMMARY:

The Law of Automation states that to be disruptive in a particular industry, you need to be disruptive within your company as well. Finding ways to automate various processes within your business—from accounting to HR—is critical in that you need to be operationally efficient to be fully competitive in the marketplace. In addition, automation allows you to focus on your disruptive solution instead of antiquated internal systems that are too manual to scale.

NEXT CHAPTER: The Law of Privilege says be bold in your business concept, but self-protective in your business operations. Assembling the capital to bring a business idea to fruition requires parallel skill sets—the ability to create a disruptive business while mastering the learning curve on how to finance it.

Chapter 17

The Law of Privilege

Capital with strings is still capital

Marion Donovan grew up in a family of inventors in Fort Wayne, Indiana. After starting her own family, she joined other busy mothers in her hatred of cloth diapers. One day, she grabbed a shower curtain and sat down at her sewing machine to create what would be her first of 11 patents—a reusable, leakproof diaper cover that unlike the rubber baby pants of the time didn't cause diaper rash. The cover—called the "Boater" because it helped babies "stay afloat"—was an instant success at Saks Fifth Avenue in 1949. But she was already on to the next idea: a durable, leakproof multi-layer paper diaper that could draw moisture away from a baby's skin and then be thrown away after use.

It wasn't to be, though. Donovan toured the nation's major paper companies trying to get them to support her research of the right blend of paper products to build the perfect diaper—only to be told her idea was frivolous. Perhaps the idea wasn't fully formed or perhaps she was a woman pursuing a bold idea at the wrong time in history. In any event, the investment capital wasn't there and Donovan's revolutionary idea was at a dead end.

Move ahead to 1956. Victor Mills, a Procter & Gamble chemical engineer who discovered how to mass-produce Ivory Soap and helped create Duncan Hines cake mixes, loved his grandkids, but also grew to hate the cloth diaper. Pursuing the same bold idea as Marion Donovan, he was able to get P&G to launch its own development effort and by 1961, Pampers was born. Disposable diapers have become so common that over 18 billion of them—nearly three times the entire population of our planet—end up in landfills every year.

Welcome to the Law of Privilege. You need resources to bring great ideas to life.

If there's anything we've learned in business, it's that disruption is costly. You need capital and you need to master the delicate choreography of raising it, managing it, deploying it and conserving it. All the previous chapters of this book have gotten you to this point. The awareness, optimism, pessimism, salesmanship and innovation you've demonstrated now depend on one thing to succeed—capital.

Raising capital is a critical component of business that is the hardest to learn any other way than through trial and error. People can give you advice all day long, but in the end, there's a wisdom that comes from doing things right and doing things wrong that is invaluable when it comes to raising and managing money.

Brad Keywell and I acquired our first company out of law school—an apparel manufacturing business in Wisconsin—with tons of optimism and absolutely no fear about borrowing money. Leveraged buyouts were the rage at that time and we didn't even blink an eye when it came to borrowing almost 90 percent of the capital we needed to buy our first company.

Soon after we acquired the business we realized that we had to begin importing products to stay competitive with the changing apparel marketplace. Our inventories began to grow dramatically. To fund this growth, we were forced to borrow more money. Within five years of acquiring the company, our debt had ballooned from roughly $4 million to over $10 million and every penny of cash we were generating was paying the interest on our existing debt.

When we launched Starbelly at the height of the Internet boom, our burn rate was growing at a dramatic pace. Our vision, like those of our peers at the time, was as grand as it could be and we needed to invest tens of millions of dollars into our technology solution before we achieved any meaningful revenues. At our peak, we were investing nearly $5 million a month in technology alone. Every dollar we initially raised was in the form of equity financing. The company had virtually no debt at the time we began discussions with Halo to sell the business. While we had many lessons to learn in business at that time, we had already learned a critical one about debt—avoid it if you can.

The contrast of these two businesses describes why we have come to favor equity over debt. In the case of the apparel company we mentioned earlier—we had a real business, with real clients, real inventory, real accounts receivable and real sales executives and yet the business was constantly crumbling under the weight of all of the debt we took on the moment we bought the company. We constantly worried about how we were going to pay the interest and principal and still invest in the growth of the business. With Starbelly, we didn't have significant clients or revenues and yet we were free to invest in our technology and invest in solutions that if deployed, were likely to have a significant impact on the market. In other words, the business was far less "real" and yet our freedom was infinitely greater because we stuck with equity financing.

Without commenting on which business was better or more likely to succeed—because both had positive and negative attributes in hindsight—we had upfront investment that allowed us to run Starbelly's business as we chose and make long-term decisions instead of focusing all of our energy on short-term cash flow. Debt is a destructive force—it keeps you distracted, focusing on making payments instead of making progress.

The Law of Privilege doesn't mean that you deserve to be in business more than the next person. But privilege, which really is another word for money, allows you to fund the development of your business and buys you the time you need to grow and evolve. This could ultimately mean the difference between success and failure.

The simple lessons

We have learned critical lessons about debt and that raising and maintaining adequate capital is an essential component of any business plan. In addition, we learned that entrepreneurs should try to focus on businesses where EBITDA can be celebrated at the point of revenue generation. As we have discussed previously, it means once you make the sale you know you are going to make a profit. There is no operational or manufacturing challenge between your order and your wallet. It's hard enough to make money in the first place, so by removing operational challenges (like running a manufacturing plant) we have reduced the number of variables that can go wrong. It might sound overly simple, but we actually sat down years ago and made a list of all of the things we liked and hated about business; our objective with each company we start is to avoid businesses that have characteristics we don't like.

We specialize in service businesses, so I can't really say we manufacture anything. But I do believe that we manufacture one thing and it's something that every business should produce.

We manufacture equity.

That single idea should drive a great majority of your thinking about capital and the development of your business. There is a simple line of organizational accountability that highlights why every business should be in the business of manufacturing the growth of its own stock. If you break down corporate governance to its simplest form, officers are accountable to directors and directors are accountable to shareholders. The common thread that should underlie all officer and director action is increasing the value of the enterprise, thereby increasing the value of each share of stock. At the center of the entire corporate structure is this very simple concept—that everyone is there for one reason—to increase shareholder equity.

When you are growing a business, especially one that is highly innovative and therefore highly disruptive, you need to constantly remind yourself that you are there for one reason—to make the company and therefore the shares of the company more valuable. At every step, you need to consider what effect your actions will have not only on the day-to-day operations of the business, but more importantly on the overall enterprise value of the business. If your actions are not increasing shareholder value, you shouldn't be taking them. It's that simple.

Understanding what the business needs

Getting a constant read on capital needs is one of the toughest things to get a handle on in a disruptive business. Funding needs are often heavy at the outset and subject to radical change over time. You can't estimate your need for money at $100,000 when it will literally take you $1 million to cover a particular stage of development. As I said earlier, this is a common flaw that I see with too many entrepreneurs who show me their business plan. They're often too optimistic about their need for capital when they should be extremely pessimistic about the things that can go wrong in the business which will cause them to burn through more money than they anticipated. This occurs not only because their concept is often untested, as most innovative ideas are, but also because there are far too many unknown variables that occur during execution even after the model has been tested. In addition, being pessimistic about the need for capital will give you a considerable financing cushion. It will keep you in the game longer.

Once you accept the chances for unpredictability in all areas of your business model, from system malfunctions to unforeseen development obstacles to erratic customer demands, then you're ready to start looking for money. You are ready to accurately assess the true amount of capital that will be required to fund your business from idea to reality.

Financing a disruptive new business idea is a bit like completing a renovation project on a house. It almost never, ever comes in on budget. For example, take the installation of a heating and air conditioning system in an old house where you need to literally retrofit the existing system to accommodate the new unit. You end up going weeks behind schedule and thousands of dollars over budget trying to make the new system work in a home with strangely placed wiring and ventilation ducts. There seems to always be an evil surprise lurking within the walls.

Consider all the various systems both old and new that need to work together within a home—heating, electric, plumbing, communications, water and more. Your internal business systems interact in much the same way. They all need to be connected. New systems need to be linked to old systems. They all need to interact with one another and exist within one framework. There needs to be a master blueprint for where they are all located and how they are all constructed and even with that blueprint, things will still go wrong. There will always be breakdowns and unforeseen complexities. The only day that your systems are not complicated and full of surprises is the first hour or two you're open for business. With each passing day, your systems and infrastructure grow more complex. This problem is not unique to start-up enterprises. The technology that eBay uses, for example, doesn't exist in a vacuum. It needs to communicate with PayPal and other key software applications that make its business function seamlessly for the end user. The process of building systems that interact is constant.

This challenge does not just create developmental or operational hurdles. It creates funding hurdles as well. The greatest similarity between building technology and building a house is the unknown. This is because so often the structure exists only on paper or in someone's mind until it is actually built. The uncertainty of this process cannot be avoided, but it can be mitigated by detailed plans, talented builders and enough capital to see the project through to completion even when it comes in over budget or takes an unforeseen turn in the middle of development.

So how do you get to more realistic funding targets at the onset of the project? One way is to develop two business plans. The first should have the most optimistic forecast possible and the second should be completely pessimistic. Afterward, take the most pessimistic plan and add 20 percent to the amount of money you think you need and go with it. As simple as it sounds, it's one approach that often gets to the right answer.

Another approach that we lean on heavily is bringing in outside experts in a variety of disciplines to question and generally disassemble your financial projections. Bring in former CFOs or people who are generally averse to risk or have significant expertise and wisdom regarding the type of business you are trying to build. Rely on their objectivity to guide you.

What you'll be asked by investors

Once you determine how much money you need to raise, the next step (and unfortunately the hardest) is to actually go out and raise it. Whether you're talking to an angel investor, a venture capitalist or a private equity firm, there's a general framework of questions the management of any disruptive business will have to wrestle with during a presentation. Your job is to determine the answers to these questions before you actually sit down with a potential investor. The good news here is that the questions are largely the same and tend to get asked over and over again by nearly every investor you meet:

1. *Describe your business model.* This is the elevator pitch. You always start out with the short and focused description of what you plan to do and why someone should invest money. This is the central theme of the presentation and will most likely get repeated throughout your meeting.

2. *Why do you need money?* This is where you need to be thorough about your financial projections and the amount of money you're really going to need to hit the targets you have laid out. It is critical to explain to someone why you are raising money and what the money will go for. We'll talk more about this below.

3. *What makes your technology proprietary?* If you walk in with a Romper Room description of your code when you're facing sophisticated investors, you'll probably walk out with nothing. Know your audience. You need to be ready to explain your technology solution at the exact level your audience is playing at and if necessary, go into great detail as to why your solution is unique and can't be easily replicated by another company.

4. *Who are your current competitors and how do you differ?* This is challenging because given the pace of technology, this is often a snapshot of the market that can change week to week, month to

month. The key is to understand the current market landscape and be prepared to talk about the strengths and weaknesses of any model that is competitive with yours.

5. *What keeps you up at night?* Investors are typically focused not only on what you are afraid of, but also that you are afraid of something. Few ideas or models are impervious to problems and so investors needs to assess your appreciation for all that can go wrong and what actions you are taking to preemptively avoid those pitfalls. Experienced investors can also pick up when an entrepreneur is trying to keep a troubled concept going, so you should highlight your worries or problems without trying to hide or minimize them.

6. *How scalable are your business model and technology?* You need to demonstrate not only how your technology will grow with demand, but also how your technology will grow with the evolution of technology itself. In addition, the critical element here is whether or not your business model and technology application can sustain growth without imploding or needing significant new investment.

7. *When do you achieve breakeven?* When your revenues are less than your expenses, you are cash flow negative and therefore you have a burn rate. A burn rate is the amount of cash you burn monthly relative to the overall amount you have—it's a measurement of how long you keep your doors open without running out of money. When you stop burning cash, you have reached a critical milestone. Your business is finally self-sustaining. Investors need to understand when and how this will be achieved.

8. *How do you expect to win customers?* Investors want to know that there's someone, anyone, out there who will be supplying the customers and revenue for the business if they provide the capital to get it off the ground. This is a general question that requires a very detailed and specific response. You have to be able to convince investors that if they fund the business, customers will want to buy the product or service that is being created.

9. ***How are you going to attract and retain talent?*** Investors want to know why you and your partners are there and they want to know the caliber of people you're hiring. They also want to know how you're going to attract and retain the human capital that is necessary to build whatever it is you are asking them to finance.

10. ***How do you plan on exiting the business?*** You need to prepare an end game. Investors put money in to get money out. There is always a timeline and a horizon at which they want and need to be paid back and earn a return on this investment. This is typically three–seven years, but you should understand what your investors are looking for before you take their money.

The baby steps of funding a business

As we go through these examples, you'll start to pick up some of the funding jargon that will become part of your life when you begin talking to angel investors, private equity firms and venture capitalists. I will try to address some of these terms as we go, though I'm assuming the audience for this book already has a familiarity with them.

Abandon wishful thinking when it comes to financing your business. In other words, if you have $300,000 in the bank and you know that you'll need $600,000 to reach a key programming hurdle in three months, you can't try to cut the cost in half by extending the time over six months and using less expensive resources to do the development as we already discussed in Chapter 15. In a world that is experiencing accelerated technological disruption, time is far more valuable than money. You must have the dollars on the table to make sure you hit your targets not only accurately, but also quickly. If you save money only by extending time, you run the risk that by the time you bring your solution to market it's become outdated or irrelevant.

You need to raise money quickly which typically means following the same predictable steps that everyone else follows:

- ✔ **Option 1:** Entrepreneurs go to friends, family and other related resources to cobble together the ground floor of money a business will need.

- ✔ **Option 2:** Angel investors come in with small amounts of capital in exchange for equity in the future business.

- ✔ **Option 3:** Larger venture capital or private equity firms come in and invest in your business in exchange for equity.

- ✔ **Option 4:** You go to the bank or some asset-based lender and borrow the money you need.

We prefer that disruptive businesses are funded with equity because it ensures that the people involved in the funding of your business will be intimately involved with and aligned with you. Debt and equity are not aligned—they typically exist at odds. When someone loans you money, all they really care about is getting paid back their principal plus some amount of interest. If they get their principal plus interest, but the rest of the business collapses (including your stock), they are perfectly content. They don't have a real stake in making your business a success.

Equity holders, on the other hand, tend to be aligned with you as a common shareholder. When you do well, they do well. While some preferred classes of stock look and smell a lot more like debt than equity, they are still far more aligned with the shareholders than a commercial lender that literally has no such connection.

In addition, having venture capital or private equity involved in your business should be your goal because you're not only welcoming capital, you're welcoming expertise and assistance. Equity investors have an unlimited upside and so they are motivated to provide assistance to your business to maximize its value, which maximizes their return. And since they invest in companies all the time, they're proficient at spotting deficiencies in your model, identifying great management that can support you and they're generally a very strong set of eyes looking at your successes and failures at every stage in the lifecycle of your company.

So here's my opinion of the optimal financing food chain. Ideally start with a well-known and well-respected private equity or venture capital fund. Private equity firms focus on bigger deals later in a company's life and venture capital firms focus on earlier stage deals when a company is starting out.

If that option doesn't work out, go with an angel investor who really understands your business and has significant relationships in the business community that can be pulled in to help you as you grow.

After that, go to friends and family. They can be and often are a good source of money for small equity financing especially in early stage businesses or with first time entrepreneurs.

As a last resort, borrow the money from an established lender.

The funding models for our technology businesses

Starbelly:

We raised $1.5 million in our Series A Preferred round in May 1999 at $8.5 million pre-money (pre-money is the enterprise value of the business before outside investment) by co-founder Rich Heise, who was essentially an angel investor; our Series B Preferred was $8 million and came from J.P. Morgan Chase in July 1999 at a $32 pre-money valuation; and we were in the middle of raising our Series C Preferred round but at that point, Starbelly was purchased by Halo Industries in January 2000.[49]

InnerWorkings:

Our Series A round in September 2001 was an investment from Incorp (an investment partnership led by Rich Heise) of $150,000 when we launched the company. We did a Series B Preferred round in the amount of $900,000 about six months later led by Rich Heise and Orange Media (an investment entity owned by my wife).

In early 2003 we raised our Series C Preferred round of $2 million led by a group of local investors, many of whom had invested with us before.

We also added the Nazarian family, one of the most successful families in the country who were initial investors in Qualcomm and have been investing with us ever since the early days of InnerWorkings. That Series C round was done at $1 a share, valuing the company at roughly $25 million. In early 2004, we completed a Series D round in the amount of $4 million at an enterprise value of roughly $90 million.

In order to get the significant step-up in valuation in less than a year's time, we had to give the Series D investors a convertible preferred security which was largely equity-based but gave them an option at some point in the future to put their stock to the company and force the company to pay them back their invested capital. While this sounds a bit like debt, it has one significant advantage. It can only be paid back in available funds, which means that if your company doesn't have the cash on hand for redemption, the security accrues a default interest rate but the investors can't force the company to redeem it. This has become our preferred instrument that we'll discuss in more detail below.

In January 2006, we completed a $50 million Series E Preferred round led by New Enterprise Associates (NEA), one of the largest technology investors in the world, at an enterprise value of roughly $192 million. And finally, InnerWorkings raised approximately $93 million in an Initial Public Offering in August 2006 at a valuation of roughly $350 million, and then completed a secondary public offering of $108 million in January 2007 at a valuation of roughly $625 million.

Echo:

Given that Echo and MediaBank are still privately held, I will discuss timing and events without mentioning specific dollar amounts. At Echo we did our Series A and Series B in February 2005. Toward the end of 2005, we raised our Series C Preferred round. We then completed our Series D Preferred round led by NEA in May 2006. Echo is currently considering an IPO that might occur sometime in mid-2008.

MediaBank:

When we came up with the idea to launch MediaBank, we did our Series A, B and C rounds at the same time in June 2006.

As you can probably tell, our financing rounds are getting compressed in terms of how fast we do them and the pre-money valuations are getting higher and higher. This is purely a reflection of our track record and the business models that we are taking to market. In June 2007, we completed a bridge financing and Series D round for MediaBank, again led by NEA.

In the midst of the round with NEA, several significant events occurred which we felt increased the value of the business exponentially. In fact, we had other investors willing to come in with money at a far greater value than NEA. We had to make a tough call. Should we proceed with the round at a substantial discount to market value because we had told them they could invest at a time when the puzzle pieces had not come together? Or should we scrap the round and risk burning a bridge with a firm that had been a great partner of ours in many of our deals? In the end, it was a quick decision. We let NEA invest even though we were selling stock at what we felt was a discount to market value.

As the cliché goes, you can win the battle and lose the war. When you have a great investor, you have to try your hardest to honor the terms of each transaction and protect the overall integrity of your relationship even as events change the landscape in which you operate. Great investors are hard to come by and some deals go well and others go badly. It's impossible to have every investment turn out to be a home run. For us, the value in protecting our relationship with a trusted investor was more important that a few percentage points of additional dilution.

We're lucky that many of the people who started with us as investors in Starbelly are still with us today. In addition, our investor base has billions of dollars of capital that can be tapped into. In addition, our investors have made over a billion dollars in profit by investing in our companies and so our track record has earned us the right to pick from among the very top investors in the country.

The value of a convertible

Today, we've moved away from conventional preferred stock in favor of convertible preferred stock in most of our equity transactions.

Convertibles are securities that convert at the option of the holder into something else, typically into either common stock or debt at some point and can therefore be manipulated as an instrument. This optionality allows you to price the instrument at a higher value and therefore suffer less dilution when you raise money because the investor has greater downside protection. The investors might have a put right which allows them to sell their stock back to the company at some designated point in the future for a specific amount of money—typically their invested capital plus a stated rate of return.

Another important point to note is that virtually every term is negotiable and a potential trade-off to the ultimate price per share at which investors will choose to invest. If you reduce the price they pay, they should be willing to give up protection. If you increase the price they pay, they are going to ask for more protection.

SUMMARY:

The Law of Privilege is all about building parallel skill sets—the ability to create a disruptive business while mastering the learning curve on how to finance it. Financing is part of the lifecycle of growing a business and it starts with finding investors that will not only fund you but nurture your ideas and growth.

NEXT CHAPTER: The Law of Risk states that risk and innovation go hand in hand. All truly disruptive models work in uncharted territory and go through the critical stages of development we've detailed throughout this book. As a conclusion, we'll review each of those stages.

CHAPTER 18

The Law of Risk

Nothing ventured, nothing gained

Taking out a $500 loan against his mother's furniture, Arkansas native John H. Johnson launched Negro Digest—*a publication based on a weekly newsletter about the black community he put together for his boss at a Chicago insurance company. Other than* The Defender, *then a chain of black-owned newspapers that were voraciously read in the North and smuggled into the South by Pullman Porters, there were no other African-American publishers of any significance in the early 1940s.*

Negro Digest *would morph into* Ebony *in 1945 and with 25,000 copies sold, it immediately became the largest circulated black-owned monthly lifestyle magazine in the United States. By 1951, Johnson's fast-rising Johnson Publishing Co. would launch* Jet, *the nation's only black newsweekly.*

Johnson's holdings—which would eventually include publishing, cosmetics, radio stations, and a TV production company—didn't stop creating breakthroughs in the black community. A consummate salesman who eventually joined the boards of Twentieth Century Fox, Chrysler, Zenith Electronics and Dillard Department Stores, Johnson single-handedly convinced Madison Avenue that there was a massive black consumer market that had gone untapped and with that recognition, Madison Avenue poured millions in advertising into Johnson Publishing's properties.

Johnson, who died in 2005, not only disrupted black media, he disrupted world media. Corporate America's viewpoint that only white consumers counted was shattered with the sheer number of readers, viewers and consumers that Johnson assembled within a mere two decades.

The fact that the world's advertisers now include all ethnic and racial minorities in devising their media plans can be traced to John H. Johnson's idea that black people deserved recognition for both their positive impact on society and their ability to spend a surprisingly large amount of money on leading consumer brands. In creating publications focusing on black success stories, he changed the minds of advertisers, Hollywood producers and major news organizations about the role of blacks in America and, by extension, other minorities similarly situated.

Today, Johnson Publishing is a $472 million media empire—all from $500 borrowed off a houseful of old furniture. Disruptive businesses require genuine innovation and sustainable business models, but they also take guts.

Welcome to the Law of Risk.

Jonathan Swift once said, "Vision is the art of seeing what is invisible to others." As you've gone through the chapters in this book, we've mapped out, stage by stage, the critical elements of bringing a disruptive idea to market and hopefully achieving widespread market adoption and success.

It's an emotional and exhilarating prospect, the idea of being the only person in the room who *gets* it, who is willing to bet everything on a belief and then make that belief a reality for a desired audience of thousands or millions. Consider that what you're about to do or are in the process of doing is exactly what Bill Gates, Steve Jobs, Sam Walton, Sergey Brin, Pierre Omidyar and thousands of other technology disruptors have dreamed about and done: Create an idea that will change the world and then keep changing that idea to keep up with the world.

Innovation can actually be a pretty lonely business with the level of risk accelerating at every stage of development. Doing something that no one has ever done is risky—Google, YouTube, Linux, Wikipedia, Apple, Microsoft, Genentech, MySpace and eBay are just a handful among thousands of companies that have been there before. With any technology business that has the potential for disruption, you are sailing into uncharted territory and you'll never really get out.

There are an uncanny number of technology entrepreneurs who have an affinity for the show *Star Trek*, present company included. I think the opening line of the original show's introduction sums up the passion of those who strive to disrupt a market or change the way we behave: "To boldly go where no man has gone before."

The Law of Risk demands you understand the level of risk involved before you take that first step, but the moment you analyze and understand the risks, you take that step.

Risk is inherent to the entire process. Your disruptive idea by its very nature is different from the way everything is being done currently in that industry. You truly have no path to follow, no road map to guide you as you build your product, service or solution. You are a pioneer at every stage of the development of the business and so you need to learn to manage the risk that goes along with discovery.

Risk is not something to fear, it is something to embrace. You need to understand what can go wrong and most likely will go wrong so you take every precaution to insure that when it does go wrong you are prepared and protected. Much like rock climbing, you will inevitably find yourself hundreds of feet up in the air clinging to a fragment of rock with your arms and legs shaking from exhaustion. But, if you are smart, the whole time you are protected by a series of ropes connected to your harness that can and will suspend you in the air if you fall. There is risk in climbing a rock, but the risk is largely mitigated if you take precautions. It works much the same in building a disruptive business in an age of accelerated disruption—there is risk, but you can manage the risk and protect your business from it.

By way of conclusion, let's go over the key messages we've shared in each chapter and apply them to the Law of Risk:

Accelerated Disruption is the state of our economy both in the present and the future. We live in an era of accelerated disruption. As technology advances in stages that are accelerating exponentially, businesses have to realize that their pace of development and progress has to parallel those advancements.

We talked about futurist Ray Kurzweil and his statement that society wouldn't experience 100 years of progress in the twenty-first century, but "more like 20,000 years of progress (at today's rate)." With the ever-increasing rate of advancement in the power of computer chips alone, there will be "exponential growth in the rate of exponential growth."

Technology is surging forward far faster than we can presently imagine. The risk here comes from a failure to realize the impact technology is having and will continue to have. The risk inherent at this stage is the risk that comes from not taking action and becoming increasingly obsolete as those that embrace technology build businesses that disrupt your model. If you are an entrepreneur looking to launch a new business, your biggest risk is that others are lurking around you with a similar idea. If you fail to act fast, you might find you have lost your first-mover advantage.

Ubiquity describes the nature in which technology surrounds us and will continue to impact every aspect of our lives. We have entered an era in which people can use wireless networks to connect computers, appliances, machines and almost any other device by using a mere mobile phone that with a keystroke can command our environment hundreds of miles away. Until recently, this kind of society existed only in people's dreams, but today it is increasingly becoming a reality.

If a business cannot adapt to the ubiquitous state of technology and figure out how to place its products and services on an expanding range of platforms and utilize the advantages that technology provides, it risks obsolescence. As a business, you can no longer avoid technology or pretend that your business is impervious to its effects. Technology in the early twenty-first century is like the air we breathe—it is all around us pervading every aspect of our lives whether we are conscious of it or not.

Need. To alleviate physical pain, one looks for a cure. To alleviate pain in business, one has to look for solutions others might have missed—or never searched for in the first place.

In each of the industries we've chosen to disrupt, we started with pain, which gave rise to need. In print, it was the lack of a central marketplace for print services at an affordable and transparent cost. In transportation, it was the inability to find the right truck moving in the right direction at the right time to fulfill our needs. In media buying, it was the lack of a centralized marketplace to tell us what media properties were available at a given moment in time and at what price.

The search for solutions to problems just below the surface of awareness is a constant task for disruptive businesses. If you can find pain and dysfunction in any business process, you have the chance to disrupt and remake an industry by developing a solution that reduces the existing pain. The risk that must be overcome is deciding to take action once you have identified both the problem and the solution. New inventions are risky, but at some stage the inventor must begin building. Taking that first step and leaving behind all that you are currently engaged in can have a significant and nauseating affect on your life, especially if you are giving up a steady job and taking time away from friends or family to launch your dream. But as we said when we opened this chapter: Nothing ventured, nothing gained.

Convention describes the current state of most entrenched industries—you'll find the dominant players in an industry typically believe their way is the only way. This provides great cover for a disruptive idea. An entrenched business practice or process shared by thousands means that most won't believe that your radically different idea has any merit or chance of success. This can often work to your advantage. If an industry insider thinks your idea makes sense, it generally means that your idea is not revolutionary enough and there are probably hundreds of other companies thinking about or doing the same thing. Truly disruptive solutions go against the grain—they go against conventional wisdom.

Risk as it relates to conventional thought is really twofold. The first is that you follow it and the second is that you don't. You need to take conventional wisdom into your thinking when creating a disruptive product because those that came before you learned something, whether you respect their business models or not. If you ignore the industry's collective wisdom, you run the risk of going down the wrong path and right off a hidden cliff. On the other hand, if you don't question conventional wisdom and go against the grain when you know your solution is right even though others are telling you it's wrong, you run the risk of never innovating. Worse, you risk being disrupted by someone who was willing to take the necessary risk that comes with innovation.

It's a bit of a Catch-22—you need to hear and respect the voice of others without being persuaded simply by the conforming opinion of the majority.

Objectivity is where you take a step away from the idea you've fallen in love with to see if it is truly worthy of exploration. When you actually launch a disruptive business, your mood needs to change from passionate to objective. This means you need to distance yourself from the vision that's in your head and stress test every element of the model you are about to deploy in the market. Your primary concern at this stage is simple: Does this idea offer true and sustainable value and can I make money at it?

There are two primary tests we apply to any business we have launched. The first is if you can't achieve EBITDA neutrality within 12 months, which means that your operating income (revenues less expenses) is equal to or greater than zero, then that's a signal that you're doing something wrong and you should either shut the doors or make a radical change. The second is you need to win customers. If you take a product to market and you can't get your key audience to respond in six months or so and buy your products or services, you might also want to consider closing up shop or making a radical change.

Risk and objectivity often exist in an inverse state. Risk is inherently an emotional characteristic driven by intangibles. Objectivity is a rational process governed by intellect and reason. During this stage of the process you need to park risk in a corner and let logic guide your actions. Too much risk and not enough logic is a recipe for disaster.

Informational Advantage is about data and the way you collect and use it in creating a disruptive company or strategy.

More that 2,200 years ago, the Chinese military strategist Sun-Tzu wrote that "intelligence is of the essence in warfare—it is what the armies depend upon in their every move…Victory indeed belongs to the commander who gets the right information in a timely way."[50]

A disruptive business requires a constant flow of data to keep its model current, evolving and continually relevant. What we can do with information and data today was impossible to even imagine a decade ago. Not only are we able to collect data faster than ever before in our history and store data at costs that are fractional to their historic rates, we are also beginning to understand and manipulate data in ways that only futurists could have predicted. The importance of information and the advantage it can provide to those who understand how to master it cannot be overstated.

Risk emerges when you fail to track, collect and analyze information and also when you fail to honor the results that come from the data you have collected. There is perhaps no greater risk to an enterprise than when it fails to learn from the information it has available; for in the evolution of businesses this may be the most common trait among all extinct companies.

Adoption occurs when a solution arrives in the marketplace and the benefit derived from switching from the existing provider is greater than the pain associated with change. It may take months or years for a marketplace to migrate to a valuable new solution, but once the tipping point has been achieved, migration occurs. The Law of Adoption takes place after you have moved through the stages we've described in the previous chapters to create a business model that offers and delivers real value on a consistent basis. During this cycle, you are soliciting customers to adopt your idea at the expense of other solutions in the market.

We're living in exponential times, but we're also living in increasingly customer-centric times. Your customer base—consumers, businesses, governments and virtually every person and institution in between—is growing increasingly impatient. They don't want to have to live with pain and yet they are slow to change and slow to adopt.

The risk inherent in this phase is not yours, but your customers'. They face risk in migrating from a process that may be inadequate but at least is currently up and running. It's predictable. Your customers also face risk in not adopting new solutions if their competitors do so and therefore gain some competitive advantage either in terms of speed or price. Your customers have risk all around them and as they consider adopting your solution, they are weighing the relative risk associated with both change and stagnation. Once you understand that *their* decision is all about risk, you can more effectively aid them in their decision process.

Space is not just the final frontier; it's the only frontier for disruptive businesses. You need as wide a space as possible to launch a business in, preferably with plenty of antiquated players that tend to be small and slow.

A common mistake we see among new entrepreneurs is that they're attacking industries that are too small, going after problems that are not relevant enough, not big enough, not meaningful enough and ultimately not valuable enough.

The way to think about size is quite simple. Do this exercise: Ask yourself if your business grew at 50 percent a year for 10 years, what percent of the market would you capture? If the answer is 20 percent, the industry is probably too small. If the answer is 2 percent, the industry is big and ultimately exciting enough for you to target.

Risk as it relates to industry size is almost formulaic. The smaller the industry you are trying to disrupt, the greater the risk you are incurring. Smaller industries are more transparent, more easily manipulated by existing dominant players and can react faster to disruptive solutions. Larger industries move slower, are much less transparent and provide you the room you need to incubate your idea and allow it gain scale before others focus on addressing and combating your solution.

Ignorance is a necessary tool to have at the start of a disruptive business. In order to learn, you need to ask thousands of very basic, almost ignorant questions in researching your market to unearth concepts and ideas that get lost in conventional wisdom. Ignorance, and as a result the pursuit of knowledge, can help you see business opportunities where others don't.

As Anthony Jay once said, "The uncreative mind can spot wrong answers, but it takes a very creative mind to spot wrong questions." The childlike pursuit of knowledge that comes from ignorance is a very effective instrument as it relates to making sure your model is sound. In addition to learning like a child learns, you can and should also bring in trusted experts and other constituencies to hear your thoughts, strategy and presentation. You'll learn an extensive amount about your markets and the structure of your business by accepting that there is a world of knowledge that you don't possess.

The Serenity Prayer has an application here: "God, grant me the Serenity to accept the things I cannot change, Courage to change the things I can and Wisdom to know the difference." The risk inherent in believing you know everything and are in control of everything is immeasurable and obvious—you will most certainly be proven wrong at some point and fail miserably.

Awareness means you're always on the lookout for self-deception. The Law of Awareness states that to keep a business disruptive, you need to constantly analyze market data and solicit feedback and adjust your model with each grain of insight you obtain. We all need input because humans are great rationalizers. Often we can't recognize our own flaws, much less the flaws in our business models. Building a mechanism for constant, constructive criticism is critical to your business structure.

Every disruptive business needs to develop a superior listening and learning infrastructure that draws immediate feedback from every key constituency you have—customers, employees, suppliers, competitors and wise outsiders willing to give you an honest point of view.

The risk of not being aware of how your solution is being received in the market should also be evident at this point. Your business exists for a reason and that reason is to win over customers and generate profits. If you are delivering an apple and your customers want to buy oranges, pretty soon you will have a fruit stand full of rotten apples.

Arbitrage is the end product of value. If your model delivers sustainable value in a marketplace, you will be able to accomplish one of the following: Either you will be able to buy something better, sell something better or clients will be willing to pay you a premium for your goods or services. In each case, you have found a reason to exist. You have found arbitrage.

I believe arbitrage contains two key elements: value and sustainable profits. As you might have guessed, the second flows naturally from the first. Unless your model delivers value to its customers and those customers are willing to pay you for that value, you have failed to create arbitrage in your business and your model cannot sustain itself over time.

Risk shows up most often as it relates to arbitrage when entrepreneurs or business leaders take a solution to market that doesn't deliver true arbitrage and end up absorbing far too much risk in developing and marketing their inferior solution. If your innovation doesn't create arbitrage and you try and market your way through the illusory value you provide to the market, you will often end up losing money as customers either don't show up or leave shortly after they have tried your product.

Velocity is a fundamental discipline you must master when building disruptive business models, especially in an age of accelerated disruption. If you can't move fast, your model will quickly become obsolete as technology forces the market to evolve around you and eventually displace you.

Businesses no longer have the option of long development times. Exponential gains in technology that are occurring in compressed pockets of time—and the willingness of customers to be a part of that advancement—make it necessary for companies to launch basic product introductions with the promise of constant and regular upgrades and updates. Organizations have to learn to react to the new technology-enriched climate and to force innovation to move at the speed of technology instead of the historic speed of research and development.

The risk in not moving fast is clear when you examine the countless market opportunities that were lost by larger companies that could not adapt quickly enough to changing market conditions.

Promotion is a skill you have to learn if your disruptive solution is to be heard above the constant noise in the marketplace. Every promoter needs a message. In the case of disruptive business models, your message has to be very tight because the concepts tend to be very broad, often unconventional and the recipient is either unfamiliar with the industry, predisposed to think your model won't work or is otherwise distracted. So, since you have a lot going against you, your message has to be sharp and your conviction has to be steadfast.

Not only do you need to master the "elevator pitch," but you also need to become as knowledgeable and informed as you can about your own operation and your industry in an effort to reach a comfort level in delivering your message.

Promotion and risk are closely related. You have to embrace risk every time you put yourself out on the line and promote your idea. The best promoters are willing to stand on the tallest mountain and shout the praises of their idea at the top of their lungs to anyone and everyone who will listen. That takes a certain level of guts.

Experience is something you can't fake. As we've said, you have to be optimistic when you sell, pessimistic when you buy and paranoid in between. This means that you have to have a positive outlook when dealing with your customers, but a negative outlook when dealing with suppliers or internal operations. In other words, you have to be waiting for the next disaster to occur at all times and you have to constantly be taking any and all actions that will help you avoid its occurrence.

The Law of Experience requires you to be compulsive about customer satisfaction while keeping an equally compulsive eye on everything that can, and inevitably will, go wrong.

Risk is mitigated by experience. The more you do, the more you learn, the more you gain insight into what can go wrong and how you can avoid problems before they occur. There is no greater weapon I know of for mitigating risk than being paranoid when it comes to the execution of your business model.

Accretion describes the state of gradual growth—putting together a whole from little parts gathered over time. This is a development strategy that technology-driven companies should follow in my opinion. The market no longer waits months or years for lengthy product cycles. The Law of Accretion states that you not only build applications at the speed of technology, but that you build at the speed of customer demand. You'll need to update your model quickly to keep up with both.

Today, we build mini working systems in small iterations where the development cycle is never more than a few months and we use every system we build day in and day out before we spend significant amounts to build long-term scalable application.

Too often, too many companies get stuck into thinking that in order to change their product they have to take a quantum leap forward and so they maintain the status quo until they are ready to release an entirely new product or system. This approach is at odds with the pace of accelerated disruption and carries with it a disproportionate amount of risk in that the innovator is putting all of his or her eggs into one basket that gets dumped into the market at one time. If you misjudge the market or other solutions come into existence in the interim, you run the risk of being the disrupted instead of the disruptor.

Automation is the process of taking every action that is repetitive within your four walls and allowing technology to enhance or perform the function to drive efficiency, speed and cost reduction. It doesn't mean forcing humans out of the business process. Automation allows an organization to choose to use staff for creative or strategic purposes and leave repetitive tasks to machines if possible.

Every point in your organization where a human touches something is an opportunity for automation. For example, in several of the companies we've launched, human hands don't touch invoices unless somebody needs a printout. Many of our systems are automated to the point where a customer's keystroke sets in motion a domino effect of actions that instigates ordering, billing, cash application and most important, data gathering at every stage of the transaction. Our systems get smarter with every call, response or keystroke that occurs because automation allows us to voraciously gather data as our back office process is largely automated.

The risk of over-automating is that machines are incapable of replicating human intellect. So if you rely too heavily on machines you could end up producing results that are numerically or procedurally accurate and yet completely wrong for the customer. On the other hand, if you fail to embrace automation, you run the risk of losing your competitive advantage as others become more efficient around you.

Privilege is the result of sound financing and a continual dedication to making sure your business has enough capital to operate and grow. Disruption is costly, so correctly estimating capital needs is one of the toughest and yet most critical elements of building a company. In a disruptive business, you have to get a handle on funding needs since they are likely to be intense at the outset. In an era of accelerated disruption, underestimating the cost of deploying your solution leads to the loss of critical momentum.

To keep this from occurring, entrepreneurs and business leaders need to be pessimistic about things that could go wrong that would have a negative effect on their cash flow. It's an overly conservative approach but one we've found is necessary in determining your financing needs as you start up and grow a disruptive business.

Raising money requires a parallel skill set—the ability to create a disruptive business while mastering the learning curve of financing. This process is part of the lifecycle of every growing business and it starts with finding investors that will not only fund you, but also nurture your ideas and add intrinsic value to your enterprise.

Risk is pervasive when it comes to financing a business. If you raise too much capital, you end up diluting your ownership in the business and reducing your ultimate upside. If you raise too little capital you could find yourself underwater and out of business before you were fully able to develop and deploy your innovation.

Parting the Red Sea

At the end of the day, building a disruptive business is all about risk—informed risk. Risk is an element at every stage of the process—from formation through execution to eventual exit. How you approach the unexpected and how you manage and mitigate the risks that are inherent throughout the lifecycle of your business will ultimately determine how successful you are. In an age of accelerated disruption, where the stakes are higher, the pace is faster and the variables are more numerous, you can't afford to shy away from risk.

According to tradition, the waters of the Red Sea did not part for the people of Israel until one single Israelite, Nachshon, the son of Amminadav, plunged headlong into the raging waters.[51]

One single risky act ended a thousand years of slavery and bondage and ushered in an era of freedom.

One single risky act.

Selected Bibliography

Alpert, Bill. 2007. "The Inner Workings of InnerWorkings/The key figure in a software company selling stock has left a trail of unhappy investors." *Barron's*. Jan. 15. http://online.barrons.com/article/SB116864725853275703.html?mod=article-outset-box (Accessed Aug. 22, 2007)

Ames, Roger. 1993. *Sun-Tzu: The Art of War*. Ballantine Books, Westminster, MD.

Ault, Susanne. 2007. "Warner touts video-on-demand/DVD simultaneous release." *Video Business*. June 4. http://www.videobusiness.com/index.asp?layout=article&articleid=CA6449011 (Accessed Aug. 22, 2007)

Bain & Co. website, CRM section. http://www.bain.com/management_tools/tools_customer_relationship.asp?groupCode=2 (Accessed Aug. 23, 2007)

Benson, Clark. 2007. "Commentary: Retail Recovery." Almighty Institute of Music Retail website. http://www.almightyretail.com/design/newpress.php?incpage=billboard6 June 9. (Accessed Aug. 22, 2007)

Bryson, Bill. 2003. *A Short History of Nearly Everything*, Broadway Books, New York.

BusinessWeek. 2007. "Trend: Innovative Services—Not Just Gadgets." http://images.businessweek.com/ss/07/05/0530_inshort/source/6.htm (Accessed Aug. 23, 2007)

BusinessWeek. 2004. "The Power of Design IDEO redefined good design by creating experiences, not just products. Now it's changing the way companies innovate." May 17. http://www.businessweek.com/magazine/content/04_20/b3883001_mz001.htm (Accessed Aug. 23, 2007)

Consumer Electronics Association, April 26, 2007 (Press Release) "CEA Finds American Households Spend $1.200 Annually on Consumer Electronics Products."

Copeland, Michael V. 2007. "What's Next for the Internet." *Business 2.0.* July 3. http://money.cnn.com/magazines/business2/business2_archive/2007/07/01/100117068/index.htm?postversion=2007070305

Christensen, Clayton M. 2007. "Simple Steps to Create Disruptive Growth Businesses." Innosight.com website. http://www.technology-reports.com:80/report.asp?id=540 (Accessed Aug. 23, 2007)

Christensen, Clayton M., Raynor, Michael E. and Anthony, Scott D. March 10, 2003. "Six Keys to Building New Markets by Unleashing Disruptive Innovation." *Harvard Management Update.* http://hbswk.hbs.edu/item/3374.html. (Accessed Aug. 23, 2007)

DiamondCluster International. 2001. "Customer Relationship Management Point of View, White Paper."

Fishman, Charles. December-January 2007. "No Satisfaction at Toyota/What drives Toyota? The presumption of imperfection—and a distinctly American refusal to accept it." *Fast Company.* http://www.fastcompany.com/magazine/111/open_no-satisfaction.html (Accessed Aug. 23, 2007)

Gates, Bill. June 7, 2007. *Harvard Commencement Speech.* http://www.news.harvard.edu/gazette/2007/06.14/99-gates.html (Accessed Aug. 21, 2007)

Gates, Bill. 1999. *Business at the Speed of Thought.* New York, Warner Books.

Gates, Bill. 2003. "The Disappearing Computer," The World in 2003 (Economist Group)

Gumbert.com website, "Shift Happens," http://www.glumbert.com/media/shift. (Accessed Sept. 18, 2007)

Henschen, Doug, Stodder, David, Crosman, Penny, McClellan, Michael McWhorter, Neal, and Patterson, David. 2007. "Seven Trends for 2007/Kicking off the new year, we're going for seven trends that represent the kind of moving and shaking in business and IT that will have repercussions beyond just the next release. Forget the little stuff—we're talking tectonic shifts." Intelligent Enterprise. Jan. 1. http://www.intelligententerprise.com/showArticle.jhtml?articleID=196603897 (Accessed Aug. 22, 2007)

InfoWorld magazine website. February 17, 2007. "Ballmer: I worry more about disruptive business models than competitors." http://weblog.infoworld.com/open-resource/archives/2007/02/ballmer_i_worry.html (Accessed Aug. 21, 2007)

Johnson, Bradley. 2007. "Top 100 Spending up 3.1% to $105 Billion." *Advertising Age.* June 15. http://adage.com/images/random/lna2007.pdf

Kim, Chan W. and Mauborgne, Renee. 2005. *Blue Ocean Strategy/How to Create Uncontested Market Space and Make the Competition Irrelevant.* Boston: Harvard Business School Publishing Corp.

Knudson, Leslie. "The Pursuit of Productivity." *Next Generation Pharmaceutical* website. http://www.ngpharma.com/pastissue/article.asp?art=270804&issue=212 (Accessed Aug. 22, 2007)

Kurzweil, Ray. 2001. "The Law of Accelerated Returns." KurzweilAI.Net website. March 7. http://www.kurzweilai.net/articles/art0134.html?printable=1 (Accessed Aug. 22, 2007)

Massachusetts Institute of Technology, Lemelson-MIT Program Inventor archive. *Art Fry & Spencer Silver: Post-It Notes.* http://web.mit.edu/invent/iow/frysilver.html (Accessed Aug. 21, 2007)

McNichol, Tom. 2007. "A Start-up's Best Friend? Failure/From Dogster to Google, Web companies are finding that mistakes can be shortcuts to success." *Business 2.0.* April 4. http://money.cnn.com/magazines/business2/business2_archive/2007/03/01/8401031/index.htm (Accessed Aug. 22, 2007)

PC Magazine website, Online Extra, Jan. 15, 2002. "Best Today, Gone Tomorrow." http://www.pcmag.com/article2/0,1895,950140,00.asp (Accessed Aug. 22, 2007)

Rothfeder, Jeffrey. November 2005. "The CEO's Role in Innovation Can a leader personally drive new ideas? Yes." *Chief Executive* magazine website. http://www.chiefexecutive.net/ME2/dirmod.asp?sid=&nm=&type=Publishing&mod=Publications%3A%3AArticle&mid=8F3A7027421841978F18BE895F87F791&tier=4&id=72BE9E54B57B4CB8A3E4AB15D5D7A72A (Accessed Aug. 23, 2007)

Strasburg, Jenny. 2005. "The genesis of discount brokerage/1975 SEC deregulation offered an opening; Schwab stepped in." *San Francisco Chronicle.* May 1. http://sfgate.com/cgi-bin/article.cgi?file=/chronicle/archive/2005/05/01/BUGT6CI0BI1.DTL&type=business (Accessed Aug. 23, 2007)

Sun Microsystems Boardroom Minutes. 2007. "Enterprise Software Development: Should You Care? Q&A with Joe Keller, Sun VP of Java Technology, Web Services, and Tools Marketing," http://www.sun.com/emrkt/boardroom/newsletter/0804leadingvision.html (Accessed Aug. 22, 2007)

TNS Media Intelligence Forecasts 1.7 Percent Increase in U.S. Advertising Spending for 2007 (Press Release: June 12, 2007). URL: http://www.tns-mi.com/news/06122007.htm

Todor, John. 2007. *Addicted Customers/How to Get Them Hooked on Your Company.* Silverado Press. Excerpt: http://www.addictedcustomers.com/excerpt.html (Accessed Aug. 23, 2007)

U.S. Food and Drug Administration, *2007 Critical Path FAQ.* http://www.fda.gov/oc/initiatives/criticalpath/faq2.html (Accessed Aug. 22, 2007)

Weiser, Mark and Brown, John Seely. Oct. 5, 1996. "The Coming Age of Calm Technology." Xerox PARC white paper. *http://www.ubiq.com/hypertext/weiser/acmfuture2endnote.htm (Accessed Aug. 23, 2007)*

Wright, Karen. 2004. *The Master's Mistake. Discover* magazine website. http://discovermagazine.com/2004/sep/the-masters-mistakes/article_view?b_start:int=1&-C (Accessed Aug. 21, 2007)

Endnotes

1. Gumbert.com website, "Shift Happens," http://www.glumbert.com/media/shift. (Accessed September 18, 2007)

2. *BusinessWeek.* 2007. "Trend: Innovative Services—Not Just Gadgets." http://images.businessweek.com/ss/07/05/0530_inshort/source/6.htm (Accessed August 23, 2007)

3. Kurzweil, Ray. 2001. "The Law of Accelerated Returns." KurzweilAI.Net website. March 7. http://www.kurzweilai.net/articles/art0134.html?printable=1 (Accessed August 22, 2007)

4. Christensen, Clayton M. 2007. "Simple Steps to Create Disruptive Growth Businesses." Innosight.com website. http://www.technology-reports.com:80/report.asp?id=540 (Accessed August 23, 2007)

5. Benson, Clark. 2007. "Commentary: Retail Recovery." Almighty Institute of Music Retail website. http://www.almightyretail.com/design/newpress.php?incpage=billboard6 June 9. (Accessed August 22, 2007)

6. Christensen, Clayton M., Raynor, Michael E. and Anthony, Scott D. March 10, 2003. "Six Keys to Building New Markets by Unleashing Disruptive Innovation." *Harvard Management Update.* http://hbswk.hbs.edu/item/3374.html. (Accessed August 23, 2007)

7. Gates, Bill. 1999. *Business at the Speed of Thought.* New York, Warner Books. Page 63.

8. Gumbert.com website, "Shift Happens," http://www.glumbert.com/media/shift. (Accessed September 18, 2007)

9. Consumer Electronics Association, April 26, 2007 (Press Release) "CEA Finds American Households Spend $1.200 Annually on Consumer Electronics Products."

10 Gates, Bill. 2003. "The Disappearing Computer," The World in 2003 (Economist Group)

11 Gates, Bill. 1999. *Business at the Speed of Thought*. New York, Warner Books. Page 143.

12 Ault, Susanne. 2007. "Warner touts video-on-demand/DVD simultaneous release." *Video Business*. June 4. http://www.videobusiness.com/index.asp?layout=article&articleid=CA6449011 (Accessed August 22, 2007)

13 Gates, Bill. 1999. *Business at the Speed of Thought*. New York, Warner Books. Page xvi.

14 Weiser, Mark and Brown, John Seely. October 5, 1996. "The Coming Age of Calm Technology." Xerox PARC white paper. *http://www.ubiq.com/hypertext/weiser/acmfuture2endnote.htm* (Accessed August 23, 2007)

15 Weiser, Mark and Brown.

16 Kim, Chan W. and Mauborgne, Renee. 2005. *Blue Ocean Strategy/How to Create Uncontested Market Space and Make the Competition Irrelevant*. Boston: Harvard Business School Publishing Corp. Page 5.

17 Ibid. Page 48.

18 Gates, Bill. June 7, 2007. *Harvard Commencement Speech*. http://www.news.harvard.edu/gazette/2007/06.14/99-gates.html (Accessed August 21, 2007)

19 Ames, Roger. 1993. *Sun-Tzu: The Art of War*. Ballantine Books, Westminster, MD.

20 Johnson, Bradley. 2007. "Top 100 Spending up 3.1% to $105 Billion." *Advertising Age*. June 15. http://adage.com/images/random/lna2007.pdf

21 Gates, Bill. 1999. *Business at the Speed of Thought*. New York, Warner Books. Page 16.

22 Copeland, Michael V. 2007. "What's Next for the Internet." *Business 2.0*. July 3. http://money.cnn.com/magazines/business2/business2_archive/2007/07/01/100117068/index.htm?postversion=2007070305

23 DiamondCluster International. 2001. "Customer Relationship Management Point of View, White Paper." P. 5.

24 Bain & Co. website, CRM section. http://www.bain.com/management_tools/tools_customer_relationship.asp?groupCode=2 (Accessed August 23, 2007)

25 Kim and Mauborgne. *Blue Ocean Strategy*. P. 118-119.

26 Ibid.

27 "TNS Media Intelligence Forecasts 1.7 Percent Increase in U.S. Advertising Spending for 2007." (Press Release: June 12, 2007). URL: http://www.tns-mi.com/news/06122007.htm

28 Wright, Karen. 2004. *The Master's Mistake. Discover* magazine website. http://discovermagazine.com/2004/sep/the-masters-mistakes/article_view?b_start:int=1&-C

29 Bryson, Bill, 2003. *A Short History of Nearly Everything,* Broadway Books, New York. P. 123.

30 Massachusetts Institute of Technology, Lemelson-MIT Program Inventor archive. *Art Fry & Spencer Silver: Post-It Notes.* http://web.mit.edu/invent/iow/frysilver.html (Accessed August 21, 2007)

31 *InfoWorld* magazine website. February 17, 2007. "Ballmer: I worry more about disruptive business models than competitors." http://weblog.infoworld.com/openresource/archives/2007/02/ballmer_i_worry.html (Accessed August 21, 2007)

32 Gates, Bill. 1999. *Business at the Speed of Thought.* New York, Warner Books. P. 5.

33 Gates, Bill. 1999. *Business at the Speed of Thought.* New York, Warner Books. P. 270.

34 Rothfeder, Jeffrey. November 2005. "The CEO's Role in Innovation Can a leader personally drive new ideas? Yes." *Chief Executive* magazine website. http://www.chiefexecutive.net/ME2/dirmod.asp?sid=&nm=&type=Publishing&mod=Publications%3A%3AArticle&mid=8F3A7027421841978F18BE895F87F791&tier=4&id=72BE9E54B57B4CB8A3E4AB15D5D7A72A (Accessed Aug. 23, 2007)

35 Gates, Bill. 1999. *Business at the Speed of Thought.* New York, Warner Books. P. 214.

36 Strasburg, Jenny. 2005. "The genesis of discount brokerage/1975 SEC deregulation offered an opening; Schwab stepped in." *San Francisco Chronicle.* May 1. http://sfgate.com/cgi-bin/article.cgi?file=/chronicle/archive/2005/05/01/BUGT6CI0BI1.DTL&type=business (Accessed Aug. 23, 2007)

37 Fishman, Charles. December-January 2007. "No Satisfaction at Toyota/What drives Toyota? The presumption of imperfection—and a distinctly American refusal to accept it." *Fast Company.* http://www.fastcompany.com/magazine/111/open_no-satisfaction.html (Accessed Aug. 23, 2007)

38 *BusinessWeek.* 2004. "The Power Of Design: IDEO redefined good design by creating experiences, not just products. Now it's changing the way companies innovate." May 17. http://www.businessweek.com/magazine/content/04_20/b3883001_mz001.htm (Accessed Aug. 23, 2007)

39. Todor, John. 2007. *Addicted Customers/How to Get Them Hooked on Your Company.* Silverado Press. Excerpt: http://www.addictedcustomers.com/excerpt.html (Accessed Aug. 23, 2007)

40. YouTube entry, Wikipedia Website. http://en.wikipedia.org/wiki/YouTube (Accessed September 18, 2007)

41. Knudson, Leslie. "The Pursuit of Productivity." *Next Generation Pharmaceutical* website. http://www.ngpharma.com/pastissue/article.asp?art=270804&issue=212 (Accessed Aug. 22, 2007)

42. Gates, Bill. 1999. *Business at the Speed of Thought.* New York, Warner Books. P. 37.

43. U.S. Food and Drug Administration, *2007 Critical Path FAQ.* http://www.fda.gov/oc/initiatives/criticalpath/faq2.html (Accessed Aug. 22, 2007)

44. Alpert, Bill. 2007. "The Inner Workings of InnerWorkings." *Barron's.* Jan. 15. http://online.barrons.com/article/SB116864725853275703.html?mod=article-outset-box (Accessed Aug. 22, 2007)

45. *PC Magazine* website, Online Extra, Jan. 15, 2002. "Best Today, Gone Tomorrow." http://www.pcmag.com/article2/0,1895,950140,00.asp (Accessed Aug. 22, 2007)

46. McNichol, Tom. 2007. "A Start-up's Best Friend? Failure/From Dogster to Google, Web companies are finding that mistakes can be shortcuts to success." *Business 2.0.* April 4. http://money.cnn.com/magazines/business2/business2_archive/2007/03/01/8401031/index.htm (Accessed Aug. 22, 2007)

47. Sun Microsystems Boardroom Minutes. 2007. "Enterprise Software Development: Should You Care? Q&A with Joe Keller, Sun VP of Java Technology, Web Services, and Tools Marketing," http://www.sun.com/emrkt/boardroom/newsletter/0804leadingvision.html (Accessed Aug. 22, 2007)

48. *Henschen, Doug, Stodder, David, Crosman, Penny, McClellan, Michael McWhorter, Neal and Patterson, David. 2007. "Seven Trends for 2007/Kicking off the new year, we're going for seven trends that represent the kind of moving and shaking in business and IT that will have repercussions beyond just the next release. Forget the little stuff—we're talking tectonic shifts." Intelligent Enterprise. Jan. 1.* http://www.intelligententerprise.com/showArticle.jhtml?articleID=196603897 (Accessed Aug. 22, 2007)

49. As an aside, there is no special designation to A, B, C, D or E when it comes to rounds of financing other than denoting sequential order.

50. Ames, Roger. 1993. *Sun-Tzu: The Art of War.* Ballantine Books, Westminster, MD.

51. Rabbi Paul Yedwab, Shema Yisrael, The Temple Israel Siddur for Shabbat and Festivals.

Index

1984 Cable Act 60

A

Aldrin, Buzz 178
Alpert, Bill 271, 278
Ames, Roger 271, 276, 278
An Inconvenient Truth 189
Anthell, George 145
Apple 15, 20, 21, 62, 68, 69, 135, 162, 184, 187, 202, 219, 257
Ault, Susanne 271, 276

B

Bain & Co. 103, 271, 276
Ballmer, Steve 138
Barnes & Noble 109
Barris, Peter 150
Benson, Clark 271, 275
Betamax 119, 120
BlackBerry 22, 23
Blank, Arthur 69
Blue Media 4
Blue Ocean 63, 64, 65, 68, 106, 121
Borders, Louis 79
Branson, Richard 178
Brin, Sergey 257
Brown, John Seely 37, 274, 276
Bryson, Bill 271, 277
Buffett, Warren 201
Burke, James 23

C

Camp Funston 175
Chase Capital Partners 17, 76
Chen, Steven 169
Christensen, Clayton 12, 19, 272, 275
C.H. Robinson 167
CNN 69
Copeland, Michael V. 272, 276
CRM 103, 104, 129, 231, 232, 271, 276

D

Datatech Software Corp. 152, 180
Dell Inc. 62
Dell, Michael 62
Desisto, Robert 129
DiamondCluster 103, 272, 276
Dolan, Charles 59
Donovan, Marion 239

E

eBay 61, 69, 184, 202, 223, 244, 257
EBITDA 5, 75, 242, 261
Echo 2, 6, 31, 49, 51, 91, 121, 123, 195
Einstein, Albert 133
EToys.com 78
Expedia.com 108

F

Fishman, Charles 272, 277
Flatiron 17, 76
Flooz.com 79
Fossett, Steve 178
Friedland, Barry 204
Friendster 181
Frisoni, Scott 232
Fry, Arthur L. 134

G

Galassi, Nick x, 191
Gates, Bill 29, 30, 37, 86, 99, 153, 156, 181, 201, 257, 272, 275, 276, 277, 278
Genentech 76, 257
Gnutella 15
Goldberg, Whoopi 79
Google 13, 34, 35, 75, 111, 163, 170, 171, 180, 183, 186, 189, 202, 208, 211, 214, 257, 273, 278
Gore, Al 189
GovWorks.com 79

GPS 128
Greenberg, Jack 150
Grove, Andy vii, 201, 203
Gumbert.com 272, 275

H
Halo 18, 241, 249
Harder, D.S. 226
Hastings, Reed 110
HBO 60
Heise, Rich 73
Henschen, Doug 272
Holden, Betsy 150
Hurley, Chad 169

I
IBM 41, 63, 109
Ideo 164
InnerWorkings 2, 4, 5, 14, 15, 30, 31, 38, 43, 45, 46, 47, 48, 49, 51, 60, 61, 65, 66, 67, 73, 88, 89, 90, 91, 105, 106, 121, 122, 123, 136, 140, 141, 142, 143, 151, 156, 165, 166, 190, 191, 193, 195, 197, 204, 207, 208, 218, 219, 220, 232, 233, 234, 249, 250, 271, 278
IntelligentEnterprise.com 236
iPhone 162
iPod 3, 15, 21, 69, 135, 162
iTunes 15
iVillage 79
IWStores 91

J
Jain, Dipak 150
Jay, Anthony 136, 263
Jobs, Steve 21, 187, 257
Johnson, Bradley 272, 276
Johnson, John H. 255
Johnson Publishing 256
Johnston, Philip 85
JVC 119

K
Kalt, David 222
Karim, Jawed 169
Kash, Rick 151
Kazaa 15
Kelleher, Herb 62
Keller, Joe 216
Keywell, Brad 6, 51, 149, 194, 240
Kim, W. Chan 63, 64, 106, 272, 276
Kitajima, Yoshitoshi 27
Knight, Charles L. 155
Knudson, Leslie 273, 278
Kozmo.com 79, 173
Kuczmarski, Tom 42
Kurzweil, Raymond 10, 11, 29, 226, 258, 273, 275

L
Lamarr, Hedy 145
Land, Edwin 25
Leavitt, Michael 176
Levitan, Ted 79
LimeWire 15
Linux 257
Lombardi, Vince 178

M
MADD 116
Marcus, Bernie 69
Mauborgne, Renee 63, 64, 106, 272, 276
MBIQ 93, 97
MBOX 93
MBXG 97
McCormack, Brian 73, 204
McNichol, Tom 273, 278
MediaBank 2, 4, 5, 6, 14, 15, 30, 33, 34, 39, 53, 56, 65, 68, 80, 92, 93, 94, 97, 106, 112, 121, 125, 126, 136, 151, 152, 167, 168, 180, 181, 185, 196, 203, 215, 219, 220, 221, 229, 234, 250, 251
MediaInfo 98, 234
Mendelow, Clive 154

Merrill, Douglas 208
Microsoft 13, 86, 87, 108, 129, 138, 152, 183, 202, 257
Mills, Victor 239
Moore, Gordon 29
Motorola 183
Murray, Brian 154
MySpace 114, 170, 180, 182, 184, 223, 257

N
Napster 14
Netflix 110, 111, 172
Nextmedium.com 130

O
Omidyar, Pierre 257
optionsXpress 108, 222

P
Pampers 239
Pauli, Wolfgang 133
Paul, Steven M. 178
PayPal 169
Peapod 79
Pets.com 78
Post-it Note 134, 135
PPM4Caster 89
Prius 135
Procter & Gamble 239

R
Rabbi Paul Yedwab 278
Research in Motion 22
Riggio, Leonard 109
Ross, Steve 153
Rothfeder, Jeffrey 273, 277
Roxio 14
Ruby on Rails 222

S
Sagan, Carl 12
Salesforce.com 129
Schmidt, Eric 111
Schwab, Charles 159, 193

Scott, Robert Falcon 178
Siegel, Noah 120
Silver, Spencer F. 134
Skinner, Sam 150
Skymeter Corp. 128
Smiles, Samuel 207
Sony Corp. 119
Southwest Airlines 22, 62, 63, 161
Starbelly 16, 17, 18, 49, 73, 76, 77, 78, 80, 147, 148, 173, 190, 217, 240, 241, 249, 251
Starbucks 79
Strasburg, Jenny 273, 277
Sun Microsystems 216
Sun-Tzu 87, 177, 261, 271, 276, 278
Sussman, Lou 150
Swift, Jonathan 256
Sylvania 146

T
Target 163
The Cambridge Group 151
The Home Depot 69, 70
ThePoint 2, 4, 7, 112, 113, 114, 115, 116, 168, 169, 170, 171, 172, 222
Tipping Point 36, 101, 102, 116, 262
Todor, John 164, 273, 278
Toyota 163
Travelocity.com 108
Trintex 109
Turner, Ted 69

V
Valery, Paul 134

W
Waggoner, Doug 198
Wal-Mart 21, 62, 63, 64, 86, 110, 161, 164, 216, 233
Walson, John 59
Walter, John 45, 60, 150
Walton, Sam 62, 257
Wanamaker, John 96

Webvan 79, 172
Weiser, Mark 37, 274, 276
White, James J. 196
Wikipedia 114, 115, 169, 170, 180, 257, 278
Wolf, Linda 150
Wright, Karen 274, 277

Y
Yahoo! 79
YouTube 114, 116, 169, 170, 171, 180, 257, 278

Z
Zell, Sam 149
Zuccarini, Steven 191